hotels • restaurants • spas • resorts • shops

dubaichic

For regular updates on our special offers, register at

www.thechiccollection.com

hotels • restaurants • spas • resorts • shops

dubaichic

text hallie campbell • brandon lee

·K·U·P·E·R·A·R·D·

publisher's acknowledgements

Welcome to *Dubai Chic*. Apart from being one of the fastest growing cities in the world, Dubai is in the process of reinventing itself as a regional and global travel hub as well as a commercial and financial centre to rival anywhere else on the planet. All of which have made this an extraordinarily difficult book to produce. A decade ago, most of the hotels, shops, galleries and restaurants in the following pages just didn't exist—and anyone who was last in Dubai even five years ago wouldn't recognise the incredible developments that have taken place since. Burj Dubai, Burj Al Arab, The Palm Jumeirah, The World, Emirates Airline, Ski Dubai—these are names that have given this spot in the Arabian Gulf a global presence to reckon with.

Hallie Campbell, the author, has done an incredible job documenting Dubai's evolution into a fashionable destination. On behalf of Hallie, I'd also like to thank Mohammed Afkhami, Farah and Vivek Ashoka, Nilou and Mitchell Abdul Karim Crites for their expert knowledge and generosity of spirit during the writing of this book. I would especially like to thank the hotels and restaurants that have supported *Dubai Chic* and have waited patiently for the end result. I truly hope that we can repay that faith by sending you even more visitors amongst our readers.

Special thanks go to the team at Editions Didier Millet led by Melisa Teo, Suzanne Wong and Janice Ruth de Belen for yet another spectacular book. My thanks also to Sharon Garrett who helped in the early days of *Dubai Chic* and seems to know everyone in Dubai. The publication of this book coincides with the opening of our Dubai office, so I look forward to thanking everyone personally in the coming months and greeting ever more visitors to this new chic destination.

Nigel Bolding
editor-in-chief

---

executive editor
melisa teo

editor
suzanne wong

assistant editor
janice ruth de belen

designer
felicia wong

production manager
sin kam cheong

first published 2008
the worlds best hotels ltd
121 telok ayer street, #03-01
singapore 068590
enquiries : nigel@thechiccollection.com
website : www.thechiccollection.com

©2008 the world's best hotels ltd
design and layout © editions didier millet pte ltd

first published in great britain 2008
kuperard
59 hutton grove, london n12 8ds
telephone : +44 (0) 20 8446 2440
facsimile : +44 (0) 20 8446 2441
enquiries : sales@kuperard.co.uk
website : www.kuperard.co.uk

Kuperard is an imprint of Bravo Ltd.

Printed in Singapore.

All rights reserved. No part of this publication may be reproduced, stored in a retrieval system, or transmitted in any form or by any means, electronic, electrostatic, magnetic tape, mechanical, photocopying, recording or otherwise, without prior written permission from the publisher.

isbn: 978-185-7334-22-7

cover captions:

1: The Great Dubai Wheel casts a striking silhouette against the afternoon sun.
2: A colourful pile of fabrics at a local souk.
3: Hijinks on ice ensue at Ski Dubai.
4: A tempting spread of Arabian tidbits.
5: Rows of exotic spices perfume the air.
6: A trio of camels in the shimmering heat.
7 AND 8: Scenes at Qamardeen Hotel.
9: The sinuous curve of a desert sand dune.
10 AND THIS PAGE: There is never a dearth of fine dining restaurants here in Dubai.
11: Interior detail at the new addition to the Wafi City complex—Raffles Dubai.
12: A suite at Al Maha Desert Resort & Spa.
13: A traditional Middle Eastern hammam.
14: BiCE is known for quality Italian cuisine.
15: An aerial view of The Palm, Jumeirah.
16: A spectacular view of the city skyline.

PAGE 2: The indoor pool at Burj Al Arab's spa.

OPPOSITE: Acclaimed chef Gary Rhodes' Rhodes Mezzanine at Grosvenor House.

PAGE 6: Five Green is one of Dubai's hippest and most popular new concept shops.

PAGE 8 AND 9: The instantly recognisable atrium of Burj Al Arab, rising in concentric layers.

contents

map of dubai 10 • introduction 12 • gourmet safari 20 • arabian nights 24 • shopping mecca 26 • in the souk 30 • oasis of culture 34 • spa sanctuary 36 • championship dubai 38 • family affair 40 • onwards and upwards 46

48 downtowndubai

Shangri-La Hotel, Dubai 56 • The Palace – The Old Town 62 • Al Manzil Hotel 64 • Qamardeen Hotel 68

72 creekside

Raffles Dubai 82 • Grand Hyatt Dubai 86 • Park Hyatt Dubai 94 • Bateaux Dubai 98 • Dubai Golf 100

104 jumeirah

Jumeirah Beach Hotel 112 • Burj Al Arab 116 • Madinat Jumeirah 120 • One + Only Royal Mirage 124 • Radisson SAS Hotel, Dubai Media City 132 • Grosvenor House 136 • Le Royal Méridien Beach Resort + Spa 142 • The Ritz-Carlton, Dubai 146 • Oasis Beach Tower 150 • BiCE Restaurant 152 • The Montgomerie, Dubai 154

158 desert+outskirts

Palm Tree Court + Spa 164 • Jumeirah Bab Al Shams Desert Resort + Spa 166 • Al Maha Desert Resort + Spa 170 • Desert Palm 172 • Hatta Fort Hotel 174 • Jumana – Secret of the Desert 176

index 178 • picture credits 181 • directory 182

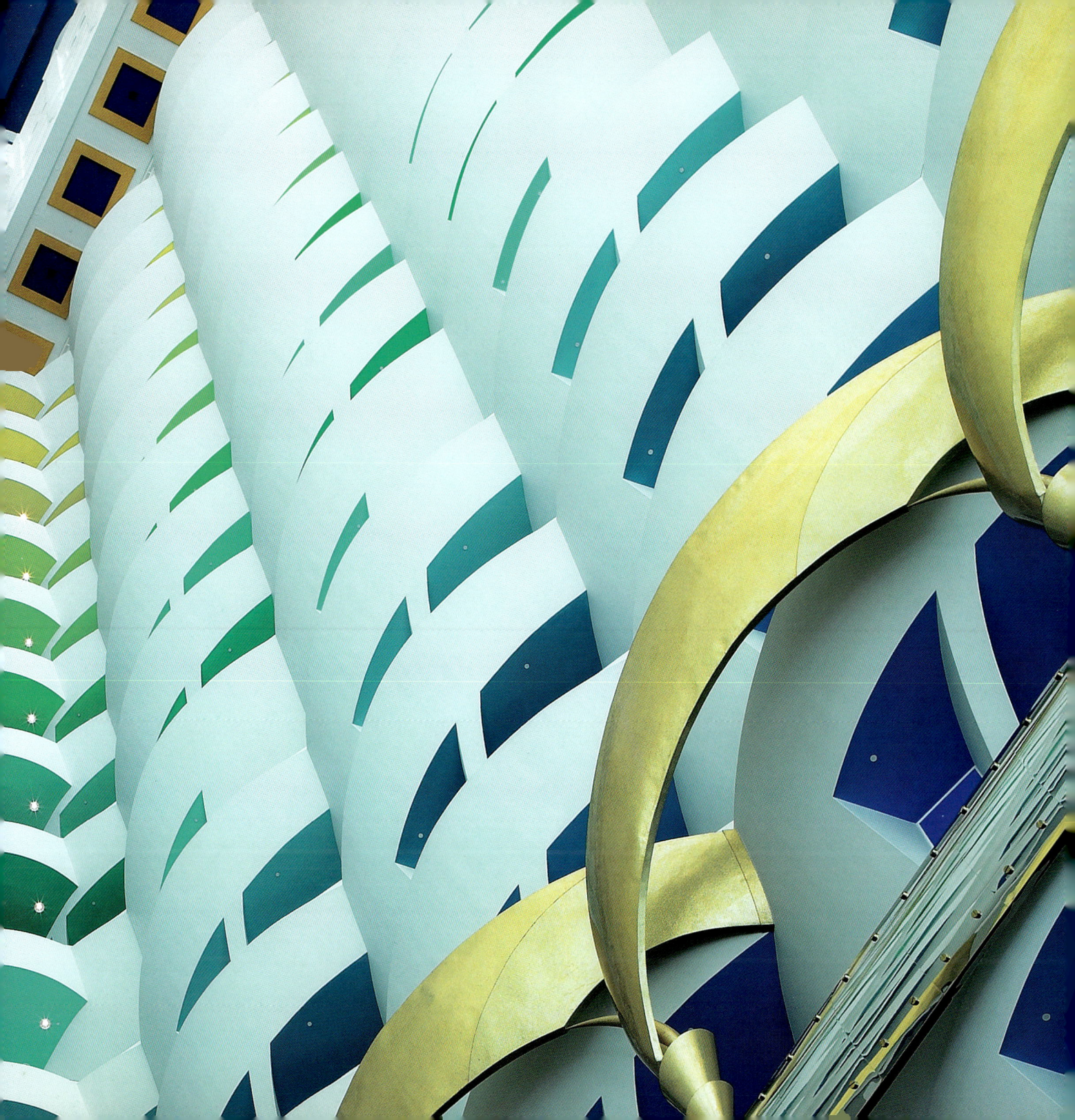

dubai

Legend
✈ Airport
◯ 0–300 m

N

0 km 20 40 80 km

introduction

from bani yas bedouins to masters of the universe

Dubai has been around in some form or other for about 4,000 years, but things didn't really take off until 1833, when the Al Maktoum branch of the powerful Al Bu Falasah clan of the Bani Yas Bedouins moved from Abu Dhabi to Dubai under the leadership of Sheikh Maktoum bin Butti. The strategic location of Dubai, at the crossroads of desert caravan routes and a seaport where trade could flourish, was irresistible. The addition of 800 ambitious new settlers changed the sleepy backwater village forever. In what has become a family pattern, the Al Maktoum aptitude for success showed itself early on.

Sheikh Maktoum bin Butti (ruled 1833–1852) was young, energetic and eager to make his mark. He sent out representatives to woo trading partners in various key markets such as India, Iran and Africa. By offering trade incentives and expanding facilities, he created the ideal of an open port city that forms the basis of Dubai today.

In the next 10 years Dubai was completely transformed. More than 350 new shops opened and the Deira souk became the biggest and busiest retail centre in the region. An influx of Indians, Arabs and Iranians—all keen to make their fortune—brought a lively cosmopolitan mix to the capital that exists today. However, the fledgling trading port's early success was marred by marauding pirates in the Gulf who plundered the richly laden dhows. A series of co-operative treaties were negotiated—cleverly cementing alliances with the British (who were eager to protect the lucrative Indian trade routes of the East India Company)—to form the 'Trucial States' in 1892. Dubai and its neighbouring emirates got the protection of the all-powerful British Navy, and trade progressed as far afield as India, Africa and Iran.

sailing ahead of the competition

However, stiff competition from bigger trading ports was still a problem. In 1894, in a masterstroke of business acumen, Dubai's leaders decided to offer what was a radical concept in the region at the time: tax exemption to traders. As a result, business flocked to Dubai. Trade in gold, silver, textiles, teak, spices, coir and dates helped create a class of prosperous merchants. Another factor in Dubai's growth was the rise of the pearl fishing industry. For hundreds of years the world's finest pearls came from the waters of the Arabian Gulf. As India and England prospered, rich Maharajas and high society matrons sought Dubai's peerless pearls, and business boomed. To meet the demand, wealthy Dubai merchants would bankroll fleets of pearling ships that earned huge revenues. Sadly this all changed in 1929, when Japan invented much cheaper cultured pearls that eventually put Dubai's pearling industry out of business. In response, Dubai resourcefully expanded its role as a trading hub between India, Africa and the Middle East.

THIS PAGE: *Desert Bedouins, in full battle regalia, solemnly enact a traditional war dance, their swords flashing reflected light.*

OPPOSITE: *Camel silhouettes turn hazy in the shimmering heat. The animals are still a large part of life in Dubai, which displays its heritage proudly, despite all its ultramodernity.*

introduction 13

THIS PAGE AND OPPOSITE: Dubai Creek—the wedge that drove open the door to the emirate's staggering economic success. All along the banks, glittering skyscrapers stand testimony to the ambition and drive that made modern Dubai what it is.

The biggest obstacle to becoming the leading port in the region was the fact that Dubai's shallow Creek waterway wasn't deep enough for the massive ships (and consequently, massive profits) that other ports like nearby Sharjah could naturally accommodate. In a daring bid to outmanoeuvre the neighbouring competition, Dubai's formidable Sheikh Rashid bin Saeed (ruled 1958–1990), widely considered to be the founder of modern Dubai, risked all by mortgaging the entire emirate to pay for the huge cost of dredging the Creek. The gamble paid off handsomely, the big ships sailed in, and Dubai never looked back.

In 1966, oil was discovered off the coast of Dubai. The news was greeted with great jubilation and the town erupted with celebrations. Sheikh Rashid, an enlightened ruler who thought of his people first, wisely invested the subsequent oil revenue into creating and reinforcing Dubai's infrastructure, building hospitals, schools, roads and a modern telecommunications network. He ensured Dubai's role as a leading trading hub by building the largest man-made harbour in the world at Jebel Ali. Foreign workers flocked to Dubai to meet the soaring demand for jobs and the population increased dramatically.

In 1968 the British announced their intention to withdraw from the region by 1971. After years of clan rivalries and squabbles over land and water rights, the rulers of the various Gulf emirates came to the realisation that they could accomplish much more by uniting together. Sheikh Rashid and the legendary Sheikh Zayed of Abu Dhabi were greatly in favour of creating a

14 dubaichic

united Arab domain. Their dreams were realised in 1971 when the independent emirates of Dubai, Abu Dhabi, Sharjah, Ajman, Umm Al Quwain, Fujairah and (in 1972) Ras Al Khaimah, came together to create the United Arab Emirates (UAE).

Supported by oil revenue and boundless ambition, the intrepid Sheikh Maktoum bin Rashid (ruled 1990–2006), the son and heir of Sheikh Rashid bin Saeed, pursued the dramatic program of modernisation and economic growth his father had started. Knowing that Dubai's oil reserves were limited, the Sheikh planned for Dubai's future by launching a bold plan of diversification, with tourism at the forefront. In 1998, the opening of Burj Al Arab, hailed as the world's most luxurious new hotel, put Dubai firmly on the map as a chic tourist destination. Today, fuelled by a skyrocketing GDP of $80 billion, Dubai's dynamic ruler, Sheikh Mohammed bin Rashid, continues to set the pace for Dubai's marathon growth that began the day his ancestors arrived.

why dubai does it better

Perched between the sparkling waters of the Arabian Gulf and the champagne-coloured dunes of the desert lies an improbable paradise. Dubai has burst onto the world stage, going from sleepy to sizzling in an incredibly short time. Dubai is a beacon of stability and prosperity in the Middle East, and one of the world's most cosmopolitan cities; 80 per cent of its population is expatriate, with people from more than 200 countries living and working together in the pursuit of excellence.

...a constantly evolving cityscape...

Dubai's residents enjoy an enviable quality of life, with one of the world's highest tax-free per capita incomes. Dubai is impressively clean, safe and civilised. It's sunny all year round, (although quite hot and humid in the summer), the sparkling clear Arabian Gulf and miles of beaches beckon, and there is every amenity, from first-rate sporting facilities to state-of-the-art hospitals and healthcare. Crime is rare (even littering is frowned upon) and business is booming, with trade alone growing nearly 10 per cent a year.

Everywhere you look there are futuristic new record-breaking developments, like the extravagantly ambitious Burj Dubai, the world's tallest building, and Dubailand, the world's biggest entertainment and leisure park. In the next five years an estimated US$30 billion worth of new projects and developments will be built. The downside to Dubai's boom are traffic jams, non-stop construction (an estimated quarter of the world's cranes are in Dubai) and a constantly evolving cityscape that can be confusing. Some residents long for the time when Dubai had more camels than Porsches, but those days are long gone. Dubai's plan to become a leading tourism destination has succeeded beyond its wildest dreams.

chic traveller's paradise

Like the ideal lover, Dubai seduces its visitors with an irresistible desire to please. It's all about you... your pleasure, your satisfaction, and your happiness. No wonder so many fall under its spell. Dubai loves nothing better than to make everyone happy, and for the most part it succeeds brilliantly. Dubai offers luxury and romance, yet also caters for families on a budget. You can find hotels, dining, nightlife and shopping to rival the world's best. Dubai combines an ancient Arabic culture and history with the latest trends. In minutes you can travel from skyscrapers to sand dunes, beach bars to Bedouin tents.

For travellers, this can be both a delight and a dilemma. Dubai is such a magnet for world-class hotels; simply selecting a place to stay becomes a challenge. Will it be a five-star desert oasis retreat like Al Maha, a sleek hotel in the heart of the action downtown like The Fairmont or a luxurious resort by the beach like One&Only Royal Mirage in upmarket Jumeirah? For all-out glamour and prestige, the iconic Burj Al Arab with its 321 m (1,053 ft) of pure unadulterated luxury still retains the top spot, but waiting in the wings are ultra-fashionable new hotels such as the eagerly awaited Armani Hotel in Burj Dubai. If the children are along, what kids' club has the most enticing forms of youth-oriented bribery? The Jumeirah Beach Hotel, with its activity-packed children's programmes and promise of free passes to the wondrous Wild Wadi Water Park, or the charming Ritz-Carlton, with its indulgent Ritz Kids Club. There are many options to choose from, each with its own special cachet.

THIS PAGE: *360° at Jumeirah Beach Hotel is a popular spot for early evening chill-outs with friends and a shisha pipe.*

OPPOSITE: *Dubai is a young city in perpetual motion—cranes are an integral part of the skyline as new developments rapidly shoot up one after the other.*

Dubai has evolved into a sophisticated destination that offers so much more than beautiful beaches and designer duty-free shopping. Dubai's winter season is tightly packed with Gulfstream glitterati off to the Polo, the Dubai Desert Classic, the Dubai Tennis Championships and of course the world's richest horse race, the Dubai World Cup. All year round, there are concerts and performances by world-class entertainers, fashion shows, art exhibitions and gallery openings—all part of Dubai's blossoming arts scene. Nightlife is also booming, with places such as Madinat Souk and Bastakiya Heritage Village attracting Dubai's affluent international set. Dining out is de rigueur. Top restaurants include Verre by Gordon Ramsay at the Hilton Dubai Creek, Gary Rhodes' Mezzanine at Grosvenor House and the Fairmont Hotel's Spectrum on One, while chic watering holes such as 360°, the ever-hip Buddha Bar, sister to the famous Paris nightclub, and Trilogy, Dubai's top disco, draw the city's gilded youth.

THIS PAGE (FROM TOP): *Jockeys astride prized horses leave the gravel flying at the Dubai World Cup; Hollywood megastars Sharon Stone and George Clooney add sparkle to the 4th Annual Dubai International Film Festival.*

OPPOSITE: *Tiger Woods tees off on the first hole of Emirates Golf Club's Majlis course for 2008's Dubai Desert Classic, which he later went on to win, after he spectacularly overcame a four-shot deficit at the very last.*

Dubai has also emerged as a sybaritic spa destination, with those seeking to de-stress and re-balance spoiled for choice among the emirate's many award-winning spas. Try the Rasul Suite in the Retreat Spa at Grosvenor House, the outdoor rain shower in the Amara Spa at Park Hyatt Dubai, Ayurvedic treatments at The Taj Palace Hotel Spa or a genuine Turkish hammam at One&Only Royal Mirage. Indulge in a caviar facial at Burj Al Arab's luxurious Assawan Spa, or get energised with crystal therapies and yoga by moonlight at Talise. Men have their own spas as well, with H_2O at Emirates Towers, a favourite for jet-lag massages for its high-flying clients. In Dubai, everything from yoga retreats to the perfect pedicure is available. Health and beauty treatments are among the best anywhere.

Shopping in Dubai is the ultimate in retail therapy: imagine a tax-free blend of Bond Street, Knightsbridge, the Rue de La Paix and Fifth Avenue. From mega malls to super souks, the selection is staggering. If you can't buy it in Dubai, it probably doesn't exist.

There must be a genie out of a bottle somewhere making Dubai's dreams come true. Does its visionary ruler, His Highness Sheikh Mohammed bin Rashid Al Maktoum, rub a magic lamp so that fairytale skyscrapers leap up seemingly overnight, and palaces rise majestically out of the sea? Dubai is an almost surreal experience. Like a fable from the *Arabian Nights*, her kaleidoscopic mix of experiences is an exhilarating adrenaline rush to the senses. But the bewitching Scheherazade, with all her storytelling powers, never dreamed up a place quite like Dubai. The creative energy powering Dubai into the 21st century is a kind of modern magic. The city is on fast-forward—blink and you'll miss it.

...Dubai's winter season is tightly packed with Gulfstream glitterati...

gourmet safari

Dining out in Dubai is like going on a gastronomic world tour. Every cuisine you can think of is available, thanks to the 200 nationalities so far who are expatriates here. So whether you crave Mexican tortillas or sushi, you're sure to find it here. Dining out is a way of life in Dubai, and there is a great deal of competition between restaurants. You'll find attentive service and good quality, whether you're at a souk café or a five-star hotel. Many of Dubai's restaurants are located in hotels so as to maintain a full wine and beverage list without running afoul of strict licensing laws, but don't miss out on some fabulous cooking just for the sake of a glass of wine. Take the time to explore beyond your hotel and you'll be very glad you made the effort.

Arabic cuisines are known for its diversity, with Lebanese food by far the most popular of them. Favourite Arabic restaurants in Dubai include the elegant **Al Nafoorah** at Jumeirah Emirates Towers, colourful **Al Qasr** at Dubai Marine Beach Resort, famous for its Thursday night mezzes and bellydancing, and the atmospheric **Bastakiah Nights**, with its flickering torches and antique furnishings. For a feast in the desert head for **Al Hadheerah** at Jumeirah Bab Al Shams Desert Resort & Spa. It's wonderfully kitsch, with live entertainment in the form of belly dancers, singers, camels, magicians—all manner of *Arabian Nights* characters—and featuring regional specialities, prepared before your very eyes in the open cooking stations. For Moroccan specialities, Marrakech at Shangri-La Hotel, Dubai is famous for its cous cous and live music, **Shoo Fee Ma Fee** in Madinat

Souk has an extensive selection of regional dishes and romantic views of the Jumeirah coastline from its rooftop terrace, while the popular **Almaz** by Momo, at Harvey Nichols in the Mall of the Emirates, is the chic offshoot of the London Momo. Sadly, if you're on the lookout for genuine Emirati or Bedouin dishes there is not very much on offer, but a good choice is **Local House** in Bastakiya, a simple but authentic restaurant where you can sit, Arabian-style, on cushions placed on the floor, while eating dishes like baked lamb with spices, from a central platter.

THIS PAGE (CLOCKWISE FROM BOTTOM): *Rhodes Mezzanine at Grosvenor House is a showcase of Gary Rhodes' cuisine; Marrakech at The Shangri-La Hotel is a premier name in Moroccan food; Vu's offers fine dining downtown.*
OPPOSITE (FROM TOP): *In Dubai, you'll find no end of novel dining experiences; Burj Al Arab's Al Mahara stuns guests with its magnificent aquarium.*

The Indian food to be found in Dubai is exceptionally good. Dubai's large Indian population means that everything from Keralan fish curries to Rajasthani tandoori is available. Top spots for Indian cuisine include Michelin-starred Indian chef Vineet Bhatia's elegant **Indego** restaurant at Grosvenor House, **Sakonis** in Karama for tasty southern Indian vegetarian at bargain prices, and the exclusive **Ashiana** at the Sheraton Dubai Creek, for Rajasthani cuisine in a colonial setting. **Khazana** in Oud Metha at Al Nasr Leisureland has a loyal following who come for India's top celebrity chef Sanjeev Kapoor's inspired recipes, such as the 'British Raj Railway Curry' while the biryanis at **Handi** in The Taj Palace Hotel in Deira are perennial favourites. If you're out and about shopping in the souks of Bur Dubai, head straight for **India House** on Al Fahidi Street for their famous thali platters.

Italian cuisine is loved all over the world and Dubai is no exception. Two superb Italian restaurants are **BiCE Restaurant** in Hilton Dubai

gourmet*safari* 21

gourmet safari

Jumeirah or **Certo**, a trendy newcomer getting top reviews, in the Radisson SAS Hotel, Dubai Media City.

Oriental cuisines are increasingly popular in Dubai. For the best Chinese dim sum, the trendy **China Club** at Radisson SAS Hotel, Deira Creek gets top marks for style and substance, while **Zheng He's** at Mina A' Salam in Madinat Jumeirah is known for the beauty of its interior and faultless cooking, winning *TimeOut Dubai*'s 'Chinese Restaurant of the Year' in 2007. The elegant **Shang Palace** at Shangri-La Hotel, Dubai is famous for its delectable Beijing Duck.

For Japanese sushi (Dubaians are deep in a sushi phase at the moment) and other specialities, try **Tokyo** at Jumeirah Emirates Towers, **Kiku** at Le Royal Méridien Dubai or **Miyako** at the Hyatt Regency Dubai, while at The Fairmont's **Café Sushi**, the selections—the super-fresh salmon, tuna and snapper sashimi (raw fish slices) are good bets—whiz past on a conveyor belt that makes its way enticingly past customers seated around the entire restaurant. For quick bite while out and about, **Sumo Sushi** (various branches) is a popular choice.

Chic newcomer **Nineteen** at The Montgomerie is getting rave reviews for its delectable Thai-French fusion cuisine. Other top Thai restaurants include the exquisite new **Thiptara** at Sofitel's The Palace – The Old Town, on Old Town Island just beneath the soaring tower of Burj Dubai, **The Blue Elephant** at Al Bustan Rotana Hotel and the exotic **Sukothai** at Le Royal Méridien Dubai. **The Noodle House**, in various locations, is Dubai's most popular place to stop by for delicious Asian fast food. Dubai's ruler, Sheikh Mohammed, is a big fan and pops in unannounced for a quick bite.

There's currently a series of what are affectionately dubbed 'Steak Wars' being waged for the hearts and fat wallets of Dubai's carnivorous crowd. There are currently about 30 soi disant steakhouses in town. The current batch of frontrunners include **The Exchange Grill** at The Fairmont, Argentinean **La Parrilla** at Jumeirah Beach Hotel, **Legends Steakhouse**, at Dubai Creek Golf & Yacht Club and **Manhattan Grill** at Grand Hyatt Dubai.

Vegetarians have a challenging time finding a full menu for their needs in Dubai unless they eat Italian or South Indian. An exception to this rule of thumb is **Magnolia**, a light and airy restaurant that caters beautifully for vegetarians. It serves sophisticated, healthy, spa-style cuisine in a secluded garden setting on the edge of the canal in Madinat Jumeirah.

Dubai's love of the dramatic and theatrical extends to dining out and there are some remarkable restaurants where the setting can be said to steal the show. **Al Mahara** at Burj Al Arab welcomes guests with a simulated submarine ride to its surreal interior where a giant floor-to-ceiling indoor aquarium, teeming with exotic fish—and even small sharks—provides the mise en scène to beautifully prepared seafood dishes. **Vu's** at the Jumeirah Emirates Towers lives up to its name by giving diners dazzling wraparound views of Dubai, while **Fire & Ice** at the new Raffles Dubai is a theatrical extravaganza, where even the food comes with special effects. **Pierchic** at Madinat Jumeirah serves award-winning seafood in a spectacular location at the end of its own pier, with panoramic views out over the Gulf and taking in Burj Al Arab. For a romantic evening for two, take a dinner cruise along Dubai Creek. Dining onboard **Bateaux Dubai** lets you enjoy Mediterranean specialties while cruising in style past Dubai's dazzling cityscape.

In terms of gourmet cuisine, Dubai just keeps getting better and better. Gordon Ramsay's award-winning **Verre**, at the Hilton Dubai Creek serves outstanding French classics accompanied by one of the best wine lists in the city.

Another top British chef with Michelin-star cred, Gary Rhodes, has launched the **Rhodes Mezzanine** at Grosvenor House, a sleek, all-white restaurant showcasing his signature style of modern British cuisine. At The Ritz-Carlton, the intimate **La Baie** is perfect for formal dining a deux. You can even go gourmet while shopping. Just pop into **Caviar House & Prunier** at Madinat Souk for their extravagant Beluga Blinis.

Don't miss going out for Friday Brunch. The latest foodie trend to hit Dubai has restaurants battling for the best brunch action. Expect anything from casual all-you-can-eat buffets to sumptuous sit-down feasts with live entertainment. Current hot spots to tuck into are **The Champagne Brunch** at Spectrum on One at The Fairmont, an elegant affair where you can sip on Moët while sampling a variety of world cuisines served from different cooking stations, followed by Madinat Jumeirah's **Al Qasr**, not to mention the ever-popular **Shangri-La**. If you want to go a bit further off the tourist trail, **Spikes** restaurant at the fashionable Nad Al Sheba Club & Racecourse is a local hot spot.

In Dubai, café society is all the rage—which doesn't mean just going to the nearest Starbucks for an iced latte. Dubai's social butterflies flit to the following coffee houses and cafés to exchange the latest gossip while checking out each other's designer wardrobes. **More**, at Al Mooraj Rotana Hotel just by Burj Dubai, is an arty addition to the café scene and earns top marks from locals for its salads and freshly baked breads. Franchise **Second Cup**, found in many of the main shopping malls, hails from Canada but has taken off in Dubai, thanks to serving the best lattes and cappuccinos in town.

On Jumeirah Beach Road, you'll find **Fudo**, a funky hangout full of beautiful people eating cutting-edge, creative cuisine served in a villa by the Mercato Mall, and **The Lime Tree Café**, the unofficial headquarters for expat high-society yummy mummies nicknamed 'Jumeirah Janes'.

In between intense retail runs, fashionista shoppers at the Mall of the Emirates love to stop by at the **Armani Caffé**, or spend some time chilling out in **Japengo**, a cool café with an Oriental twist. Also worth checking out are the many fresh juice and smoothie bars where you can choose from a mouthwatering array of exotic fruits, like guavas and mangosteens. Wherever you go in Dubai, a good meal isn't far. You can eat melt-in-your-mouth Shawarma wraps from a street vendor, or dine like a sheikh in a palace.

THIS PAGE (FROM TOP): *Fire & Ice at the new Raffles Dubai is the latest hot restaurant to hit this vibrant scene; Thiptara at Sofitel's The Palace – The Old Town serves up piquant Thai.*

OPPOSITE: *Pierchic sits at the end of its very own private jetty, taking in the great views of the Arabian Gulf and Burj Al Arab from its vantage point.*

gourmetsafari 23

arabian nights

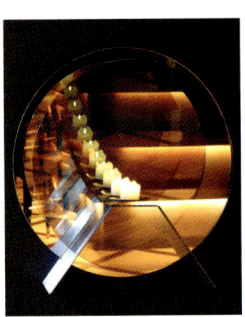

THIS PAGE (FROM TOP): Terrace Bar at Park Hyatt Dubai has an enviable view; The Apartment at Jumeirah Beach Hotel is done up with subtle hints of Moroccan-accented interior style; a flickering candle is reflected into a replicating multitude by a mirror.

OPPOSITE: Buddha Bar at the up-and-coming area of Dubai Marina is a opulent shrine to exotic Chinoiserie; the Buddha Bar menu reflects the club's modern Far East aesthetic.

In the last few years Dubai's nightlife has exploded on to the scene, with a dazzling selection of places to party. The weekend starts Thursday night, when the city's many clubs and bars begin to buzz. Start your evening off well with an al fresco sundowner at one of Dubai's many sea-view rooftop lounges such as **Shoo Fee Ma Fee** in Madinat Souk, the **Rooftop Lounge** at One&Only Royal Mirage, the **Barasti** bar at Le Royal Méridien or **360°** at Jumeirah Beach Hotel. If you happen to be Creekside, head straight for the **Terrace Bar** at Park Hyatt Dubai; or if you're downtown, try Shangri-La Hotel, Dubai's stunning outdoor pool bar.

Crossroads, at the newly opened Raffles Dubai, has a dramatic Balinese-style interior which opens out onto an outdoor terrace, and boasts an impressive array of special cocktails including the Dubai Sling, inspired by Raffles' legendary Singapore Sling. The breathtaking (and appropriately named) **Vista** bar at the swish new InterContinental Dubai Festival City makes the most out of its Creekside setting, with a view terrace outside overlooking the yachts at the marina and the everchanging downtown Dubai skyline. Other great bars for stupendous views of Dubai are at Burj Al Arab's retro-chic **Skyview Bar**, **Vu's** at Emirates Towers and **Bar 44** at the top of Grosvenor House.

The moment the sun sinks out of sight, and the first cocktail slips down thirsty throats, Dubai comes alive. Up until recently the biggest drawback of nightlife in Dubai was the distance between venues. If you wanted to try a few different places in an evening it meant plunging into Dubai's non-stop traffic just to get to the next hot spot. Happily, however, this has changed with the launch of Madinat Jumeirah. Now it is possible to have a big night out within a short stroll. This Arabian-themed souk is a favourite watering hole for both locals and visitors.

Dubai's atmosphere at night is—in a word—magical. The moon sails over the traditonal wind towers of Mina A' Salam and shines on the sea, as people pop in and out of the many restaurants, clubs and bars. Some of the best spots include **Trader Vic's**, a Polynesian-style bar and restaurant where Tiki isn't tacky and where you'll always find a crowd of Dubai's bright young things sipping brightly coloured super-sized tropical cocktails. Nearby is **The Agency**, a sleek, sophisticated wine bar where you can sample a range of serious vintages and enjoy nibbles. Another stellar choice for drinks is **BarZar**, a popular cocktail bar with a modernist interior spread over two floors, that attracts a young and trendy crowd. If you have a fondness for jazz, be sure to check out **Jam Base**, Dubai's top jazz club, where live acts perform nightly. **Left Bank** has a hip following, with lots of young fashion and media types, who come for the stylish interiors and chance to pose. **The Madinat Theatre** often has live performances of top bands or comics, make sure and check with your hotel concierge to see what's on the agenda. If you're feeling in the mood to dance the night away, look no further than **Trilogy**. Considered Dubai's leading disco, there are three floors of non-stop action as top DJ's create a party vibe that has everyone on their feet until the wee small hours.

Dubai's clubs are hassle-free and offer everything from the latest DJs to live jazz. The beats of Arabic pop are big on the dance floor and dressing up is de rigueur. Jeans and trainers won't get you past the velvet rope, and forget the shorts, even if it is hot. Unlike the drug-fuelled raves in other cities, Dubai's party scene is clean, and drunken behaviour is considered bad form Popular Dubai clubs include the **Peppermint Club** at Habtoor Grand Hotel, the exotic Moroccan **Kasbar** at the One&Only Royal Mirage, and the recently revamped, always jam-packed **Zinc** at the Crowne Plaza Hotel.

In Dubai, many nightclubs also serve food. One of the best is the stunningly beautiful **Buddha Bar** at Grosvenor House. If you only get to one club when you're in Dubai, let this be it. The dramatic Oriental interior, presided over by a massive bronze Buddha beaming down at the crowd, is a riot of colour and texture. There are intimate nooks to lounge in, huge crystal chandeliers, floor-to-ceiling windows overlooking the water and Dubai's gilded youth at their designer-clad best. Even the waiters look like models as they go around serving delicious Asian fusion cuisine from dim sum to sushi. Celebrities from Bollywood superstars to famous footballers can often be spotted in VIP splendour surrounded by minders and chilled bottles of Cristal.

At Dubai Marine Beach Club in Jumeirah, there are currently two hot spots; **Boudoir**, a sizzling late-night Parisian restaurant and club with dancing after 11.00 pm, which attracts a glamorous group who come for the opulent interiors and the music—which can be anything from R&B to Latino—and **Sho Cho**, a sushi bar with a fabulous outdoor terrace overlooking the marina, that also doubles as a nightclub for Dubai's fashionable set. Nearby at Jumeirah Beach Hotel, **The Apartment** is a French restaurant and bar done up in Moroccan style with house DJs that create a chilled-out vibe. Downtown, **Lotus One**, with its chrome, glass and wood interiors, chairs hanging from the ceiling and buzzing atmosphere is fun for drinks. Further afield at Al Nasr Leisureland in Oud Metha, **Chi** at The Lodge is a brilliantly designed club with four huge, lavishly appointed rooms (each has a different style) that has a hip, young following who come for the exciting live bands and top DJs. The neon-bright **Submarine Bar** at the Dhow Palace Hotel is a hot new club for late-night dancing, with live bands playing well after midnight and a pop art interior with a sliding roof that rolls back for dancing under the stars. For a complete contrast to Dubai's sophisticated night spots, stop by the **Rock Bottom Café**, at the Regent Hotel in Bur Dubai, where you'll find garage rock bands playing old Led Zeppelin hits to a party-on crowd. The bar's lethal Bullfrog cocktail is a Dubai rite of passage. For a late-night snack to fill up after all that clubbing, try the mouthwatering Shawarma wraps at various **Saj Express** outlets.

There is so much going on here at night that you're sure to have an exciting evening. Or just forget the bright lights and go for a moonlit stroll on the beach. Like a mirage rising from the desert sand, Dubai promises an oasis of pleasure.

arabian nights

shopping mecca

Dubai has come a long way since the days when the airport duty free was the height of retail sophistication. With its cosmopolitan population, high per capita income and love of luxury, Dubai has very quickly evolved into one of the world's most exciting shopping destinations.

From Armani to Zegna, Dubai has it all. Shopping is as natural to a Dubaian as breathing so if you like to shop, you've come to the right place. And even if you hate it, somehow Dubai's glittering emporiums and seductive souks has you buying on impulse. In Dubai, if you mention that you are desperate to find a certain pair of designer stilettos that you saw in *Vogue* a month ago, or that 'must have' mobile phone, no one laughs—they join your quest. In Dubai no retail request is too obscure or too extravagant. After all, this is a nation built by traders. They don't call it 'Do Buy' for nothing, so come with an empty suitcase and a full wallet.

If the thought of shopping malls seems rather dull and pedestrian, rest assured—in Dubai, the malls are state-of-the-art lifestyle centres that are an integral part of the scene. In Dubai, malls are a way of life, not just a place to buy things. So you'll find great restaurants, cafes, a variety of entertainment, exhibitions—all sorts of diversions—along with a brilliant array of shops.

The **Mall of the Emirates** just off Sheikh Zayed Road is the mother of all malls, home to **Harvey Nichols** and designer-filled **Via Rodeo**, and 400 other shops that sell everything under the sun from designer brands to teen fashion, furniture, electronics, accessories, jewellery, shoes, bags, toys, books—you name it! With its stores grouped in themed precincts and the two levels of the mall interconnected by a vast network of escalators and travelators, shopping is made easy. If you want to stay near the shops there is the five-star Kempinski Hotel. You'll also find **Magic Planet**, an indoor amusement arcade, **Ski Dubai**, a mini-ski resort with real snow, runs and a chairlift, a 14-screen cinemaplex, and more than 50 places to eat and hang out while your cash vanishes. For a complete set of store listings, visit www.malloftheemirates.com .

Ever since its expensive new makeover, **Wafi City Mall**, the elegant, Egyptian-themed mall by the Creek off Sheikh Rashid Road has become an upmarket favourite, with excellent cafes and restaurants, galleries and superb shops. Spend a day investing in a whole new wardrobe. Wafi's shops include the classic luxury of **Chanel** and **Escada**, the chic lines of **Nicole Farhi**, the glamour of **Versace**, and trendsetting new designers at cutting edge boutiques such as **Ginger & Lace**, **Tiger Lily**, **Etoile**, and **Desert Rose**—as well as popular UK high street brands such as **Monsoon** and **Topshop**. There's also the new souk style Khan Murjan wing, which features Arabian products, and the first Raffles Hotel out of Singapore, Raffles Dubai. The entire Wafi complex is a Dubai institution that just keeps getting better.

BurJuman Centre on Trade Centre Road, near the Dubai Creek on its Bur Dubai side, is excellent for fashion, cosmetics, perfume and footwear. America's **Saks 5th Avenue** leads the way, and there are designer boutiques such as **Louis Vuitton**, **Prada**, **DKNY**, **Ralph Lauren**, **Hermès**, **D&G**, **Just Cavalli** and **Cartier** adding their own brand of glamour.

Boulevard at Jumeirah Emirates Towers is small but beautiful, with only the best designers. The shopping Boulevard links the Emirates Hotel and Office towers, and is mapped out over two floors. As befits the location, this is a place for some serious, smart shopping. Designer-label boutiques include **Gucci**, **Giorgio Armani**, **Yves Saint Laurent**, **Jimmy Choo** and jewellers such as **Bulgari**, and **Cartier**. After all that shopping, rest your feet with an iced tea or something stronger at **The Agency**.

Exotic and only a short hop from Jumeirah on Sheikh Zayed Road near Interchange 6 is **Ibn Battuta Mall**, a wonderfully artistic shopping and entertainment complex is divided into six themed zones based on the countries visited by the legendary 14th-century Arabian explorer. It's worth a visit just to see the full-sized Chinese Junk and Al Jazar's Elephant Clock. Visit the opulent **India Court** for fashion, **Persia Court** for lifestyle shops, **China Court** for entertainment and food, and **Egypt Court** for sporty items. **Tunisia Court** has a **Fun City** arcade for the kids while **Andalusia Court** has more everyday shops and services such as drycleaners and DVD rentals. The mall is home to the 21-screen **Grand Cinema Megaplex**. This the largest cinema complex in the Middle East and also features an IMAX screen for specially formatted films. For a complete listing of shops and services, visit www.ibnbattutamall.com .

THIS PAGE (FROM TOP): *Emirati women spend an afternoon shopping at the Mall of the Emirates in Jumeirah; Five Green is Dubai's most cutting-edge concept store and a breath of fresh air from all the megamalls.*
OPPOSITE: *The curved glass dome of the roof of the Mall of the Emirates.*

shopping mecca

THIS PAGE (FROM TOP): *Via Rodeo at the Mall of the Emirates is a collection of high-end designer boutiques; jewellery is a big deal in Dubai, and jewellers do a roaring trade here; colourful scarves flutter in the wind.*

OPPOSITE (FROM TOP): *A wide range of traditional Arabic wares are found at shops such as Arabian Treasures; Global Village is a showcase of food and fashion from all over the world.*

Mercato Mall on Jumeirah Beach Road is a favourite for Jumeirah's upscale residents who pop in to the airy, Renaissance Italianate-style mall for the latest CDs at **Virgin Megastore**, **Topshop** top-ups and **Armani** must haves. A good boutique for swimsuits and resort wear is **Beyond the Beach**. If you're shopping for gifts, **Pride of Kashmir** has a superb selection of pretty pashminas and interesting Indian objets d'art. For a bite to eat between shops, try the coffee and Parisian patisserie at **PAUL**, or salad and a sandwich at the popular **Fiesta Café**. Mercato Mall is smaller and easier to navigate than the rest of the mega-malls, which makes it a good choice if you don't want to do an all day shop-a-thon. For details, visit www.mercatoshoppingmall.com.

Dubai Outlet Mall on Al Ain Road in Dubailand is off the beaten path, but can't be beat for bargains on a wide range of fashions, from high-street staples to designer frocks, celebrated perfumes and one-off gems for a fraction of the usual prices. The selection changes frequently so visit www.dubaioutletmall.com for all the latest details.

Dubai Festival City, the latest retail extravaganza in Dubai, has just opened and is already getting rave reviews for its range of shops and wide variety of chic places to 'see and be seen' including the stunning new InterContinental Dubai. When it is complete, the retail resort will have 600 shops, as well as many new speciality boutiques and international brand names. There will be over 100 international restaurants, bistros and cafés throughout the resort including 40 al fresco dining venues along the scenic waterfront. Although still under construction, new stores are opening all the time. For details visit www.dubaifestivalcity.com.

In terms of speciality shopping, **Fab India** in Bur Dubai is as good as a trip to Delhi for trendy Indian kurtas, linens, and colourful fabrics. **Boom & Mellow** at the **Mall of the Emirates** is the place for accessories. **Five Green** is currently Dubai's most cutting edge 'concept store' and a must stop for fashionable trendsetters. It combines a gallery, club, and shop within its minimalist, light-filled space, with floor-to-ceiling windows, frosted glass room dividers, and poured concrete flooring. There are CDs, edgy style magazines, quirky art objects and a stunning selection of clothes by such hot local designers such as **Manabu Ozawaand**, **Pink Sushi**, **Shirtaholics Anonymous**, and **Saadia Zahid**.

Ginger & Lace, **Etoile**, **La Boutique**, **Luxecouture**, and **S*uce** are among the leading boutiques bringing exciting young talent, established designers and a fresh hip vibe to Dubai's fashion scene. In a city where you are what you wear, the clothing competition among Dubai's socialite set can be intense. These are the shops that make all the difference to the men and women whose perfectly groomed, glossy faces smile out from the pages of *Ahlan!* and *Society Dubai*.

Jewellery is a top status item here, and there's a great range to choose from, including top names such as **DeBeers**, **Graff**, **Cartier** and **Tiffany's**— all at duty-free prices. **Damas** has affordable jewellery and a wide range of designs, including Indian sets that will make you feel like a Bollywood princess. If you are put off by the crowds at the Gold Souk, try the **Gold & Diamond Park** on Sheikh Zayed Road—it's air-conditioned and there are 90 retailers selling gold, precious gems and the latest collections.

An impressive range of Islamic arts and textiles (pricey but lovely Kashmiri shawls) are displayed at **Miraj Islamic Art Gallery** in Jumeirah.

For exotic Arabic perfumes in stunning bottles that make excellent gifts, visit **Arabian Oud** and **Ajmal Perfumes**. Ajmal Perfumes has its main showroom at Deira City Centre on Al Garhoud Road, while Arabian Oud has various outlets in malls around Dubai, including Wafi City Mall and BurJuman Centre.

For a superb selection of books on Dubai and the UAE, **Magrudy's** (in various locations) is the top bookshop in town, while **Arabian Treasures** at Deira City Centre offers a selection of Arabian wares, showcasing everything from traditional coffee carafes to ceremonial daggers. For Arabic dates and sweets **Bateel** (various locations) and **Wafi Gourmet** (Wafi City) has the best selection of regional goodies to take home and enjoy.

Dubai loves shiny new things: skyscrapers, Ferraris, Rolex watches and hot new gadgets. So if you're looking for the latest laptop, iPod incarnation or mobile phone check out **Al Ain Mall** in Bur Dubai, and **CompuMe** and **Plug-Ins** (both have outlets at various places in the city) for hi-tech at low prices. **CompuMe** has its main showroom at Zalfa Building on Al Garhoud Road, while **Plug-Ins**' newest outlet is off Al Rebat Road as part of Dubai Festival City. For good deals on electronics such as digital cameras, it's well worth a stroll along **Al Fahidi Street** in Bur Dubai.

The **Dubai Shopping Festival** in January is when knock-down bargains and events attract fashionistas from around the world. Don't miss **Global Village** in Dubailand on Emirates Road, a showcase for food and fashion from exotic locations. If you don't mind the heat, **Dubai Summer Surprises** runs from June to September. For details on Dubai's various shopping events, visit www.mydsf.ae . Whatever you're looking for, if you can't find it in Dubai, it probably doesn't exist.

in the souk

Souks are traditional markets with a genuine flavour of Arabia where the prices are significantly lower than at the malls and the atmosphere more local. Quoted prices are almost always negotiable so make sure and bargain. Cash is king so don't expect traders to take credit cards. Take note that most of the stalls will be closed in the sleepy afternoon hours from just past noon to about 5.00 pm, and then proceed to stay open throughout the whole evening well past dinner.

Dubai has a number of wonderful souks where you can wander around and soak up the atmosphere and find something special to take home after your holiday. Traditionally Deira and Bur Dubai are the areas where the souks are, but a new wave of modern souks based on the traditional Arab concept have recently been launched with great success.

The **Spice Souk** is fun and exotic, a real treat for visitors eager for a look at Old Dubai. In constant use for more than a century, it gives a real feeling of how marketing used to be done in Dubai before the superstores moved it. The scents, colours and characters are redolent of Arabia. Nuts, dried fruits, sweets and of course spices are all good buys. With the supermarkets beginning to take over, the souk is one of the few places in Dubai where you can still find such rare and exotic spices as frankincense and myrrh; fragrant handfuls of pink and red dried rosebuds, bundles of cinnamon bark, the prized vanilla pods from Madagascar, saffron from Kashmir, star anise and cardamom from Kerala—all overflowing from sacks, boxes and ornate containers.

At the **Perfume Souk** you can literally follow your nose to find just the right scent for you. At almost any of the stalls, the shopkeeper will happily make up a blend according to your tastes using his many aromatic essential oils. Arabic perfumes, called attar, are stronger than the lighter floral-based perfumes in the West. Typically oil-based, (watch that they don't stain your clothes) they last longer and are equally popular for both men and women. There are also many European perfumes for sale as well, and prices are lower than in the department stores. Many of the perfume shops in the souk also sell Arabian incense, called oud, which can come in the form of compressed powder, crystal, rock or scented wood. Frankincense is probably the most common type of incense.

You'll find stunning fabrics from around the world at shops such as **Meena Bazaar** and **Rivoli** in Bur Dubai's **Textile Souk**. The skillful tailors here can whip up beautiful bespoke outfits in a few days — bring something you want copied or a good picture of a design you'd like tailored to your exact measurements. **Deepak**'s fabric store in Satwa is a hot favorite with expats. **Dream Girl**, **Lobo Tailors** and **Kachins Tailors** are good choices for expert tailor-made clothes.

It may look slightly seedy, and it's more modern in form than a traditional souk, but as any seasoned Dubai bargain hunter will tell you, the tightly packed alleyway of shops at the **Karama Complex** can't be beat for its array of knock-off designer watches, sunglasses, handbags, shoes and clothes. The good stuff is usually

THIS PAGE (CLOCKWISE FROM TOP): *A row of perfume bottles sparkles in the souk; a stack of colourful fabrics in the sun; exotic spices are piled high at a stall.*

OPPOSITE: *Souks have an authentic local flavour that is worlds apart from that of gleaming megamalls.*

inthesouk 31

in the souk

THIS PAGE (FROM TOP): *A shop sells richly woven carpets and colourful lamps; the glitter of Dubai's famous Gold Souk is a lure for bargain hunters .*
OPPOSITE: *Madinat Souk is a modern souk selling traditional Arabic wares.*

kept tucked away, so don't worry if you are escorted into a store room as it will inevitably turn into a treasure trove of faux Fendi, Tods, Chanel, Chloe, Prada and more. The quality is usually excellent, but give the goods a subtle once-over before forking over the cash. If there is a specific model you want and you don't see it make a request—chances are that it will somehow materialise, genie-like. In Karama you'll also find knock-offs of Rock & Republic and Seven for All Mankind jeans (very popular and impossible to tell from the real thing). Hidden gem Sana Fashion is great for brand name clothes at laugh-out-loud prices for men, women and children.

You'll also find Arabic kitsch like Mosque alarm clocks and battery-operated dancing camels. **Gift Tent** has great souvenirs for a fraction of your hotel's gift shop, and a rainbow assortment of pashminas. Shopping in Karama is hot, crowded and tiring, but if you're a true retail warrior, it's a great Dubai tradition. Never admit you're a tourist. Haggling is the order of the day, and a smile does wonders when you're hoping for extra discount. Go soon before the government finally cracks down on the most fab fakes you'll ever see.

Dubai's most famous souk—the **Gold Souk**—is a 24-carat Aladdin's Cave where all that glitters is the real thing. Dubai is the worlds leading re-exporter of gold and prices are set by weight. That said, you can negotiate per piece depending on how much workmanship is involved—simpler pieces should always be cheaper. One of the special things about the Gold Souk is that you can get jewellery made up to your own design here. Craftsmen are on site and can create a unique piece usually in 24 hours or less. They can alter the composition of alloys in the gold to create pink, white, yellow or green hues in one piece, as well combine the gold with silver, platinum, precious and semi-precious gems or pearls. It's best to visit in the evening when it is cooler.

Madinat Souk, the charming shopping enclave by the popular Madinat Jumeirah resort is done up like a traditional bazaar, but much more glamorous. Meander along its pathways to find gifts and clothes from all over the Middle East and India, with a great atmospheric buzz and fascinating people watching. It is just as popular with Dubai locals as tourists. The emphasis is on specialist boutiques and the souk is excellent for art, carpets and crafts. There are lots of places to eat and drink as well, making this one of Dubai's most enjoyable shopping experiences.

The stunning new **Khan Murjan** souk at Wafi City is an authentic re-creation of a 14th century souk. Khan Murjan is an historical and cultural haven for craftspeople. More than 150 stalls exhibit traditional arts and crafts. Visitors can watch as talented artisans blow glassware, weave rugs, make pottery and more. With an area of 4,650 sq m (50,000 sq ft), the Khan Murjan project includes shops, cafés and restaurants all within the two-level subterranean souk.

Souk Al Bahar is a new waterside shopping and entertainment complex on Old Town Island, in Downtown Burj Dubai, part of the 'New Dubai' being developed around the spectacular Burj Dubai tower. A charming blend of traditional architecture set within a modern context, Souk Al Bahar has over 100 shops, with trendsetting new shops such as **50°C** (by the same people who started Dubai's hip lifestyle shop, Five Green), and fashionable designer **Roccobarocco** alongside shops selling traditional Arabic furniture and art, as well as excellent carpet galleries such as **Pride of Kashmir**, **National Iranian Carpet** and **Emad Carpets**. With views of the iconic Burj Dubai tower, and a wide array of waterfront restaurants, stylish bars and cafés set along the scenic promenade, Souk Al Bahar is a delightful new addition to Dubai's leisure and shopping scene.

oasis of culture

Not long ago Dubai was considered a cultural as well as physical desert. But with its phenomenal growth, Dubai is now attracting creative talent from across the Arab world, India and Turkey, making this an exciting time for emerging artists. Political and economic problems in other Middle Eastern countries have resulted in artists seeking refuge in Dubai's creative atmosphere and booming economy. Fuelled by the vast amounts of money flowing into Dubai, its blossoming arts movement shows no sign of a slowdown.

In addition, visitors are becoming more sophisticated. More people are looking for a cultural experience as much as a holiday. Dubai has some excellent galleries, small museums and heritage areas. **Bastakiya**, on the Creek in Bur Dubai, is one of Dubai's only pedestrian areas devoted to culture and tradition; a place where 100-year-old wind towers rise above galleries showing the latest modern art. Along its winding, cobbled streets and alleyways you'll find fascinating artisan studios and galleries.

One of the best of these is **XVA**, a pioneering gallery at the epicentre of the Dubai arts movement. XVA is considered unique because it is a gathering place where artists from the Middle East and beyond meet, sleep, work and exhibit. It has been hugely influential, a hotbed of ideas and inspiration, with various exciting exhibitions. Along with the gallery, there is a delightful courtyard café as well as a shop and a boutique hotel.

Nearby, in a restored wind tower, **Majlis** is a charming, well-established gallery that helped put Bastakiya on the map. It features a collection of fine art, pottery, glass and unusual souvenirs such as art postcards.

In Jumeirah, the recently opened **Meem Gallery** has already earned a reputation as having some of the finest examples of Arabic calligraphy in the region, from modern masters such as Iraq's Taha Al-Hiti to rare masterpieces of ancient Islamic art. The gallery has major exhibitions of the world's leading contemporary Arabic artists, such as Ali Omar Ermes, whose work is collected by museums such as the Tate Modern in London.

Also in Jumeirah, the **Green Art Gallery** features paintings by up and coming local talent, while **B21** is the place to see the latest work by top Iranian contemporary artists. **Traffic**, (located just behind the Mall of the Emirates) is the first gallery in Dubai to have an exclusive focus on design. **The Courtyard Al Quoz**, in Bur Dubai, started out as an industrial space but has attracted cutting edge galleries such as **Total Arts** and **The Third Line**, who love the white cube open spaces for exhibiting large-scale installations.

If you want a thorough overview of Dubai's contemporary arts scene, don't miss **The Creek Art Fair** and the **Dubai Art Fair**, held in March. It is a glittering showcase of regional talent that attracts dealers from around the world. With auction houses such as Christie's and Bonham's coming to Dubai and setting new bid records for Middle Eastern contemporary art, now is the time to start collecting.

Artists such as Tehran's Farhad Moshiri started exhibiting in Dubai; now his paintings are selling for over US$100,000. To find a comprehensive listing of reputable galleries, enquire with your hotel concierge or Dubai Tourism for The Art Map, or simply visit www.artinthecity.com.

Other emirates in the UAE are following Dubai's lead. In nearby Abu Dhabi, only a short day-trip away, the **Guggenheim** and **Louvre** museum projects on Saadiyat Island have been increasing local awareness of the importance of fine art. Sharjah is also attracting a strong colony of artists, and is well worth visiting for its many museums and galleries.

The performing arts are taking off as well. Dubai is bringing world-class entertainment to the desert. Stars from Elton John to José Carreras have performed to sell-out crowds. Along with these concerts you'll find comedy, theatre, opera and ballet. Even **Cirque du Soleil** will soon have a permanent performance space at The Palm development in Jumeirah.

Dubai has grown so quickly, it is hard to imagine what it was like only a generation ago. To get a glimpse of traditional Emirati life before the oil boom, visit **Dubai Museum** at the Al Fahidi Fort in Bastakiya. Built in 1787, it is one of the oldest buildings left in Dubai and is now a public museum dedicated to revealing Dubai's past to visitors. The **Heritage and Diving Village**, on the Creek at Al Shindagha, is a fascinating 'living museum' where you can watch craftspeople at work and also learn about Dubai's maritime history as a regional centre of the pearl industry. Nearby and also worth visiting is the beautifully restored **Sheikh Saeed Al Maktoum House**, home of the former ruler and now open to the public as a museum.

THIS PAGE (CLOCKWISE FROM BOTTOM): *XVA is one of Dubai's very first art galleries; Traffic focuses mainly on design; the Arab influence is strongly seen and felt in the region's modern art.*
OPPOSITE: *Bastakiya's traditional Arab architecture has been conserved.*

oasis of culture 35

spa sanctuary

THIS PAGE (FROM TOP): *At Al Maha Desert Resort & Spa, the main draw is the chance for total submersion in luxury in an eco-friendly environment; traditional Arabian spa treatments use saffron, dates and frankincense.*
OPPOSITE (FROM TOP): *The Ritz-Carlton, Dubai offers inner tranquillity and wellness with its spa treatments; natural materials in the treatment rooms give off a harmonious vibe.*

From dreamy desert oasis retreats to beachfront bliss-outs, Dubai's spas are a destination in themselves. The emirate has become a holistic heaven of top treatments, luxurious surrounds, exotic therapies, caring staff—in short everything for a top spa holiday.

Dubai, with residents from 200 countries is one of the world's most diverse cities. This is good news for spa goers because there is a wealth of treatments available, with specialists from as far afield as Sweden, Thailand, India, the Philippines, Bali and more. The ancient healing benefits of Indian Ayurveda sit side by side with the latest high-tech La Prairie facial. You'll find Arabic Rasul, Turkish hammam, Greek Thalassotherapy, American canyon hot stone massage, French body wraps—only Dubai offers such a world of wellness wisdom in one place. Spas in Dubai come in a variety of settings. Happily, Dubai is small enough that you can stay at one spa resort, and try a tempting treatment at another. Many of the top resorts are located on fashionable Jumeirah beach. The Balinese **Ritz-Carlton Spa** has an elegant beachfront setting, and emphasises personal service. The resort also has the excellent Ritz Kids Club, so you can go to the spa guilt-free while the children are amused. Further down on the coastline, the One&Only Royal Mirage on Al Sufouh Road is an award-winning five-star resort with spa accommodation at **The Residence & Spa**. The resort's superb **Health & Beauty Institute** has both a Givenchy Spa and a gorgeous Oriental Hammam, where guests are steamed, washed with traditional black soap, scrubbed with a loofah and then given an invigorating massage on a heated marble table.

At the popular Madinat Jumeirah resort, you can book treatments at the impressive **Talise Spa**, Jumeirah's exclusive brand. The spa is the biggest in Dubai, with separate men's and women's wings, and is set in a lovely garden. Talise has a comprehensive range of holistic treatments, such as its Crystal Facial, and features all-natural products from Sodashi. In up and coming Dubai Marina, the chic new Grosvenor House has **Retreat**, an entire floor devoted to spa services, with a hip hair salon, Jetset, and men's grooming at 1847, as well as a nail bar. It also boasts the best Rasul therapy suite in town.

In Dubai's dynamic city centre you'll be spoilt for choice. Men will love the stress-busting massages available at **H$_2$o**, the male spa at the Jumeirah Emirates Towers. Just a few minutes away at The Fairmont, a sleek modern skyscraper hotel, the **Willow Stream Spa** takes up an entire floor, offering advanced options such as their signature detox Phytomer Body Relax Treatment. Shangri-La Hotel, Dubai has a tropical garden setting, with its **CHI** spa inspired by China's philosophy of traditonal medicine.

The Orientalist theme continues at Grand Hyatt Dubai's **Grand Spa**, with its minimalist Zen interior and range of soothing treatments like their signature Hot Stone massage. There's an indoor pool and jacuzzi, as well as a lavish outdoor pool and recreation area. Its trendy Creekside sister hotel, Park Hyatt Dubai, is in a secluded location on Dubai Creek. Its **Amara Spa** made it onto *Condé Nast Traveller's* Hot List when it first opened, for luxurious treatments like the Anne Semonin herbal facials, and outdoor rain showers. Fans of Indian Ayurveda will find treatments like Shirodara at **The Taj Palace Hotel Spa**. The new Raffles Dubai has launched its **Amrita Spa**, with special packages like the 'Dubai Decadence', a six-hour pampering session that promises to leave you feeling totally refreshed.

Day spas, usually located at one of Dubai's many shopping malls, are an excellent option, with treatments costing far less than those at a five-star resort spa. Combine spa therapy with retail therapy at **Cleopatra's Spa**, located in the Wafi City mall; it's a hot favourite among Dubai's beauty-conscious women, who come here for one-of-a-kind treats like the delicious-sounding Frangipani Body Nourish Wrap. Other good day spas include **Paris Gallery** (their chocolate facial is a current hit) and **SensAsia**, for its innovative massages.

Dubai is so exciting it's easy to forget that in less than an hour's drive, you'll find a complete contrast to the fast pace of town in the desert. At the Jumeirah Bab Al Shams Desert Resort & Spa you can stay comfortably ensconced in an Arabian-style fort and enjoy the lush pampering of the **Satori Spa** when you aren't soaking up the sunshine by the pretty palm-fringed pool. Further afield, Al Maha Desert Resort & Spa offers total luxury in an all villa, eco friendly haven. Their **Timeless Spa** boasts a comprehensive list of Emirates' own signature treatments, inspired by traditional Arabic beauty secrets and using local ingredients such as dates, saffron and frankincense. The peace, total privacy and timeless calm of the desert makes it an ideal retreat.

Whichever hotel or resort you choose for your Dubai spa escape, you can relax knowing you are in good hands. Dubai's spa hotels win many of the world's top awards and attract the most sophisticated level of spa goers, who know they will find a true oasis of well-being.

spa sanctuary 37

championship dubai

If you want to start a conversation in Dubai, just mention sports—traffic is another ice-breaker, but that's a different story. Dubaians are sports mad and F1, rugby, cricket, football, golf or tennis will all get you off to a flying start. Dubai has **Sports City**, a 4.6 million sq m (50 million-sq-ft) development that will have four stadiums, as well as an International Cricket Council Academy, Manchester United Football Academy, Butch Harmon School of Golf and a David Lloyd Tennis Academy, as well as an Ernie Els 18-hole championship golf course, fitness centres and state-of-the-art swimming complex. Sports City may be the future home of the Olympics if Dubai realises its goal of one day hosting the Games. Visitors who like the active life ought to take full advantage of the remarkable array of activities Dubai has to offer.

It's a little-known fact that Dubai is a thrill-seeker's paradise. Visitors can indulge in adrenaline rushes such as skydiving, microlight flying, hot air ballooning, paragliding, quad-biking, rock-climbing, dune-bashing, polo and endurance riding, to name but a few. Car-crazy Emiratis love Dubai's **Autodrome**, with its FIA approved Formula One track. You can take a lesson in high speed driving or enjoy white-knuckle Go-Kart rides. Extreme sports are fast becoming a national pastime. Dubai's **Victory** powerboat racing team, which was unbeaten for several years in Europe's Class 1 UIM championship, brought offshore racing to the region.

The Arabian love of horses is still very much part of the culture. Riding is a great way to see the desert, or you can go for a hack on the beach. The **Emirates Riding Centre** and **Jebel Ali Equestrian Club** both have options for visitors. Go the races at **Nad Al Sheba** for a thrilling day watching the world's finest thoroughbreds in full action. For schedule and details visit www.dubairacingclub.com.

The **Dubai Tennis Championship** brings the world's top players in each year, so if you love seeing live matches you can get tickets to top events here for a fraction of Wimbledon or US Open prices. The tennis facilities in Dubai are superb and your hotel can provide details on coaching and courts.

Get wet. Every imaginable water sport is on offer, from windsurfing to water-skiing. Better yet, learn to dive. With its warm, clear waters, abundant tropical fish and many dive centres, Dubai is a great place to get your PADI certificate. The **Pavilion Dive Centre** at Jumeirah Beach Hotel has an excellent range of PADI courses. Visit www.thepaviliondivecentre.com for details. **Al-Boom Diving** (254 Al Wasl Road) at ww.alboomdiving.com is another reputable company that provides instruction for all levels.

When Dubaians want to cool off in style they gather a group of friends and charter a boat for a day of fishing, snorkelling, swimming and cruising along the crystalline Gulf. Prices are reasonable, and usually include soft drinks and a picnic or barbecue lunch (you can bring your own beer or wine). Many beach hotels offer charters, or check the listings in *TimeOut Dubai*. Sailing has taken off in Dubai and there are many marinas to choose from. Visit **www.uaeyachting.com** for a wide selection of cruise options.

38 dubaichic

Golf is Dubai's status sport of choice. The **PGA Tour Dubai Desert Classic** brings golf gods such as Tiger Woods to the prestigious Emirates Golf Club. Other top golf clubs here include the stylish **Montgomerie** in Jumeirah, which boasts one of the world's longest 18th holes at 650 yards. The **Dubai Country Club** has sand golfing, the newly renovated **Nad Al Sheba Club** provides floodlit night golf until midnight and a 'Learn to golf in 7 Days' course. The **Dubai Creek Golf & Yacht Club** boasts a beautiful Creekside location and a par 71-championship course. **The Four Seasons Golf Club** at Dubai Festival City is a recent arrival and features a 72-par golf course designed by Robert Trent Jones, as well as a stunning club house and a world-class academy showcasing the region's one and only TaylorMade Performance Lab and MATT swing analysis system, one of just six in the world. Another exciting new championship course that is quickly gathering attention is **The Dunes** at Victory Heights. Designed by none other than golf legend Ernie Els, the 18-hole, links-style course is 7,538 yards of neatly manicured Bermuda grass whilst five sets of tees, generous fairways and closely cropped rough make it playable for all standards. It's also environmentally friendly. Solar panels are being tested to power golf buggies, and trees and shrubs have all been sourced from sustainable forests or carbon-neutral nurseries. Your hotel can arrange golf flights for you, or you can book ahead at any course in the emirate using **Dubai Golf**'s excellent reservations system on www.dubaigolf.com. It is highly important for golfing visitors to note that all golf courses in Dubai have been designated spike-free.

Because Dubai has a dearth of homegrown international sporting stars or teams, it imports overseas teams to play in friendly exhibition matches, which are hugely popular. Dubai also lures the big name stars with glamorous events and serious prize money. Dubai's social scene revolves tightly around the sporting calendar, so check ahead to see what's on. The biggest sporting events of the year are the **Polo**, the **International Rugby Sevens**, the **PGA Dubai Desert Classic**, the **Dubai Tennis Championships** and the world's richest horse race, with US$6 million in prize money, the **Dubai World Cup**. If you thought Dubai was just about hanging out at a pool all day, think again.

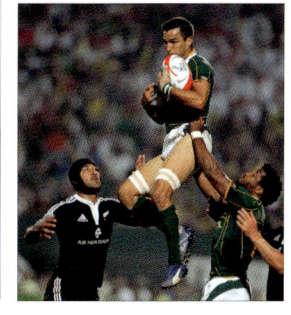

THIS PAGE (FROM BOTTOM): *Get in on some gear-crashing action at Autodrome; the International Rugby Sevens is one of Dubai's high-profile events; tennis is popular in Dubai as both a spectator sport and also a pastime.*
OPPOSITE: *Yachting has an enviable spot in Dubai's social scene, with its growing affluence and its prestige.*

championship dubai 39

family affair

Travelling with the family is a risky business. Like Oscar Wilde said about marriage, it can often be 'the triumph of hope over experience'. After all, nothing ruins a holiday faster than a miserable child. Blissful bonding between relaxed, glowing children and patient, adoring parents—with an album full of happy snaps to prove it—is every parents' holiday dream. In Dubai, one of the most kid-friendly places on the planet, you have a good chance of making that dream come true.

Dubai's beach resorts appeal to kids of all ages and most will have children's clubs with supervised activities, primarily for ages three to 14. There is usually an indoor playhouse with all sorts of arts and crafts, games, and toys. Older children will find there are videos, Playstation game consoles and computer games. There will also be a range of outdoor activities, watersports like banana boat riding and often a separate swimming and play area as well. Some kids' clubs will keep children all day and give them lunch or tea, but others require parents to pick up children for meals.

If your child is younger, check for crèche or babysitting options at your hotel before you go. If it's high season it makes more sense to book a sitter in advance. Don't be shy about emailing ahead with your requirements for things such as cots, high chairs and baby monitors. The more you can sort out ahead of time and the less kit you have to bring along, the better. A brilliant service for visitors is **Rent-A-Crib** (www.rentacrib.ae) who hire out all manner of baby gear, from push chairs to car seats and will deliver and pick up for free. Babies and toddlers hate the high heat and humidity of summer, so unless you want to spend your holiday in an air conditioned environment it's better to travel with very young ones between October and April.

Whether you stay on the beach or in town, you and your children will be well looked after. In Dubai, all the hotels are engaged in an ongoing competition to be the best and this has real benefits for families. Hoteliers know that parents will stay where their kids are happy. So if you want children's room service menus, in-room gaming, kids' videos, kid-sized bathrobes, apple juice instead of champagne in the mini bar, just ask, and you're likely to get it.

Dubai offers a dazzling choice of family and child friendly activities. Culturally, Arabs are exceptionally family-oriented and children are treated as minor royalty. Don't be too surprised if your little ones get a few admiring looks and indulgent comments—it's all very much a part of the warmth that makes Dubai such a nice place. Another plus is that Dubai is extremely safe, so you can let your teenagers loose in the malls without worry. Just about the biggest danger kids can or will face is getting sunburnt, so make sure everyone has a hat and sunscreen on when you go outside. As far as sightseeing with children in tow goes, remember that Dubai is not paradise for pedestrians and there is very little public transport. Take taxis to your destinations; they are cheap and safer than trying to go about on foot in Dubai's traffic.

Another option is to hire a car and driver so you can come and go as you like. It sounds indulgent but chauffeur-driven cars are so common in Dubai that prices are actually reasonable.

Dubai is always changing and it can be confusing to figure out the latest geography. To get oriented, it's a good idea to have a tour. There are plenty of Dubai city tours, but out of all of them **The Big Bus Company** (www.bigbus.co.uk) and **Wonder Bus Tours** (www.wonderbusdubai.com) are the most fun for kids. The Wonder Bus is an amphibious craft that even the most jaded young jetsetter will be delighted by when it suddenly plunges into the waters of the Dubai Creek. The tour takes two hours and covers Dubai's main sights with informative commentary. The Big Bus is a British-style, open double-decker affair with witty guided commentary in English covering all the main sights and providing lots of fascinating local trivia such as the number of cars in Dubai in 1968 (only 13). You can hop on and off to explore, a great benefit if you have restless little ones.

Wild Wadi Water Park in upscale Jumeirah (www.wildwadi.com) is one of Dubai's favourite cooling off places and a joy for kids of all ages. There are 23 rides set within a 5-hectare (12-acre) park, to choose from—including the white-knuckle ride on the 33-m (108-foot) drop 'Jumeirah Sceirah'. There are winding lazy river rides you can take perched on your rubber ring, a beach complete with surf created by wave machines, a faux shipwreck to explore (it even has canons that squirt water) and lots more. Parents can work on their tans at Breaker Bay

THIS PAGE (FROM TOP): The beach is one of Dubai's fun zones—don't hesitate to bring the whole family along; Jumeirah's Wild Wadi Water Park can be a full afternoon's outing; children love the beach, but don't forget to bring the SPF15 sunblock.

OPPOSITE: Dubai is considered young by most standards—it has a playful side that makes it a favourite of kids.

familyaffair 41

family affair

while the kids have fun. Loads of vigilant lifeguards keep it safe. Wild Wadi is the place kids always want to return to. Other places that also offer watery fun include **Al Nasr Leisureland**, an amusement park providing such distractions as bowling, squash, go-karting, ice-skating, swimming, rides and more. There's also **Wonderland**, which has a range of water rides and fun games for children.

Ski Dubai at Mall of the Emirates (www.skidubai.ae) tops the list of all the surreal places one finds only in Dubai. You could be forgiven for thinking it was a mirage cooked up by the desert. Outside it may be hitting the high 30s but in this man-made winter wonderland it's closer to zero. Snow swirls around as skiers fly down the five slopes (including the world's first indoor 'black run'), ride up to the top again in their chairlifts, or frolic about throwing snowballs. Ski Dubai provides 6,000 tons of snow, plastic fir trees, faux igloos, and a Zermatt-style Avalanche Café with a balconied chalet where you can sip mugs of hot chocolate and watch the fun. There's even a bobsled run, tobogganing and attractions such as a 3,000-sq-m (32,000-sq-ft) ice cave, an ice maze and dedicated spaces for building snowmen. All levels of skiers and snowboarders are catered for and all your equipment hire (except hats and gloves) is included in the price.

Also at the Mall of the Emirates is **Magic Planet**, the biggest indoor amusement park in the region. You'll find everything from rollicking rides like the RoboCoaster, to the latest high-tech arcade games, dedicated to the philosophy that Kids Rule. There is Cosmic Bowling, bumper cars, and pool and billiards tables. Younger children will love the soft play area, and there is a professional childcare service so you can drop kids off while you shop. There are also a number of tempting kid-friendly restaurant options. A smaller version of Magic Planet is also at the Deira City Centre shopping mall.

Malls in Dubai are brilliant for providing places where the kids can hang out in supervised surroundings while parents shop. **Wafi City** is one of Dubai's most popular malls with good reason. It has an excellent range of retailers, very good food courts, and a family-friendly vibe. Kids flock to the **Encounter Zone** to escape the tedium of shopping with adults. There are two fun zones here offering lots of exciting options. **LunarLand** caters for the under-eights with suitable rides and games while the older kids can hang out in **Galactica**. It has cool rides like the Komet, which takes children around the top of the building, an anti-gravity simulator, a 3D cinema and the challenging Crystal Maze. Best of all, you can drop kids off while you shop, knowing they will be safe while having a great time. For details visit www.waficity.com.

Another mall that has excellent children's facilities is the exotic **Ibn Battuta Mall**. It has a 21-screen **Grand Cinema Megaplex**—the largest cinema complex in the Middle East—which also features an IMAX screen, as well as **Fun City**, which provides supervised entertainment, rides and games. If you've got a baby along, you will find the Nursing Room offers a discreet ambience for breastfeeding, nappy changing and so on. There are also Fun City branches at BurJuman Mall and Mercato Mall. For shopping with the family away from the malls, try one of the outdoor markets such as the very popular **Marina Market**, that happens on the weekends in the fashionable brand new Dubai Marina walkway, opposite Grosvenor House hotel. There are lots of stalls selling creative and original art, toys, clothes and souvenirs. Pop in for burgers and shakes at **Johnny Rockets**, an American style diner.

When the kids have had enough thrills and want some quieter fun, **The Jam Jar** in Bur Dubai is perfect. A hit with local kids and off the tourist trail, at this lively arts studio children and adults can create their own artistic masterpieces. The kid-friendly staff provides everything from paints to easels and are on hand to help. Another option is **Café Ceramique** in Jumeirah, which lets grownups enjoy a needed caffeine break while kids can choose their own pottery creations (mugs are popular) to paint.

Children's City at Creekside Park is a highly creative and innovative centre devoted to educating through entertainment. It works for toddlers as well as teenagers. Visit zones such as the **Nature Centre** or **Planetarium**. There's a section on Arab culture too. Interactive displays, tasty burgers at the café and a gift shop make this one of the most enjoyable places to go with kids—especially if (for some unusual reason) the weather isn't perfect for the beach and you can't bear the thought of another mall. Visit www.childrencity.ae for the latest exhibitions.

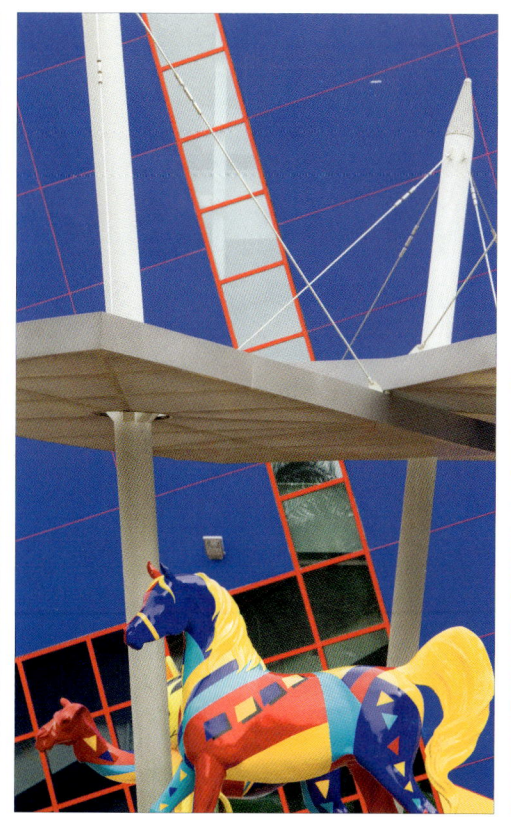

THIS PAGE (CLOCKWISE FROM BOTTOM): Wafi City Mall is a kid-friendly zone, with specialised play areas for children; the bright colours of Children's City are instantly appealing to all kids; parents can leave young ones to watch a film while they go shopping. *OPPOSITE (FROM TOP):* Lots of shopping malls have facilities to keep kids busy; Ski Dubai can provide hours of fun.

family affair 43

family affair

For active older kids, check out the **Dubai Kartdrome** at the Dubai Autodrome, which offers a fleet of Karts that delivers an excellent racing experience and ensures high safety to satisfy those aged seven and up. Visit karting@dubaiautodrome.com for more details.

There's indoor ice-skating at the **Galleria Ice Rink** at the Hyatt Regency Hotel in Deira. For skateboarders and in-line skaters there's **Rampworks Skatepark**, an indoor, air-conditioned bit of skateboard heaven. For details visit www.rampworks.com

Alternatively, if the kids want to catch a movie while you shop, there are multiplex cinemas at most of the major shopping malls screening all the latest blockbusters.

For a more Arabian experience try going to the **camel races**. The sport is a Dubai institution, and just about everyone from the ruler, Sheikh Mohammed, to the newest expat turns up for a piece of the action. Top racing camels can fetch more than US$1 million, and the races are always jam-packed with fans cheering on their favourite. The kids will love the innovative robot jockeys. Locations change so check with Dubai Tourism or hotel concierge for race details.

Spend a morning exploring the heritage areas by the Creek at Bur Dubai. The **Dubai Museum**, **Heritage and Diving Village** and the **dhow boatyards** are all there and you can take the kids across the Creek on a traditional abra—these small boats are still used today to ferry Dubaians around and you can even hire one for private sightseeing tours down the Creek at the abra station.

Although Dubai is known more for fun zones than culture, it's worth seeing what's playing at the **Dubai Community Theatre and Arts Centre** (www.ductac.org) at the Mall of the Emirates, as they often have plays and musicals that will appeal to the whole family. **Madinat Theatre** (www.madinattheatre.com) in the exciting Souk at Madinat Jumeirah has a range of programmes, from concerts to comedy.

Dubai is more than its dynamic capital city. For outdoor adventure in the rugged wadis, along the coast, or amidst the rolling dunes of Dubai's desert, companies like **Desert Rangers** (www.desertrangers.com) specialise in providing families with an adrenaline-fuelled assortment of activities such as camel trekking, rock-climbing, dhow cruising, dune bashing in a four-wheel-drive, desert camping, sand boarding, deep sea fishing, helicopter tours, and hot-air ballooning. **Arabian Adventures** (www.arabianadventures.com) and **Gulf Ventures** (www.gulfventures.org) are also reputable and experienced tour companies providing a huge range of outdoor activities.

For the latest in children's events and activities in Dubai drop by the website www.dubaikidzbiz.com, go through the Children's Listings in *Time Out Dubai* magazine or just simply visit www.timeoutdubai.com. Dubai is evolving rapidly, so it's best to check with Dubai Department of Tourism (info@dubaitourism.ae) or with your hotel concierge about new events and openings near you. One thing is for sure; the kids will have an amazing time in Dubai, and as a result, so will you.

THIS PAGE (CLOCKWISE FROM BOTTOM): Dubai Kartdrome offers young ones the chance to speed around a track in rented go-karts for the afternoon; sand boarding is like snowboarding except at far higher temperatures; robots are fastened to camels in order to control them during races.

OPPOSITE (FROM TOP): Hop in an abra for a sightseeing tour of Dubai Creek; dune bashing is a popular activity in the desert, riding over the sands.

familyaffair 45

onwards and upwards

Dubai is the world's fastest growing city, so if you wonder why parts of town resemble a giant building site, here's why: as Dubai accelerates into the future, a series of mind-boggling projects are being launched. In 10 years the emirate will evolve into the greatest tourist destination on earth, the financial centre of the Middle East and a dynamic global presence. The sheer scale of these projects, involving billions of dollars and the creative energy of some of the world's most talented designers, architects and futurists, is extraordinary.

'Anything you can do, I can do better' is Dubai's brave message to the world. An example is **Burj Dubai**, the world's tallest building; yet before it is even opened, rumour has it that a new tower, **Al Burj**, will be even taller. The answer to Dubai's shopping mania is the 1.1 million-sq-m (12 million-sq-ft) **Dubai Mall**, opening soon, yet already it is destined to be eclipsed by the upcoming **Mall of Arabia**.

Dubai's upbeat government, with its 'nothing is impossible' mantra, has given the green light to such building extravaganzas as the **Bawadi Project**, nicknamed 'DuVegas', which consists of 51 new hotels with 60,000 rooms, including the world's biggest hotel, the 6,500 room **Asia-Asia**, due for completion in 2010.

Off Dubai's coastline, **The Palm Jumeirah**, has just opened. It will be followed by two more developments just off the coast of Jebel Ali and Deira. Then there's **The World**, a map of the earth created from 300 man-made islands 4 km (2.5 miles) off the Dubai coast, destined to be a US$1.8 billion super-exclusive development

THIS PAGE (FROM TOP): *The Great Dubai Wheel cuts a striking profile at dusk; an Emirati businessman brokers an important deal while overlooking the rapid downtown developments.*

OPPOSITE (FROM TOP): *Visitors examine a model of The World, a US$1.8 billion development of stupendous scale; the Bawadi hospitality and tourism project is due for completion in 2010.*

reachable only by boat or helicopter. The Middle East hasn't seen building on this scale since the Pyramids.

Dubailand, the most ambitious tourist destination ever created, with its theme parks (including exclusive deals with Universal Studios), leisure and entertainment facilities, and its exhibitions, will make Florida's Walt Disney World Resort look like a kids' playground in comparison. The entire complex will be the size of Singapore, and (you guessed it!) the world's largest multi-use theme park. One of its more wacky attractions will be the **Falcon City of Wonders**, a recreation of the world's greatest architectural wonders infused with 21st century features. Imagine the Pyramids, the Eiffel Tower and the Taj Mahal all in one place, all full-scale and you begin to get the idea. Don't miss **Restless Planet**, a Jurassic Park extravaganza complete with an animated T-Rex and other scary beasties created at a cost of over US$1 billion. Also coming soon is **The Great Dubai Wheel**, even bigger than the London Eye. Dubai is even setting up in space, with the launch of its first satellite, called **DubaiSat-1**.

To handle the millions of visitors to these exciting new ventures, **Dubai World Central International Airport** is being built. It'll be the world's largest airport, with a capacity for more than 120 million passengers a year. As the Middle East, India and China prosper, more people will be travelling—and Dubai wants to be their favourite destination. Getting around town will be much easier with the launch of the **Dubai Metro** and **Al Sufouh Tram**. Already 70 km (44 miles) of light railway have been developed, and by 2020 there will be more than 300 km (186 miles) of Metro line in full service, vastly easing the heavy congestion on Dubai's crowded roads.

What sets Dubai apart from other developing nations is the imagination to think not just big, but brilliant. For example, one day you may be able to stay at **Hydropolis**, the world's first five-star underwater hotel. It's being built off the coast of Dubai Marina, 20 m (66 ft) below the waterline, at a cost of roughly US$600 million. The hotel will be a surreal vision out of Jules Verne. Guests will stay in state-of-the-art, bubble-shaped suites, surrounded by sheer Plexiglas walls for optimum fish watching. But the hotel is more than just an attraction—its creators are pioneering the concept of living under the sea.

Not all investments in Dubai's future are material. The government has recently launched a US$10 billion education fund so as to create higher standards of learning at all levels. Huge investment has also been made in **Dubai Healthcare City**, making it a global hub of research, specialised healthcare and education. Ecological investment in such projects as the Emirates Green Building Council, a legislative body created to make sure all builders and developers comply with Dubai's new 'green building' directive, recycling, water management and solar energy, will also contribute to a bright future for this rising star. As Sheikh Mohammed puts it, 'To dream of the future is one of the most beautiful things in life. We are not content only to dream, we also work hard, because our ambitions are great and so are our dreams'.

onwardsandupwards 47

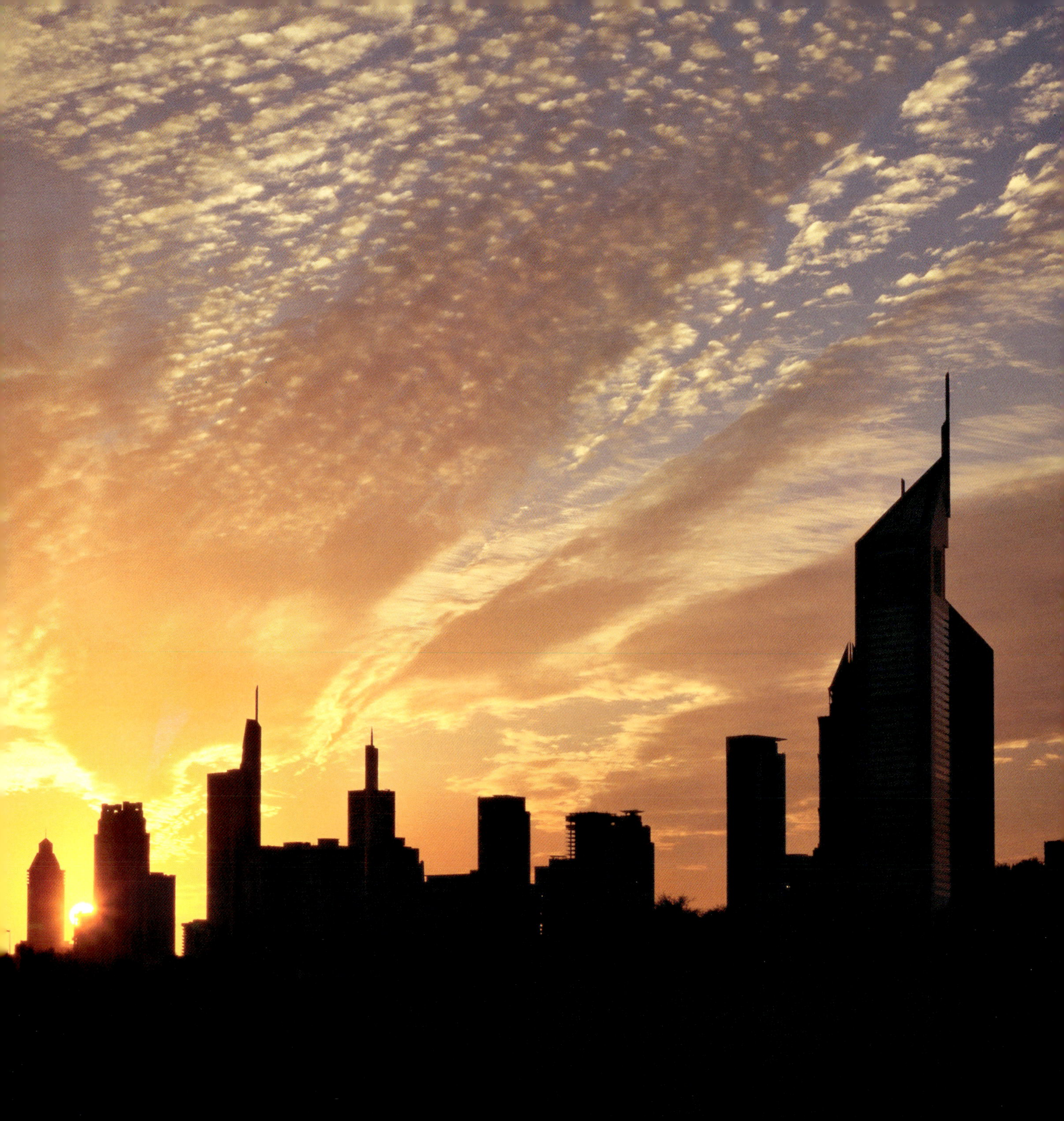

downtowndubai

- Mercato
- Jumeirah Mosque

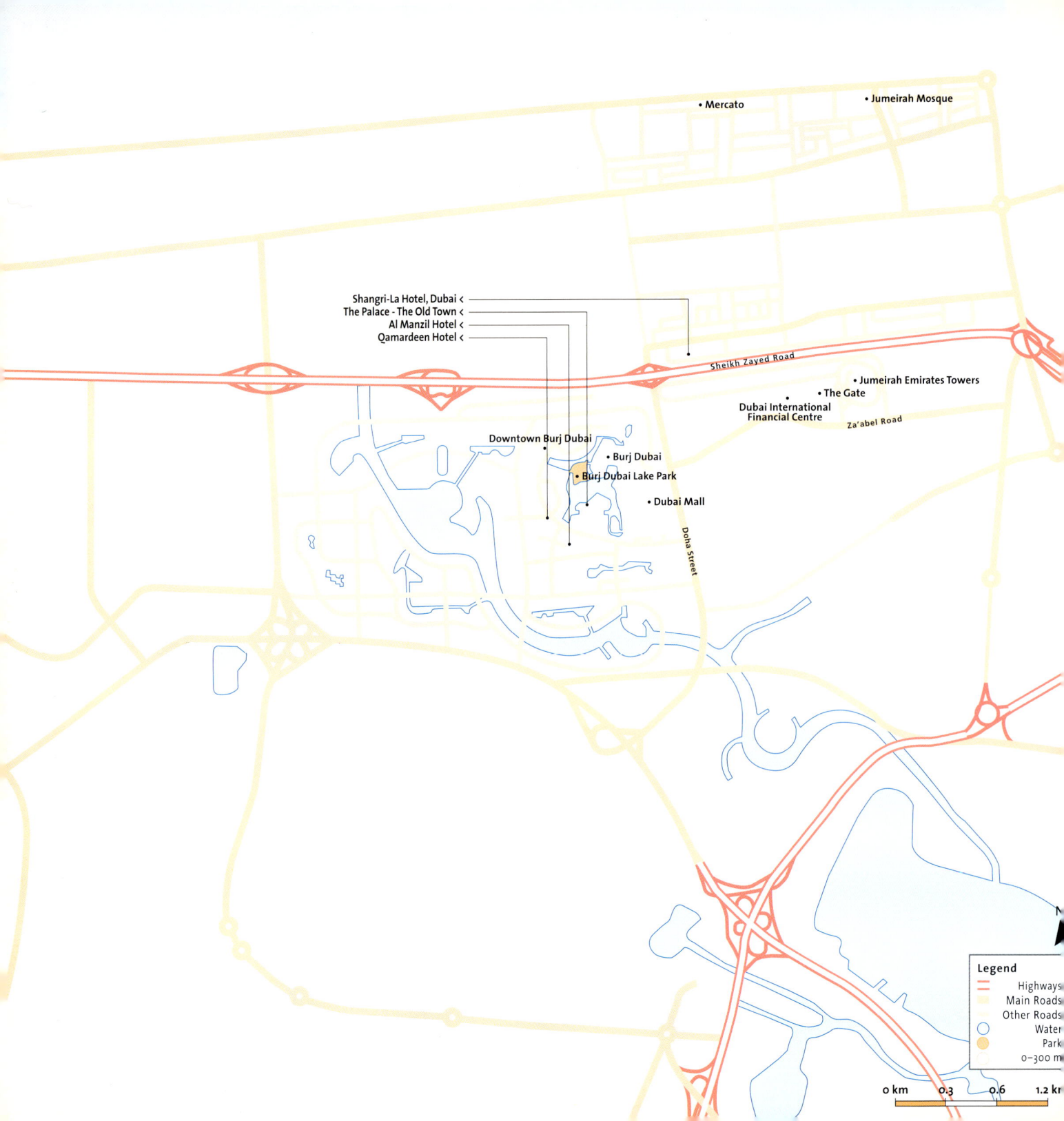

Shangri-La Hotel, Dubai
The Palace - The Old Town
Al Manzil Hotel
Qamardeen Hotel

Sheikh Zayed Road

- Jumeirah Emirates Towers
- The Gate
Dubai International Financial Centre
Za'abel Road

Downtown Burj Dubai
- Burj Dubai
- Burj Dubai Lake Park
- Dubai Mall

Doha Street

Legend
Highways
Main Roads
Other Roads
Water
Park
0–300 m

0 km   0.3   0.6   1.2 km

downtown dubai

gulf glitterati

Dubai is breathtakingly new. Unlike most capital cities, which have layers of history and architecture, Dubai's entire infrastructure was developed in the last few decades, an incredible feat of urban planning. The heart of Dubai's downtown runs along the arterial Sheikh Zayed Road between Trade Centre Roundabout and Interchange One (soon to be renamed Burj Dubai Interchange in honour of the new landmark tower). Although it's only about 0.5 sq km (0.2 sq miles), the area is easy to find. Just look for the soaring twin blades of Jumeirah Emirates Towers, one of Dubai's most famous landmarks. Downtown Dubai is a glittering showplace of dramatic architecture as each new building vies for supremacy through style, scale or sheer splendour. Downtown is where the money is made, the epicentre of Dubai's skyrocketing success as a player in the world's financial markets.

The Gate is home to the Dubai International Financial Centre (DIFC) and the bullish young DIFX stock exchange. Behind its imposing exterior of gleaming glass, steel and stone, the wealth and future of Dubai is being forged. Since its launch in September 2005, it has attracted many of the top international investment banks, including big players such as Citigroup, Credit Suisse, HSBC and Morgan Stanley, bringing substantial clout into Dubai's economy. In accordance with Dubai's successful strategy of making investment attractive through incentives, foreign firms operating in the DIFC are eligible for benefits such as a zero tax rate on profits, 100 per cent foreign ownership, no restrictions on foreign exchange or repatriation of capital, operational support and business continuity facilities. Dubai has led the way in the region for greater transparency and openness and its daring spirit and risk-taking have paid off. As a result of all these factors, investors are seeing Dubai's potential as the hub of the lucrative Middle Eastern market. Right now, foreign investment in Dubai is at an all-time high, and the DIFC can proudly take its place as a fully fledged onshore capital market, alongside those of New York, London and Hong Kong. As bankers tumble out of their offices at Jumeirah Emirates Towers, jostle for early-morning coffee at Caribou and grab a fast lunch at the Noodle House there is the unmistakable energy and exciting optimism of ground-breaking deals being done. Around The Gate, the buzz you hear is the happy hum of money being made.

after hours

As night falls over Sheikh Zayed Road, the jewel colours of the sunset fade into the electric glow of Dubai's pulsating cityscape. Far beneath the skyscrapers, the sound of throbbing engines fills the air as the crowds of commuters wend their way home through the relentless rush hour traffic, while fun seekers come out to play.

THIS PAGE: *The construction of Burj Dubai, set to be the tallest building in the world, lights up the surrounding area for miles.*

PAGE 48: *Dubai's iconic skyline, punctuated by the twin spikes of Jumeirah Emirates Towers, is bathed in a fantastic show of colours—an Arabian sunset.*

...Dubai's neon-bright cityscape...

Downtown has a high proportion of Dubai's favourite bars, nightclubs restaurants and hotels. Each has its own style and appeal. To see Dubai's movers and shakers in action, head for Scarlett's, a lively bar and restaurant famous for its burgers, or Vu's, aptly named for its panoramic vistas, at Jumeirah Emirates Towers, Spectrum On One at The Fairmont hotel, with its four illuminated towers adding to Dubai's neon-bright cityscape, and the Shangri-La—popular with international celebrities. Latin American pop star Enrique Iglesias and his glamorous entourage recently stayed and loved the glitzy suites and nonstop nightlife.

Dubai's cash-rich young professionals can be seen out partying at a variety of downtown watering holes, such as Fibber Magee's at Trade Centre 1, a rollicking Irish pub favoured by expats and a longtime stalwart of Dubai's night scene, or The Agency, a glamorous wine bar with a European vibe, a favourite gathering place for after work drinks. As the evening progresses, Dubai's partygoers flit between nightclubs and swish bars, dancing to the latest beats at Zinc at the Crowne Plaza and posing with cocktails at Lotus One or The Loft. Late nights are typical, and it's not uncommon to see a bevy of designer clad bright young things at 3.00 am eating mouthwatering Lebanese shawarma wraps hot off the grill at casual local places such as the ever-popular Saj Express, and Automatic. Off the beaten five-star hotel path, there are little-known gems for authentic Arabic food such as Arabica and Zyara, or cafés such as the wonderfully eccentric Shakespeare & Co, famous for its fruit smoothies.

reigning retail

For serious shopping, the Boulevard, located in a sophisticated setting between the two spires of Jumeirah Emirates Towers, has the cream of international designers such as Cartier and Gucci, in a series of chic boutiques that are arrayed in aristocratic splendour along a spacious marble walkway. The Boulevard is Dubai shopping at its most extravagant, an exclusive platinum card paradise far removed from the madding crowds of the city's mega malls. Further along Sheikh Zayed Road, the popular new Times Square Centre has an array of shops selling clothes, accessories and housewares at much more down-to-earth prices. While here, look out for Chillout, a trendy new addition to Dubai's more extreme themed cafés. Chillout's interiors and furnishings are made entirely from 40,000 tonnes of specially manufactured crystal-clear

THIS PAGE: *Partygoers dance all night at a Dubai club—the energy here never lets up.*
OPPOSITE: *Sheikh Zayed Road, at the heart of Dubai's economy, comes alive in a million bursts of electric light after sundown.*

THIS PAGE (FROM TOP): *Boulevard, at Jumeirah Emirates Towers, is a sleek retail complex boasting only the best designer brands; Emirati women enjoy a day out of shopping and leisure.*

OPPOSITE: *Camels stand at the ready for a race—a traditional Arabian sport—while soaring towers of modern downtown Dubai loom in the distance.*

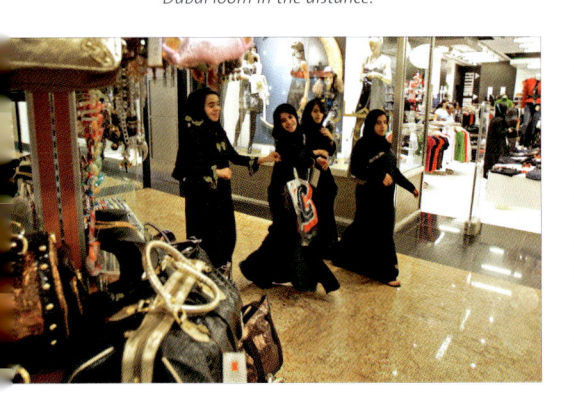

Canadian ice, bathed in a frosty purple and blue light. Visitors are kept warm by Chillout's signature designer parkas and gloves. The intimate interior seats just 45 so there is often a queue to get in, but the wait is worth it for the fun of popping in for a snack or drink served on ice plates and glasses, while sitting on sculpted ice chairs above ice chandeliers, while an illuminated ice sculpture of Dubai's skyline glows in the background. It's Dubai's ultimate place to cool off.

city of superlatives

As so often happens in Dubai, the scene is rapidly changing. New developments such as Downtown Burj Dubai, a 1-sq-km (0.4-sq-mile) business, retail and residential district radiating out from the extraordinary Burj Dubai, are adding a dynamic new element to the downtown mix.

Burj Dubai, planned to be the tallest building on the planet, is set to become a major attraction in its own right. Desert Bedouins can see the tower shimmering in the distance like a mirage from 100 km (62 miles) away. It is a feat of both engineering and aesthetics, inspired by the delicate grace of the Hymenocallis flower, which blooms in the region, and traditional Islamic architecture. Burj Dubai's fascinating design by über architect Adrian Smith (famous for his remarkable towers like Jin Mao Tower in Shanghai and NBC Tower in Chicago) has it being hailed as a modern masterpiece. For Dubaians, it is more than an amazing record-breaking new building; it is a symbol of their highest aspirations. Inside the Burj Dubai is the world's first Armani Hotel, bearing Giorgio Armani's signature style of simple elegance achieved at great expense. There are also super-luxurious private apartments, shops, restaurants and meeting places all striving to be the best in Dubai. Certainly no expense has been spared to create a space that will set a new standard in a city that loves nothing more than setting new standards. In Dubai, oneupmanship is a game that is played to win

Along with the tower will be Burj Dubai Square, an outdoor pedestrian shopping and leisure area, and in keeping with Dubai's love of superlatives, Dubai Mall, the world's largest retail complex. The Guinness Book of World Records should have a chapter dedicated to Dubai. Just across from the tower, the Burj Dubai Lake has been created where there was once just sand. In the middle is an island, ironically called 'Old Town Island' although it is brand new— which will feature an attractive residential area with market squares, waterfront restaurants and traditional Arabian architecture—along with Souk Al Bahar, a series of shops showcasing Dubai's cultural heritage. Sofitel's new five-star The Palace – The Old Town, a resplendent vision of Arabian architecture, is already attracting a glamorous crowd. The hotel's Ewaan restaurant has fabulous views of Burj Dubai from its charming outdoor terrace. As it evolves, Downtown Burj Dubai is destined to emerge as one of the emirate's most luxurious hotspots

...*destined to emerge as one of the emirate's most luxurious hotspots.*

shangri-la hotel, dubai

THIS PAGE: *At night, the stunning pool is an ideal backdrop for intimate conversations.*
OPPOSITE: *The ambience at Dunes Café is casual and contemporary.*

Like the Himalayan utopia of James Hilton's seminal novel *Lost Horizon*, from which the hotel takes its name, Shangri-La Hotel, Dubai rises like a perfect image of paradise from what was once a forbidding desert landscape. Complementing the hectic pace of life in downtown Dubai—which seemingly quickens by the day, if not the hour—this five-star hotel is equipped to provide travellers with a much-needed haven of luxury and respite.

Across Asia, the Shangri-La name has always been associated with first-class service, as well as Oriental-style charm and hospitality. In Dubai, those values meet the famed warmth of Arabian hosts. The result

...a much-needed haven of luxury and respite.

is a hotel that has won the world and the tourism industry over. Accolades received by Shangri-La Hotel, Dubai over the past four years include 'Best New Hotel of the Year', 'Business Hotel of the Year' and 'Interior Design Excellence' at the DEPA Middle East Hotel Awards, and the prestigious 'Best New Business Hotel in the World' title in 2005 from *Business Traveller*.

This proud architectural icon stands 200-m- (656-ft-) tall, overlooking the emirate's finest real estate. From its position on the corner of Al Safa Street and Sheikh Zayed Road, guests are minutes away from the landmark Burj Dubai development, the Dubai International Convention Centre, and the Dubai World Trade Centre. Housed within Shangri-La Hotel, Dubai's walls are 43 storeys of grand opulence, superlative spa treatments and recreational facilities, magnificent dining venues and all the comforts of home.

The refined hotel lobby draws the eye down its length with a series of sweeping, curved walkways from the upper levels that hang in the air like terraces. Throughout the property, the Arabian-inspired organic design elements of gentle curves and large circular forms hold together a stunning aesthetic that incorporates the use of premium metallics, glass, marble, plush fabrics and pearlescent finishings. This look extends to all 301 guestrooms and suites, as well as the hotel's 126 furnished serviced apartments for guests desiring longer stays.

The most popular choice at Shangri-La Hotel, Dubai is the Deluxe Room. The 231 rooms are located on the 29th to 39th floors, and offer 45 sq m (463 sq ft) of stylish comfort. From the entrance, guests are led along a curved wall before encountering the room proper. Large, spacious and decorated in earth tones with sycamore veneers, the Deluxe Rooms have panoramic views of either the business district or the Arabian Sea. Modern furnishings, minimalist appliances, designer light fixtures and local works of art complete the picture of a room to remember.

For those looking for a little more room to stretch out, 11 Executive Rooms each offer 48 sq m (517 sq ft) of comfort designed to the same specifications as the Deluxe Rooms. Both room options feature generous en suite bathrooms with deep soaking tubs and walk-in rainforest shower units. An example of Shangri-La Hotel, Dubai's dedication to details can be found in the exclusive Aigner designer bath amenities replenished daily. High-speed Internet access, satellite TV, IDD telephones with voice mail, minibars and a pillow menu make these rooms a cut above the rest

Shangri-La Hotel, Dubai is especially popular with business and frequent travellers, because of its understanding of the little differences that mean a whole lot more than what others might assume. In service of these special guests, the hotel created the Horizon Club. In some ways a hotel of

...every room at Shangri-La Hotel, Dubai is impressive...

its own over two levels, guests at the Horizon Club enjoy privilege check-in, late check-outs and personalised services. The centrepiece of the Club is the exclusive Club Lounge on the 41st floor, where books, newspapers, board games, high-speed Internet access and complimentary drinks are provided to enable both work and play. A Horizon Floor Health Club on the 42nd floor reserved for the exclusive use of Horizon Club guests boasts an infinity-edge pool, sun deck, gym and wet areas. Other features of the Club are the complimentary buffet breakfasts at the Lounge, daily deliveries of fresh fruit, suit press and shoeshine services, and a purser that sees to special needs and arrangements.

Spread over the 40th and 41st floors, the rooms of the Horizon Club all provide fantastic views. The Horizon Deluxe and Horizon Executive Rooms offer the same comforts as their regular counterparts, with the Horizon Executive Rooms being slightly larger at 55 sq m (592 sq ft). Unique to the Club are eight Horizon Premier Rooms, the hotel's largest non-suite guest rooms, offering an unparalleled 66 sq m (710 sq ft) of richly appointed sophistication each. There are also Horizon Suites that feature a spacious sitting room separate from the bedroom, allowing guests to work and entertain comfortably.

Putting stopovers and business trips aside, the ultimate Dubai holiday experience begins with a stay at one of the city's most celebrated suites. Large enough for entertaining guests, each of the 29 One Bedroom Suites fulfills every need with a host of incredible extras like Bang & Olufsen TV and entertainment systems, powerful computers with printers, fax machines, and electronic safes. The spacious and comfortable 83-sq-m (893-sq-ft) rooms incorporate fine wood panelling, detailed rugs and an array of colours chosen to suggest the long and rich history of Arabic architecture, and yet do so with contemporary simplicity. The suites have separate sitting and dining rooms, and the bedrooms have large en suite bathrooms with Aigner and Trussardi bath products.

THIS PAGE: *Helpful and attentive staff ensure the success of any meeting or conference at Shangri-La Hotel, Dubai.*

OPPOSITE (FROM TOP): *The bedrooms are havens of relaxation; for the most luxurious and impressive accommodation, book the Presidential Suite.*

THIS PAGE: *Shang Palace serves supremely delectable Cantonese dishes.*

OPPOSITE (FROM TOP): *Deep soaking tubs are standard features in the luxurious bathrooms; CHI, The Spa helps guests achieve a balance between vitality, fitness and beauty.*

While every room at Shangri-La Hotel, Dubai is impressive, the very last word in luxury comes in the form of a single Presidential Suite occupying two floors. An impressive 343 sq m (3,692 sq ft) of floor area is comprised of a master bedroom, large bathroom, lounge area, dining room, and kitchenette—all presented in elegant fashion with premium furnishings. The Presidential Suite and the One Bedroom Suites all come with access to the Horizon Floor Health Club on the 42nd floor.

Reflecting the multicultural spirit of modern Dubai, the hotel's five restaurants serve up an international feast, with both local and international cuisines represented.

Amwaj is a seafood restaurant with startlingly original modern décor. For casual dining, Dunes Café offers an international à la carte menu and three buffet meals daily with the added flair of an open kitchen that lets diners participate in the excitement of creating culinary masterpieces.

Throughout Dubai, one place is renowned for providing an authentic Moroccan dining experience. The menu at Marrakech has been designed by Chef Khadija Manar to succinctly capture all the nuances of her native cuisine. Chef Khadija had the illustrious title of Head Palace Chef to the King of Morocco.

The two East Asian restaurants, Hoi An and Shang Palace, bring a flash of exoticism to the mix. Hoi An serves traditional Vietnamese cooking, long inspired by and intertwined with French cuisine, under the direction of Chef de Cuisine Nguyen Trong Phu. Fantastic Cantonese cuisine may be hard to come by in the Middle East, but Shang Palace brilliantly delivers. The signature restaurant of the Shangri-La hotel group, Shang Palace is no less ingenious, and no less mouthwatering here than it is anywhere else in the world. Chef Ken Huang brings with him a lifetime of experience from China, so be sure to bring a worthy appetite. Afterwards, retreat to the Balcony Bar for the second part of one's Asian journey. Decorated in a decadent style reminiscent of Old Shanghai, the bar serves coffee, cigars, fine wines and cocktails in the romantic haze of a bygone era.

...true utopia in Dubai.

Continue the nourishment of mind, body, and spirit at Shangri-La Hotel, Dubai's superb health and leisure facilities, which include a health club and spa. The Health Club & Spa on the fourth floor is both a place to work out and relax, with a gym, outdoor pool, jacuzzis, plunge pools, an aerobics studio, sauna and steam rooms, full-sized tennis and squash courts, and hair salon. The Health Club is open daily from 6.00 am to midnight, with spa treatments available from 10.00am until 10.00 pm. Options range from full body massages to scrubs, wraps and facial therapies. Indulge in a Back, Neck and Shoulder Massage, or try Balinese and Thai variations for something different. A number of treatment packages are also offered, such as the Executive Escape massage and facial treatment for the 'man on the go' and the Shangri-La Experience, which incorporates a Biodroga Milk & Honey Wrap, moisturising facial and Swedish massage.

If a hotel and its staff are measured by the strength of their desire to please, then the weight of Shangri-La Hotel, Dubai's achievements may be off the scales. At every turn, one is met by sincerity—from the provision of thoughtful services, both large and small, to the inclusion of functional designs that were no doubt created with real people in mind. Seeing how serenely everything comes together here, it is not hard for guests to believe that they have found true utopia in Dubai.

rooms
301 rooms and suites • 126 serviced apartments

food
Amwaj: seafood • Dunes Café: international • Hoi An: French-Vietnamese • Marrakech: Moroccan • Shang Palace: Cantonese

drink
Balcony Bar • Lobby Lounge

features
high-speed Internet access • business centre • conference facilities • Horizon Club • shopping arcade • gym • spa • tennis court • squash court • sauna • jacuzzi • steam rooms

nearby
Burj Dubai • Dubai International Airport • Dubai World Trade Centre • Dubai Convention Centre • Za'abeel Park • Jumeirah Mosque

contact
Sheikh Zayed Road, PO Box 75880, Dubai, UAE • telephone: +971.4.343 8888 • facsimile: +971.4.343 8886 • email: sldb@shangri-la.com • website: www.shangri-la.com

the palace – the old town

One of the most exciting new developments in Dubai is Old Town Island, a neighbourhood in a lakeside setting centred around Burj Dubai, the world's tallest skyscraper. The Palace – The Old Town is the jewel of this new neighbourhood, rising from the lake like a vision from the short-story collection *One Thousand and One Nights*. The Palace's romantic Arabian architecture, with its arches, balconies, fountains and charming garden courtyards, is welcoming in the true tradition of the region.

The hotel, managed by Sofitel Luxury Hotels, has 242 rooms and suites with generous balconies that offer stunning views of Burj Dubai or Old Town Island. The spacious 51-sq-m (550-sq-ft) rooms are a harmonious blend of contemporary style and Arabic tradition in warm colours and luxurious fabrics. The 81 suites, on the other hand, have apartments ranging from 65 sq m (700 sq ft) to just over 93 sq m (1000 sq ft), while the spectacular Imperial Suite, measuring more than 465 sq m (5,000 sq ft), encompasses four apartments on two floors. All bedrooms feature Mybed, the exclusive Sofitel bedding concept that promotes a good night's sleep.

The Palace offers an array of first-class services with the most advanced hotel technology. There is a butler assigned to

THIS PAGE (FROM TOP): *Rediscover the meaning of 'sweet dreams' at any of The Palace – The Old Town's deluxe rooms and suites; the hotel shines like a jewel in the night.*
OPPOSITE (FROM TOP): *Ewaan will satisfy cravings for sumptuous food any time of the day; LeSpa boasts luxurious changing rooms.*

...get used to living a royal lifestyle.

each room, limousines at guests' beck and call, and wireless Internet access in all rooms. For business trips and seminars, The Palace offers a full-service business centre with conference rooms, as well as secretarial and computer facilities. Guests can also enjoy a ride across the lake on the traditional abra service to the excellent shops and restaurants in Downtown Burj Dubai.

The central location of Old Town Island allows for easy access to all the major attractions of Dubai. The Palace is in an ideal position close to the new Dubai Mall, the biggest shopping centre in the world, with 1,200 shops and attractions such as the exotic Souk de l'or, an aquarium and an Olympic-size ice rink.

There is a wealth of pleasures within the hotel, including superb entertainment and dining. The enchanting lakeside setting of Thiptara sets the scene for the best Thai food this side of Bangkok. The Asado is a genuine Argentinean steakhouse, where meat is cooked asador criollo on an open grill. Live entertainment adds to the festive atmosphere and recreates the style and sophistication of Buenos Aires. For all-day dining, Ewaan serves a blend of Mediterranean and Middle Eastern cuisine. A favourite gathering place is the Lounge Bar, which offers a selection of freshly baked pastries, tea, coffee and cocktails.

One of the highlights of The Palace is its exquisite Oriental spa. LeSpa is a 929-sq-m (10,000-sq-ft) space dedicated to the well-being and relaxation of hotel guests. It has a splendid range of massages, treatments and wellness therapies from around the world, as well as products and techniques catered to the different seasons. There are six treatment rooms, four spa rooms, an Oriental bath house with a hammam table, a gym, a relaxation area and a beauty salon.

Activities at The Palace include swimming and sunning at the hotel's stunning pool, tennis at a nearby facility, golf at neighbouring championship courses and a series of tours and excursions happily organised by the concierge. With so much provided for guests' comfort, amusement and well-being, The Palace – The Old Town certainly makes it easy to get used to living a royal lifestyle.

rooms
242

food
Thiptara: Thai • Asado: Argentinean • Ewaan: Mediterranean and Middle Eastern

drink
Lounge Bar • Asado Bar • Thiptara Bar

features
wireless Internet access • butler service • Mybed bedding concept • limousine transfers • business centre • meeting rooms • spa • gym • hammam • outdoor heated pool • sauna • massage • jacuzzi • private beach access

nearby
Burj Dubai • Dubai Mall • Dubai World Trade Centre • Dubai Museum • Nad Al Sheba Racecourse • Ski Dubai • Dubai International Financial Centre

contact
The Old Town Island, Downtown Burj Dubai
PO Box 9770, Dubai, UAE •
telephone: +971.4.428 7888 •
facsimile: +971.4.428 7999 •
email: h6230-re@accor.com •
website: www.sofitel.com

al manzil hotel

Opened in December 2006, this four-star, deluxe business hotel is conveniently situated on the outer rim of Burj Dubai Boulevard, a lively stretch that encircles the emirate's newest treasure, the Burj Dubai development. Within walking distance is a wealth of dining and entertainment options at new and upcoming developments such as Old Town Island, the Burj Dubai Lake Park and the Dubai Mall. Guests not only find themselves on the doorstep of the world's tallest tower and the largest retail complex in the world, but also at the centre of Dubai's charm, in a hotel that embodies the artful union of old and new.

Al Manzil's commanding exterior features traditional Arabic architectural forms, where lattices and minaret-style arches combine with understated ornaments to give the 10-storey building a classic presence in the heart of downtown Dubai. The view once inside the lobby, however, often takes visitors by surprise. Modern designer furnishings in relaxed earth tones and the judicious use of wood and glass elements take the interplay between East and West to another level altogether. But for all its concessions to modernity, the atmosphere at Al Manzil remains warm and intimate. Refined touches

THIS PAGE (FROM TOP): *Exquisitely crafted Arabic lanterns add interest and colour to rooms and suites; Al Manzil offers top-notch service at reasonable rates.*

OPPOSITE: *Marvel at the hotel's stunning exterior.*

...a hotel that embodies the artful union of old and new.

and exemplary Arabic hospitality elevate the experience at this hotel to what could easily be called five-star anywhere else in the world.

The relationship between ancient tradition and modern innovation is seen throughout the property's rooms and suites. Amid fine, luxury appointments and stylish designs lie undeniably old-world comforts. Clean and modern lines complement the colours and textures of the Middle East. In every bedroom, intricately cut lanterns cast patterned motifs along the walls. Spacious desks make room for business travellers' laptops and papers, while complimentary wireless Internet access keeps them connected to offices and contacts beyond. All rooms feature air-conditioning, minibars, coffee and tea making facilities and revolving flat-screen TV.

The 155 Standard King rooms offer plenty of space to stretch out after a long day of meetings, shopping, or both. The large, premium beds showcase fine Egyptian cotton linens and soft, fluffy pillows for a perfect night's rest. The Standard rooms are spacious at approximately 36 sq m (388 sq ft), but are made to look even larger through clever interior design and layout. Glass partitions separate the beds and living areas from large open plan bathrooms, giving a sense of continuous space. Each bathroom features a large freestanding bath, perfect for relaxing and unwinding, as well as a separate shower and toilet. Also available are 32 similarly equipped Standard Twin rooms.

THIS PAGE: *Have a blissful night of sleep in this stylish and comfortable room.*

OPPOSITE (FROM LEFT): *Wash away the stresses of the day with a swim at the inviting pool; tuck into a sumptuous meal at the Courtyard.*

For a stay with a difference, the hotel offers eight Junior Suites. Each one has an even more spacious floor plan, complete with a generous sitting area and a balcony that looks out over the surrounding districts. Two physically challenged rooms are available for guests with disabilities. They are single rooms, with passages to adjoining rooms for caregivers.

True to the hotel's aim of meeting all of its guests' needs, Al Manzil has three world-class dining establishments under its roof. The Conservatory is open from the early hours of the morning until just before midnight. It serves a full buffet breakfast with delectable croissants, fresh fruit and an 'a la minute' juice bar, and various international dishes, with à la carte and a buffet available at lunch and dinner. Diners can choose to take their meals and evening drinks at the Courtyard, which also offers its own menu. This restaurant is a good place to admire the building's architecture and enjoy a shisha under the night sky. At other times of the day, Mokaroma, a trendy coffee shop with an open-air terrace, is perfect for casual meetings and lazy afternoons. Its bright and breezy atmosphere complements the freshly baked cakes and pastries on offer, which are best enjoyed with a steaming cup of gourmet roasted coffee.

Nezesaussi is a speciality restaurant with a name and menu inspired by three countries: New Zealand, South Africa and Australia. It combines sports entertainment with a grill and bar concept that seats 120 people. Explore the extensive wine and beer selection, with dozens of imported brews and bottles from the three countries. Satisfy appetites on a large scale with Nezesaussi's southern hemisphere meals like succulent steaks, chops, and boerewors sausages.

For those who like to mix business with pleasure, Al Manzil gets it right. Arrange a conference here, and take advantage of the three meeting rooms that can seat up to 136 people theatre-style. There is also a boardroom for 10. All of these rooms have access to natural light, and some even have outdoor terraces. A 24-hour business centre with complimentary Internet connectivity is available.

...offering warmth, comfort and value for money.

In addition to being a first-class business facility, Al Manzil also caters to health and leisure needs. An inviting outdoor pool is temperature controlled, so any time is a good time for a relaxing dip. The health-conscious can opt for a workout on state-of-the-art equipment at the airy Fitness Centre, which is open 24 hours, and everyone else can enjoy no end of nearby shopping options. World-class retail is just down the street, while a taste of the traditional local shopping experience is even closer. An array of 30 shops and boutiques, named the Souk Al Manzil, is directly connected to the hotel. When the Dubai Mall is completed, both the past and present of shopping malls will literally stand side by side, building on each other's strengths.

In rapidly developing Dubai, known for its superlatives and extravagance, it is comforting to discover an establishment that prides itself on offering warmth, comfort and value for money. Al Manzil is a retreat that is delightfully uncomplicated, letting one luxuriate in the free time and freedom that is the mark of any true holiday. In this regard, the hotel is truly an oasis within that greatest of all oases, the Burj Dubai.

rooms
197

food
Conservatory: international • Nezesaussi: New Zealand, South African and Australian • Mokaroma: coffee shop • Courtyard: traditional Arabic

drink
Nezesaussi • Mokaroma • Conservatory • Courtyard

features
pool • fitness centre • business centre • complimentary wireless Internet access • limousine service • meeting rooms • boardroom

nearby
Burj Dubai Shopping Complex • Old Town Island • Mall of the Emirates • Dubai World Trade Centre • Ibn Battuta Mall • Mercato Gold and Diamond Park • Jumeirah Beach Park • Dubai World Trade Centre Exhibition Grounds

contact
PO Box 114822, Burj Dubai Boulevard The Old Town, Dubai, UAE •
telephone: +971.4. 428 5888 •
facsimile: +971.4. 428 5999 •
email: reservationsalmanzil@southernsun.ae •
website: www.almanzilhotel.com

qamardeen hotel

As Dubai prepares itself for the grand opening of the world's most ambitious building project, the Burj Dubai, guests at an exclusive four-star hotel just across the street might very well have the best seats in the house. Located in the Old Town area of the Burj Dubai commercial and residential district, Qamardeen is a deluxe establishment with 186 rooms and suites generously spaced over its six expansive floors. Despite appearances—Qamardeen has a majestic Arabian façade the color of sandstone which, by night, is illuminated like a castle's ramparts—one can expect a thoroughly modern and sophisticated hotel with dining and leisure facilities worthy of this Middle Eastern capital of luxury.

Throughout the hotel, Arabic traditions merge with 21st century sensibilities for a refreshingly different experience. In the lobby's reception area, stylish designer furnishings in bold shades of red rest on rugs with traditional latticework designs. Elsewhere, these shapes and patterns reappear in subtle forms all over Qamardeen. Helpful staff, dressed in flowing, traditional attire, see to one's every need. The quality of service here is impeccable, as is the hallmark of properties operated by Southern Sun Hotels, South Africa's leading hotel brand.

Inspired by the spice trade, each one of the 123 Standard Queen rooms, 48 Standard Twin rooms, 13 suites and two rooms for the

THIS PAGE (FROM TOP): *An elegantly arranged table setting, fit for a celebration or a simple meal; unwind with friends while sipping a piping hot brew from the coffee bar.*
OPPOSITE: *Sit down to have relaxed conversations amid soaring ceilings.*

...*a thoroughly modern and sophisticated hotel*...

physically challenged are dressed in rich materials and elegant embellishments conveying the full breadth of Middle Eastern warmth and variety. Comfort is ensured by a host of standard amenities that are anything but. The TV is large, and of the flat-screen variety. The Internet access is more than just high-speed, it is unlimited and complimentary. Add a generous work desk for writing anything from postcards to presentations, a well-stocked minibar, premium tea and coffee making facilities, and the result is a delightful stay for couples, families, and globetrotters.

Standard Queen rooms are designed to feel open and spacious, with large glass-walled bathrooms that include a bath tub, separate shower, and separate toilet. With layouts that allow the eye to be drawn to free spaces without restrictions, they make one feel at home immediately. Standard Twin rooms are similarly sized, but feature open plan bathrooms with separate showers, double vanities and separate toilets. There are also two wheelchair-accessible rooms with doors leading to adjacent rooms for caregivers.

At twice the size of regular rooms, the 10 Executive Suites promise a very special stay at Qamardeen. Roomy at over 62 sq m (667 sq ft), they are ideal places for guests to relax in perfect luxury with friends and visitors. Each bedroom is draped in relaxed earth tones with plenty of throw cushions and traditional-style pillows on each king-sized bed. They have separate baths and

THIS PAGE: *Each suite comes with a separate living space.*
OPPOSITE (FROM LEFT): *Simple, stylish furnishings are a hallmark of this deluxe hotel; order a fresh fruit smoothie from the Pool Café.*

showers, and the tastefully furnished lounge areas have guest toilets of their own. Complete with large sofas and lots of natural light from French windows, the living areas are liable to put one right at home.

The three Deluxe Suites offer 93 sq m (1,001 sq ft) of space. Featuring bedrooms with en suite baths and showers, the suites also come complete with dressing rooms for trying out the fruits of one's Dubai shopping labours. Connected to the bedrooms are plush, inviting lounges and study areas for entertaining. There are also separate butler's kitchens, dining areas, and guest toilets. These spacious suites are perfect for large families, extended stays, or whenever luxury absolutely must come first.

Qamardeen's relaxed mood extends to its casual dining experiences, which place pleasure and convenience above all. Esca, an all-day dining restaurant, serves a wide range of authentic and inspired Mediterranean and Italian cuisine. Enjoy a freshly made pizza or pasta dish, and bring adventurous tastebuds on a journey with Esca's exotic cuts of meats, unusual salads, and scrumptiously rich desserts guaranteed to pique your interest. Dine in the comfort of its apricot-hued walls and rosewood tables, or move outdoors onto an airy terrace in view of the pool and gardens. The restaurant offers an à la carte menu throughout the day and into the night.

The Lobby Lounge, decorated in modern furnishings, serves a selection of hot beverages and gourmet brews to go with its delicious, freshly baked breads, cakes and pastries. Guests are drawn in by the rich aromas, but it is the soothing décor, high ceilings and soft music that keep them lingering. It is an ideal place to find oneself at the end of an exciting day, recounting adventures over a hot shot of espresso and a warm biscotti. A traditional ladies' majlis, or seating area, is also available.

Alternatively, stretch out by the beautiful pool with a long, cool drink from the Pool Café. The large outdoor pool is uniquely shaped and bordered by palm trees. Health enthusiasts may also want to make use of the hotel's new and very well-equipped fitness centre, which is open 24 hours. Cool

...a true find for visitors to Dubai...

and well-ventilated, the gym sees a lot of activity in the mornings and evenings, but is easily large enough to accommodate all workout regimes.

While business travellers are expected to make full use of the 24-hour Business Centre and complimentary wireless Internet access in the hotel's public areas, everyone else is likely to be at the shops—and what a pleasure it is to have them all close at hand. The Dubai Mall, soon to be the world's largest retail mall; the Mall of the Emirates; and the Old Town Souk—30 exquisite boutique shops—are all near. Free, pre-scheduled transfers to the shops, the beach and back to the hotel are available. Upcoming attractions like Old Town Island and the Burj Dubai Lake Park will soon make Burj Dubai Boulevard an even more exciting location, with dining, retail and entertainment options that easily compare to those on other world class shopping streets such as Oxford in London and the Champs-Élysées in Paris.

With remarkably stunning old-world architecture that promises to hold its own even against the marvel that is the Burj Dubai development, impeccable and friendly hotel service that surpasses expectations of a four-star establishment, and a superb location, Qamardeen offers excellent value for money. The hotel is a true find for visitors to Dubai, and certainly no visit to it is ever the last.

rooms
186

food
Esca: Mediterranean and Italian

drink
Lobby Lounge • Pool Café • Esca

features
pool • fitness centre • business centre • complimentary wireless Internet access • limousine service • boardrooms

nearby
Burj Dubai Shopping Complex • Old Town Island • Mall of the Emirates • Dubai World Trade Centre • Ibn Battuta Mall • Mercato Gold and Diamond Park • Jumeirah Beach Park Dubai World Trade Centre Exhibition Grounds

contact
PO Box 11788, Burj Dubai Boulevard
The Old Town, Dubai, UAE •
telephone: +971.4. 428 6888 •
facsimile: +971.4. 428 6999 •
email:reservationsqamardeen@southernsun.ae •
website: www.qamardeenhotel.com

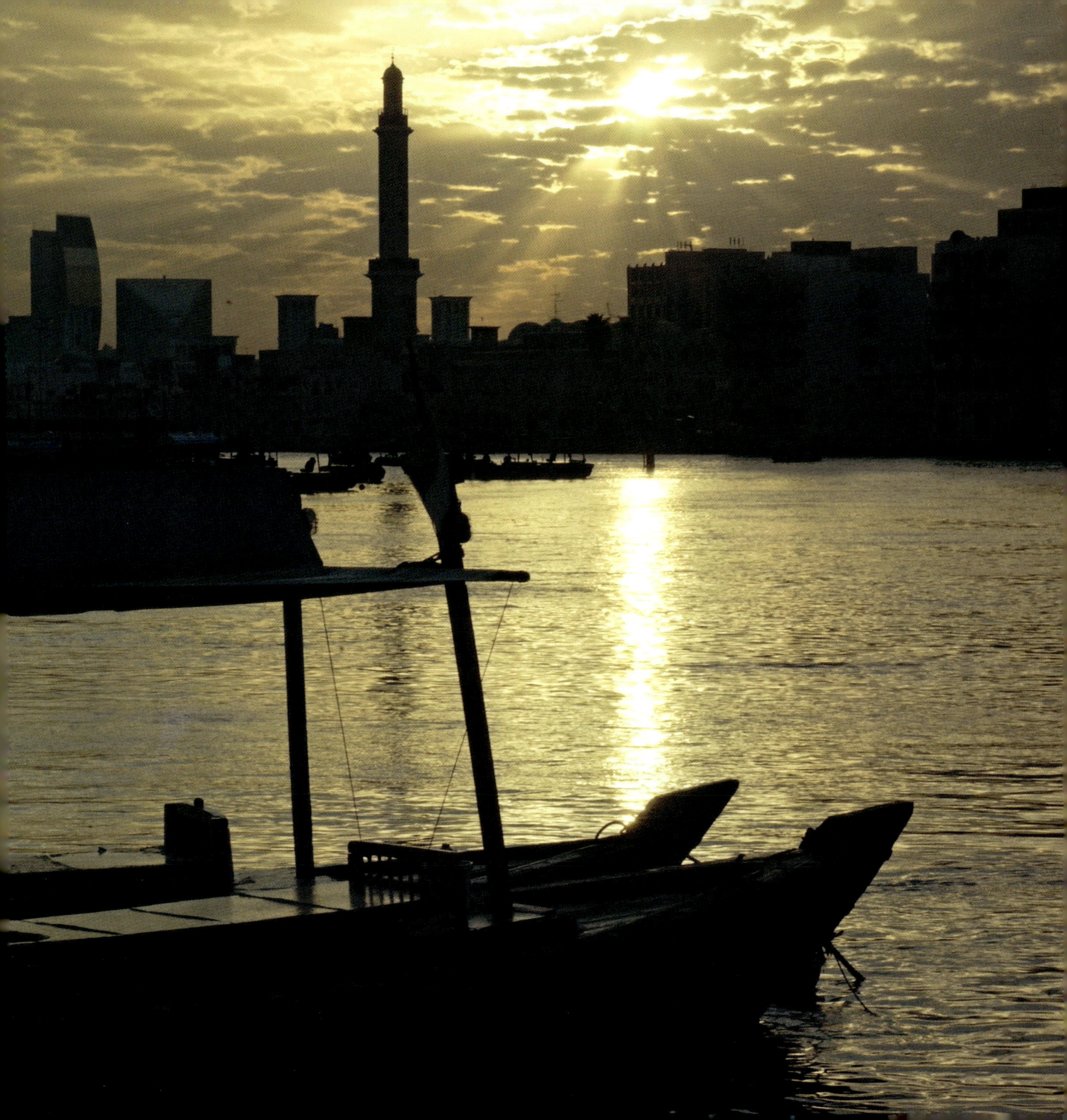

creekside

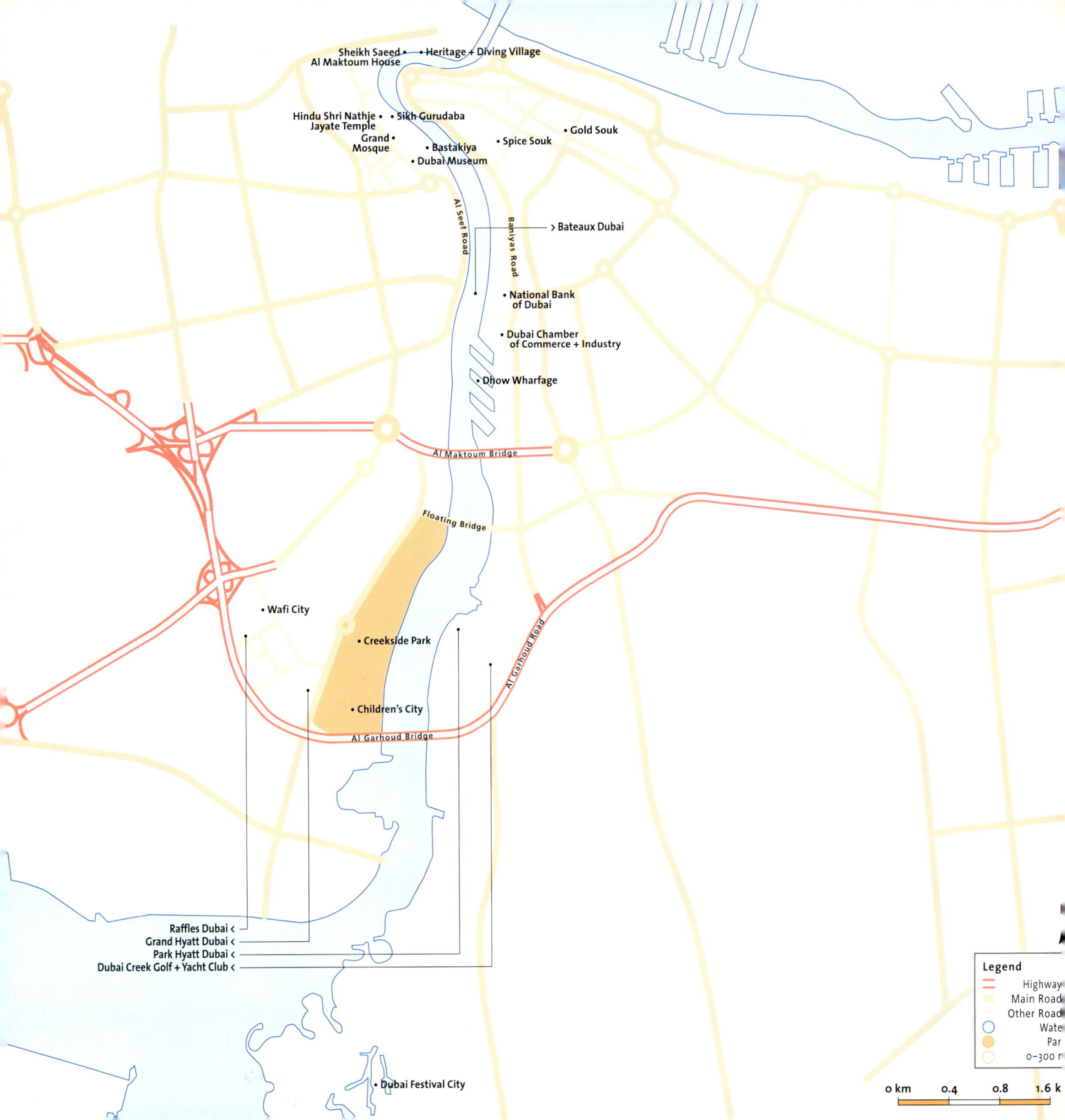

creekside

two sides of a river
Dubai is traditionally divided by the Creek, a spectacular waterway that was the lifeblood of Dubai's maritime trading for many generations, and still provides a vital artery for shipping today. The Creek retains much of Dubai's heritage, and is a fascinating place to embark on a sightseeing tour of what is generally considered to be Old Dubai. The two sides of the Creek are Bur Dubai on the south, and Deira on the north.

bur dubai: an early headstart
Bur Dubai got off to a flying start when the Al Maktoum family and their clan settled there after moving to Dubai, and offered tax-free trading in order to woo merchants to its shores. Bastak in Southern Iran was a trading partner and soon adventurous fortune seekers set up shop. The area became known as 'Bastakiya' and many local families who are descended from the early settlers still live there. As Dubai developed, much of the original architecture was lost in the process. For instance, the local barasti houses, made from palm fronds, are completely gone.

Happily Bastakiya has been made a heritage preservation area—one of the very few places where you can wander about and get a feel for what life was like generations before the oil boom. Bastakiya's distinctive limestone and coral houses are about 100 years old, and have high walls, intricately carved wooden doors and windows, wind towers to help cool the interiors with a flow of air, and gracious, shaded courtyards. Stroll along the maze of winding lanes, now flourishing with chic galleries like Majlis, in a charmingly restored merchant's house that has an excellent selection of pictures inspired by the region, and XVA, which exhibits the latest contemporary art and has a guesthouse, shop and café as well. The Ostra Gallery, FAE boutique, and Eye Art Gallery are also well worth an afternoon's visit. After all that sightseeing, stop for a meal at one of Bastakiya's atmospheric restaurants, such as Basta Art Café, Bastakiah Nights or Local House, a restaurant serving Emirati cuisine.

heritage on the waterfront
The Al Fahidi Fort is the oldest building in Dubai, built in 1787, and since being restored in the 1970s, home to the Dubai Museum. This rather quaint museum has many diorama displays featuring life-size figures in traditional dress, from richly embroidered bridal finery to basic Bedouin robes, along with photographs illustrating Dubai's 'rags to riches' history. Nearby is the Grand Mosque, with the highest minaret in Dubai, also the Hindu Shri Nathje Jayate Temple, as well as a Sikh Gurudaba. Bur Dubai's rich multicultural mix is part of its charm. The Bur Dubai souks have everything from tacky souvenirs (sequined belly dancing outfits, anyone?) to the

THIS PAGE: *Across the Creek, the twin Rolex Towers dominate the glittering city skyline in a tranquil evening view of Deira.*
PAGE 72: *The Creek, lifeblood of trade in Dubai's younger days.*

latest electronic gadgets in Al-Fahidi Street. Historically, the area was settled by traders from southern India, and their influence is pervasive, with Bollywood film soundtracks blaring, sari shops on every corner and spicy curries from roadside stalls adding to the atmosphere—at times you feel you could be in a street in Mumbai. Bur Dubai's souks are at their best at night, when it's cooler and quite lively. Join in the energetic bargaining and don't be shy about asking for a discount. Although the street is best known for electrical products, there is an eclectic selection of goods—from sublime pashminas to ridiculous singing camels.

About a 10-minute stroll past the Bur Dubai Abra Station along the Creek brings you to the waterfront heritage area on Al-Shindagha Road. Here you'll find the beautifully restored Sheikh Saeed Al Maktoum House, the former home of the brilliant ruler who helped establish Dubai. Built in 1896, the spacious 30 room residence, with its main courtyard, four wind towers, balustrades, teak doors and spacious majlis, is a classic example of Arabic architecture in the Gulf. It is now a museum showcasing a rare collection of vintage photographs that eloquently reveals life in Dubai before the oil boom.

Nearby is the Heritage and Diving Village. This is a living museum, where you can see craftspeople involved in such traditional arts as weaving and pottery. Emirati women were known for their skillful needlework and it is still a popular pastime for ladies, who gather together to sew, have tea and exchange the latest news. There is also an attractive recreation of a Bedouin tented camp, which provides insights into their fast-vanishing way of life. Dubai's colourful history as a pearl-trading centre is also explored in exhibitions, and during the holidays there are live performances of traditional dances. There are shops selling souvenirs and food stands selling snacks like savoury fried doughnuts—a chance for visitors to try local home-made food.

For a peaceful place to watch the water ballet of dhows, pleasure boats, abras and container ships as they go about their business, visit Creekside Park by the Al Maktoum Bridge. The striking contrast between the gleaming steel skyscrapers and ancient wooden dhows reflects Dubai's respect for the past in its pursuit of the future. Hire a bike or just wander along the well-landscaped pathways. If you're feeling brave take the 2.5-km (1.5-mile) cable car ride for bird's eye views of the Creek. If you're travelling with the kids pop by Children's City, an interactive blend of amusement and education, with a planetarium, play area and nature centre.

atmospheric deira

Once you've explored Bur Dubai, do as the locals and hop on an abra to get to the Deira side. These traditional water taxis have been ferrying passengers to and fro for years and around 15,000 commuters use them every day. The abra stations are always busy but just line up with everyone and you'll soon have your place on board. It's great fun, if a bit bumpy.

If you prefer a more luxurious craft there are companies such as Bateaux Dubai, which offer Creek cruises in style. It's enchanting at night, when the lights of the city are reflected in the water. Along the Creek are many Dubai landmarks, such as the towering blue glass triangle of the Dubai Chamber of Commerce & Industry, the sloping tablet of the National Bank of Dubai,

THIS PAGE (FROM TOP): *Sunlight pours through ventilation gaps in the roof of one of Dubai's oldest open souks—the Textile Souk; colourfully embroidered slip-on shoes put on a bright show.*

OPPOSITE: *Abras, or water taxis, are part of ordinary public transport in Dubai—take a ride down the Creek to get a real feel of everyday life here.*

...the eclectic buzz that makes the Creek waterfront one of the most enjoyable places in Dubai.

which turns to a golden ingot in the light of the setting sun, and the Dubai Creek Golf & Yacht Club, whose soaring white roofs were designed to resemble the sails of an Arab dhow. There are palaces and warehouses, floating restaurants and fishing boats, majestic mega yachts and rusty trawlers—all adding to the eclectic buzz that makes the Creek waterfront one of the most enjoyable places in Dubai.

Deira was settled early in Dubai's career as a trading port, and while it can appear rather run-down and chaotic in comparison with the gleaming shopping malls of exclusive Jumeirah, its many souks have more authentic charm. The most atmospheric of them is the Spice Souk (just across from the abra station), an exotic showcase of commodities traded since the dawn of commerce. You see trays of frankincense, saffron, rose petals, cardamom and nuts—a cook's tour of the region all in one spot and going strong since the 1830s. Massive burlap bags brimming over with cumin seeds, cardamon pods, cashew nuts, yellow and green lentils, burnt orange turmeric, cloves, star anise and more are strewn about the dusty, close-packed shops. The traders come from Africa, India, Iran and throughout Arabia, and the hum of many dialects fills the air as buyers come and deals are made.

down in the souk

Just down the street, the seductive scents of traditional Arabian perfumes, oud (scented wood burned as incense) and attar (fragrant oils, often made from rose petals) waft through the air at the Perfume Souk. Float along on a scented cloud of jasmine, ylang ylang, sandalwood, rose, neroli, pathouli, vetiver and musk. Try one of the popular Arabic perfume brands, like Ajmal, or have a perfume mixed specially for you. The decorative bottles make pretty souvenirs.

The biggest and flashiest of all the markets is the Gold Souk, which attracts thousands of bargain-hunters to its glittering interior. It's an Aladdin's Cave of treasures, with every sort of gold jewellery imaginable. It is always busy and it can get hot and crowded, but the Gold Souk is one of Dubai's most popular sights, and a must for anyone who likes jewellery. The prices are very competitive. Gold is sold by weight, with the quality of the workmanship adding to the basic price. Be sure to haggle, staying cool and determined, but ready to walk away if the deal isn't right. There's always another shop waiting to tempt you. Gold charms and chains are particularly good buys. Jewellery is a huge business in the Arab world and very much a part of the culture. Traditionally, a women's wealth was in her jewellery, so the more bling, the better.

THIS PAGE (FROM TOP): *A jungle of ships and smaller boats crowd the cacophonous wharves; all that glitters is gold—here at the Gold Souk in Deira.*

OPPOSITE: *New man-made islands just off Deira are an upcoming development that will totally revitalise the area.*

Along with its atmospheric souks, Deira has off-the-beaten-track places to explore, such as the dhow wharves, where you can see these ancient craft being built and serviced. Ships still ply their wares from India, Africa and the Middle East. You can watch as they unload their cargo, as they have for centuries, although now it is more likely to be the latest electronic goods rather than exotic bolts of silk. For a glimpse of what life was like for the wealthy merchants of Dubai at the turn of the century, visit Heritage House. Completely restored, it dates from 1890 and is typical of the homes of prominent families at the time. The majlis, or meeting room, is an essential part of Arab house design and such families had a separate ladies' majlis as well as a special 'bride's room'. Behind the house is the Al-Ahmadiya School, the oldest in Dubai (the current ruler, Sheikh Mohammed, is a distinguished alumnus) and is open to visitors, with displays showing how education was achieved before formal schooling was established in 1956.

coming up

The eastern section of the Creek, just over Al Garhoud Bridge, is having a massive makeover with the launch of Dubai Festival City, an ambitious and exciting multi-billion dollar project that will completely revitalise the waterfront. Although the development is still under construction, there are enough venues open to make it well worth a visit. There are scenic Creekside views, with walkways, canals, fountains, restaurants and designer boutiques—as well as major retailers like Ikea and Marks & Spencer. With a variety of venues opening, the area is set to be popular for concerts and live entertainment. There is also a marina and a lively boating scene.

New hotels such as the InterContinental Dubai are adding glamour to the new neighbourhood. At 35 floors, the hotel has panoramic views over the Creek. Nearby, the new 18-hole championship Four Seasons Golf Club, with its dramatic, modernist clubhouse, based on the arc of a golfer's swing, is already a landmark, and the completion of the Four Seasons luxury resort hotel is keenly anticipated. With so much happening in this part of town, Dubai Festival City promises to be the most exciting new development on the Creek, giving Deira a sophisticated new image.

THIS PAGE: *A striking panorama of the Creek and its surrounds.*
OPPOSITE: *For bird's eye views of the Creek, hop on a cable car ride from Creekside Park.*

There are scenic Creekside views...

raffles dubai

Dubai's inhabitants have come to expect their city to change without so much as a moment's notice, rarely batting an eyelid at the emergence of some man-made island or desert miracle. However, one new landmark on Sheikh Rashid Road has turned more than a few heads. Perhaps it is the boldness of its pyramidal structure with a glowing peak of glass and steel, rising from the sand like an Egyptian mirage. Or perhaps, knowledge of its otherworldly spa and 11 dining establishments has finally escaped upper-class circles. Whatever may be the case, few hotels in recent memory have made as impressive an appearance in the emirate as Raffles Dubai.

From the moment one sets foot into the hotel, a vision of opulence unfolds. The reception area overwhelms the senses with its size and the richness of its construction. Black marble flooring and intricately carved pillars the colour of sandstone unite the atrium, while a cascading water feature serves as the centre of attraction.

The Grand Stateroom is Raffles Dubai's standard guestroom, offering 70 sq m (753 sq ft) of space. With a private balcony that other hotels would only build into a suite, the Grand Stateroom defies the conventional definition of standard accommodation. The living area is large and open, with a lounge

THIS PAGE: Raffles Dubai draws design inspiration from the great pyramids of Egypt.
OPPOSITE: The lobby is awe-inspiring.

...a vision of opulence unfolds.

area complete with sofa, widescreen wall-mounted TV, work desk and an incredible view of the city. The bathrooms feature walk-in rainfall showers, soaking tubs and an array of premium toiletries.

Business travellers may prefer the Raffles Inc Staterooms, designed to match luxury with modern amenities. In addition to wireless Internet access, these rooms include convenient services such as airport transfers, 24-hour check-in and check-out and access to the Raffles Inc Lounge, which serves breakfast, drinks and canapés in a serene environment conducive to work.

Furnished with an abundance of wood, cream fabrics and warm lighting fixtures, the corner Diplomatic Suites give first-time travellers to Dubai a powerful sense of place. Featuring separate bedroom and lounge areas, guests can simultaneously make full use of the living and dining spaces, as well as a work alcove. Landmark Suites, on the other hand, offer a different take on interior decoration with dark wood highlights and the judicious use of leather. Their master bedrooms are oversized, and the inclusion of well-stocked minibars make them perfect for both business and social entertainment.

Those on the lookout for extraordinary creature comforts will find them plentiful in the remaining three suite options. Each of the four Presidential Suites spans 301 sq m (3,240 sq ft), and boasts an intriguing design concept that revolves around the

THIS PAGE (FROM LEFT): *The Middle Eastern Royal Suite boasts a princely master bedroom; the Grand Stateroom allows guests to relax in spacious comfort.*

OPPOSITE (FROM TOP): *Unique accent pieces, such as this lamp artwork, are prominent throughout Raffles Dubai; The Noble House blends striking Chinese motifs with clean Scandinavian design.*

four elements: earth, wind, fire and water. They are represented in wall coverings, fabric prints, art pieces and even exclusive designer furnishings. The overall effect calms the spirit; so does the panoramic view of the city below. Penthouse Suites are perfect for those seeking a home away from home, or perhaps a romantic getaway or honeymoon. Lavishly designed in every way, their interiors feature red highlights that hint at a playfulness beneath the surface. Large four-poster beds form the centrepiece of the bedrooms, which also share access to the private balconies.

However, everything pales in comparison to the Royal Suites—and those fortunate enough to enjoy them can choose between a majestic Middle Eastern-style suite and an exotic Asian one complete with Buddhist statues. The bedchambers are enhanced with touches of soft lighting and silk. Beyond the bedroom doors, spacious majlis-style entertainment rooms, full kitchen facilities and dining rooms large enough for 10 easily accommodate any informal business meeting or gathering of friends.

Those wishing to entertain guests outside their suites will find no shortage of options. The major cuisines of the world are well-represented at over 11 restaurants and bars. Asia alone is served by several: The Noble House, a fine dining Chinese restaurant; Asiana, which specializes in favourites such as dim sum and noodles; the Crossroads Cocktail Bar, featuring an authentic Balinese design and atmosphere; and the exquisite China Moon Champagne Bar, which redefines luxury dining with champagne and caviar.

Egypt's presence is felt in the spectacular Raffles Botanical Garden, a 1-hectare (2-acre) garden planted with rare tropical blooms and

This sense of magic, of finding something new beyond every corner...is everywhere...

orchids on the third floor of the hotel. Divided into four themed areas representing the four elements, nearly 130,000 plants converge on a central glass dome dubbed the 'Eye of Horus'. As part of the award-winning RafflesAmrita Spa, enjoy a soothing body treatment in the Garden Pavilion, or choose one of seven other treatment rooms for a relaxing experience to savour. The Spa is one of few places in the world to explore a bold new concept—the Egyptian Gold, a facial treatment that uses a mist of 24-karat gold.

Be prepared to adjust your sense of scale while at Raffles Dubai. Large and impressive as it is, venture out and you will find that the hotel is part of the Wafi development, which includes the adjacent Wafi City Mall. As a shopping and leisure destination, Wafi City Mall has no equal. With over 350 international stores and a recreation of a 14th-century crafts souk, the mall has everything one could desire in a single convenient location. It also succeeds on an artistic level: shoppers are greeted by Egyptian motifs embedded in stained glass, carved surfaces and mosaics everywhere they turn. The entire mall is enveloped by lush greenery, giving it the appearance of a hidden oasis. This sense of magic, of finding something new beyond every corner—whether an artefact from an ancient civilisation or some pleasure one never knew existed—is everywhere at Raffles Dubai.

rooms
248

food
Fire & Ice – Raffles Cellar & Grill: trans-ethnic • Azur All Day Dining: international and pan-Arabic • The Noble House: contemporary Chinese • Asiana Restaurant: Far Eastern • Raffles Salon: light fare • Pool Restaurant & Bar: light fare • Café Raffles: coffee shop

drink
China Moon Champagne Bar • New Asia Bar & Club • Crossroads Cocktail Bar • Juice Bar

features
Raffles Inc Lounge • butler service • wireless Internet access • fitness club • RafflesAmrita Spa • pool • meeting rooms • library • Botanical Garden • business services

nearby
Wafi Mall • Deira City Centre • Mall of the Emirates • Ibn Battuta Mall • The Creek • WonderLand family theme park • golf • desert safari • museums • Dubai Zoo

contact
Sheikh Rashid Road, Wafi City
PO Box 121800, Dubai, UAE •
telephone: +971.4.324 8888 •
facsimile: +971.4.324 6000 •
email: dubai@raffles.com •
website: dubai.raffles.com

grand hyatt dubai

Grand Hyatt Dubai manages to be very clever at bringing guests the best of both business and leisure facilities, making it one of the top places in town for those who like to play hard and work hard. It is conveniently close to the main Dubai attractions, such as the shopping mecca of Wafi City, the financial district on Sheikh Zayed Road, and the heritage areas of the Dubai Creek—a city landmark whose futuristic, undulating curves can be seen from many miles away. Grand Hyatt Dubai looks big, and it is—with 674 deluxe rooms and suites, the region's most high-tech conference centre, 15 hectares (37 acres) of lush landscaped gardens, a 450-m (1,476-ft) jogging track, one of the biggest outdoor pools in Dubai, a tennis centre, and a top spa and health club. Grand Hyatt Dubai has everything to ensure

THIS PAGE (FROM TOP): *Relax at the Manhattan Grill lounge after a satisfying steak meal; these orchids provide a touch of the tropics and beckon guests to The Grand Spa.*

OPPOSITE: *Any time is a good time for a refreshing dip in the large indoor pool.*

...*a top-notch option.*

a successful business trip or holiday. No matter what the event or occasion, the hotel is a top-notch option.

However, 'big' at Grand Hyatt Dubai does not mean impersonal. The staff are exceptionally proactive, helpful and genuinely friendly. They really do hope guests have a nice day and will go out of their way to make it happen. The ambience is buzzy and upbeat, with a lively lobby that is one of the most glamorous in town. The huge chandelier—made from over 150,000 Swarovski crystals—that greets visitors as they walk into the Al Nakheel Lounge in the lobby is typical of the attention to detail that makes Grand Hyatt Dubai so popular.

Two light sculptures, made from glass and 24-carat gold, adorn the walls of the lobby. The sculptures reflect the sea and the desert—two quintessential features of the Dubai landscape. The hotel is also famous for its full-sized Arabian dhows suspended from the ceiling of its atrium lobby. Handmade in New Zealand, each dhow weighs 5 tonnes and is actually part of the structural support for the building. Below the dhows is a unique 345-sq-m (3,714 sq ft) indoor tropical garden on two floors, complete with running streams and little bridges, cascading flowers and towering palms. There is nothing else like it in Dubai.

Accommodation at Grand Hyatt Dubai provides a variety of options to suit individual preferences. All the 674 deluxe guestrooms,

Abdul Elmubarak and Mohammed Hossen. The Grand Rooms, divided into King and Twin rooms, offer 42–54 sq m (452–581 sq ft) of space. Situated on the 1st to 16th floors of the hotel, these rooms have interactive satellite TV, minibars, personal safes, walk-in wardrobes, coffee and tea making facilities and luxurious marble bathrooms with separate bath and shower, twin washbasins and hairdryers. The Grand Club rooms, located on the 11th to 16th floors, have the added benefit of access to the 24-hour Grand Club Lounge. The Lounge provides an elegant meeting space, complimentary Continental breakfast, beverages throughout the day, and evening cocktails and canapés. If the family is in tow, they will not feel left out because there is also an additional family lounge with entertainment options for the kids. Add to this complimentary suit pressing, express check-in and check-out, high-speed Internet access and free airport transfers, and it is easy to see why the Grand Club rooms are so popular.

Guests desiring even more space can stay at the 66-sq-m (710-sq-ft) Grand Deluxe Room. The 88-sq-m (947-sq-ft) Grand Suites are another option, offering a living room and a separate king-sized bedroom. The Emiri Suites, meanwhile, provide 132 sq m (1,421 sq ft) of space and feature living and dining areas with kitchenette, a guest bathroom, and a separate bedroom with an en suite bathroom. Located on the 13th to 16th

THIS PAGE: *The Prince Suite offers an elegant sitting area.*

OPPOSITE: *The Creekside King Room combines comfort with views of Dubai's historic Creek.*

Grand Club rooms and suites have sweeping views of either Dubai's distinctive skyline or the historic Dubai Creek. They are decorated in understated chic tones of soft cream and beige, and feature original artwork of Arabian themes by three of the Middle East's top contemporary artists: Zohra Moideen,

...one of the city's favourite hotels for wining and dining.

floors, the 196-sq-m (2,110-sq-ft) Prince Suites have the same facilities, plus a work area and dual views of the Creek and the Dubai skyline. Finally, the 264-sq-m (2,842-sq-ft) Royal Suites on the 15th and 16th floors feature two bedrooms and bathrooms, a work area-cum-library, and a dining room and kitchen. Handcrafted rugs, crystal chandeliers and one-off pieces of furniture liven up the décor of the Royal Suites. All the rooms and suites have amenities that business travellers will love, including two hands-free, dual-line IDD telephones with handy options like call waiting and conference call, voice messaging, high-speed Internet access and fax hook-up.

The Grand Hyatt Business Centre gives executives the advantage of an office away from home. It provides a complete range of business support services, such as secretarial help, translation, travel and conference arrangements, courier service, fax machines, private offices for meetings, and private workstations equipped with the latest computers, software, high-speed Internet access, printers and scanners.

The hotel also boasts the largest and most sophisticated conference facilities in the region. The Convention Centre has 4,340 sq m (46,715 sq ft) of flexible space with its own lobby area, grand entrance and private driveway. There are two pillar-less ballrooms, which can be partitioned into three soundproof sections, each with their own designated pre-function areas. The Baniyas Grand Ballroom can accommodate 2,000 delegates theatre-style, or 1,500 for a banquet. The Al Ameera Ballroom, on the other hand, can accommodate 800 guests for cocktail events or up to 550 for dinner. The Media Room, with its cutting-edge communications and multi-media technology, provides all the technical support services for the two venues. In addition to the ballrooms, there are 11 meeting rooms of different sizes, and two boardrooms. A

THIS PAGE: *Wox serves Southeast Asian cuisine and noodle dishes in a casual setting.*

OPPOSITE: *Located in the hotel's atrium, Sushi's Japanese food is prepared right on the spot.*

multi-lingual support team for conferences, separate delegate check-in, VIP rooms and other benefits make Grand Hyatt Dubai one of the most sought after conference and meeting venues in the region. Indeed, its world-class facilities justify Grand Hyatt Dubai's moniker as the city's premier luxury conference hotel.

Grand Hyatt Dubai is one of the city's favourite hotels for wining and dining. There are an impressive 14 restaurants and bars within the hotel. For fine dining, choose the gourmet Lebanese restaurant Awtar, with its flowing tented interiors and exotic belly dancers, or the sleek Manhattan Grill, serving mouthwatering steaks and fresh seafood. Lovers of Indian cuisine have been giving rave reviews to iZ, the hotel's Indian restaurant, serving traditional north Indian tandoor grills and spicy curries. At Grand Hyatt Dubai, the flavours of the Orient are well-represented, with Sushi serving the freshest sushi and sashimi, while Wox delights guests with its creative selection of noodles and traditional Southeast Asian hawker stall nibbles. Seafood fans will enjoy the delights of Peppercrab, a family-style restaurant inspired by Singapore's vibrant cuisine.

For those who prefer a more European ambience, Andiamo! is a stylish northern Italian restaurant. It has an open-plan kitchen so diners can see all the chefs creating delicious pizza, pasta and regional favourites. Complementing the restaurant is Vinoteca, an Italian wine bar that gives an authentic Mediterranean flavour. For lighter fare or snacks, guests can visit Panini, an Italian deli and café. Enjoy a tempting selection of homemade breads and pastries, artisan chocolates and speciality olive oils. Guests wishing to take advantage of Dubai's sunny weather can dine al fresco at the Pool Bar. All-day dining is also available at The Market Café, an international venue featuring five open kitchens with cuisine from Arabia, India, and Italy, as well as a rotisserie and grill. Nightlife revolves around the intimate Cooz cigar and piano bar and MIX, the hotel's well-

...feels like a country club, yet lies in the heart of the city.

known club, where dancing the night away to music spun by top DJs is all part of the scene. Whatever the hour, guests can find a warm welcome and light refreshments at the hotel's elegant Al Nakheel Lounge.

The unrivalled range of activities at Grand Hyatt Dubai makes it a perfect place to combine leisure and business. It feels like a country club, yet lies in the heart of the city. Unlike many business-oriented hotels, which can have a sterile, corporate atmosphere, Grand Hyatt Dubai radiates warmth and flair. The landscaped gardens, with their winding pathways, cascading waterfalls and tropical lagoons are a delight. The highlight of the outdoor leisure area are the three lovely freeform pools, which encompass a children's pool complete with water slides and games, and a shaded toddler pool. A dedicated team of lifeguards is on duty to keep younger ones safe and amused. The hotel's Kidz Club offers a range of fun activities for children up to 12 years of age. Babysitting is also available.

Grand Hyatt Dubai also boasts a stellar leisure and exercise complex called The Grand Spa, which is located on the lower ground floor of the hotel. Unwind with a game of tennis on one of the four outdoor floodlit courts, with pros from the Clark Francis Tennis Academy on hand to coach upon request. Go for an early morning run on the 450-m (1,476-ft) jogging track, which winds its way through the hotel's scenic gardens. Indoors, the state-of-the-art, 24-hour fitness centre

THIS PAGE: *The Kidz Club has plenty to keep children entertained for hours.*

OPPOSITE: *Greenery creates a calming spa atmosphere; the hotel stands majestic and resplendent at night.*

features the latest TechnoGym equipment, a sophisticated range of exercise machines that use 'smart key' technology to monitor the user's fitness and progress. Personal trainers are available to create individualised workouts. Guests can also take advantage of the two squash courts, an indoor 20-m (66-ft) lap pool complete with underwater sound system, a jacuzzi, sauna and steam rooms. Golfers can tee off at the world-class Dubai Creek Golf & Yacht Club and Emirates Golf Club, which are just a short drive away.

After all these sporting options, a relaxing massage or pampering body treatment is in order at any of the Spa's six treatment rooms. The sound of running water is dominant throughout the hotel and this continues to the Spa, complementing the

...a top resort with everything in place to do business.

Zen-inspired interior and creating a calming atmosphere. Guests can choose from a variety of rejuvenating therapies to help balance mind, body and spirit, featuring exclusive products by cult New York skincare companies Bella Lucce and June Jacobs. Try the signature Arabian Incense Cocoon treatment, which uses sandalwood, spices and rare oils like jasmine and neroli to exfoliate, detoxify, massage and moisturise the body. Manicures and pedicures are also available, as well as different types of massages such as Hot Stone, Thai Massage and the Businessman's Detox to melt away the pain and tension of tired muscles. Treatments can also be enjoyed in the privacy of one's room, or amid the lush landscaped gardens in the cooler months.

Grand Hyatt Dubai benefits from its proximity to Dubai's main attractions. Visit the Gold and Spice Souks, the Dubai Museum and Heritage Village, the fashionable Dubai Festival City, and the Egyptian-themed shopping complex Wafi City, which boasts a wide array of fashion boutiques, as well as top restaurants and cafés. Travellers looking for a top resort with everything in place to do business should look no further than Grand Hyatt Dubai.

rooms
674

food
Awtar: Lebanese • Peppercrab: Singaporean • Manhattan Grill: grill cuisine • Andiamo!: Italian • The Market Café: international • Sushi: Japanese • Panini: Italian • iZ: Indian • Wox: Southeast Asian

drink
Vinoteca • Cooz • MIX

features
high-speed and wireless Internet access • childcare centre • limousine service • spa • pools • jogging track • tennis courts • gym • business centre • meeting rooms • conference ballrooms • events lawn • technology concierge

nearby
Gold and Spice Souks • Dubai Museum • Heritage Village • Dubai Festival City

contact
PO Box 7978, Dubai, UAE •
telephone: +971.4.317 1234 •
facsimile: +971.4.317 1235 •
email: dubai.grand@hyattintl.com •
website: dubai.grand.hyatt.com

park hyatt dubai

THIS PAGE: *A stay at Park Hyatt Dubai ensures magnificent views of the Dubai Creek.*

OPPOSITE: *Surrounded by tall palm trees, the pool is cool and inviting, perfect for swimming or plain frolicking on the water.*

Cool, calm and captivating, this luxury hotel established in 2005 has received excellent reviews, making *Condé Nast Traveler's* coveted Hot List in its first year. Park Hyatt Dubai is a chic, sleek and secluded hotel with a boutique feel, located at the Dubai Creek Golf Club, in a stunning spot overlooking the city's historic Creek.

It is not easy to create a sense of tranquillity in this city. Yet when guests enter Park Hyatt Dubai's lovely circular lobby, they find themselves in a peaceful, unhurried and harmonious world. There are no noisy crowds of just-arrived holidaymakers, no brash braying into mobile phones, no gold-plated glitz, no hoi polloi milling around and spoiling the views—everything is as tasteful and understated as an Armani suit.

Park Hyatt Dubai has 225 guestrooms, including 35 suites, but thanks to its clever design and garden setting, the hotel feels intimate. The size and style of the rooms echo the spacious elegance that pervades the hotel. Guests will find an airy 52-sq-m (560-sq-ft) waterfront retreat featuring a balcony terrace with marina and Creek views. Relax on a chaise longue and enjoy the action on the Creek as traditional Arabic dhows and abras sail past

...a peaceful, unhurried and harmonious world.

the latest multi-million dollar yacht. The room interiors make the most of natural light, with large windows that let in the breeze and sunshine. The sleek, contemporary design features a king-sized bed with Egyptian cotton linens and fluffy goose down duvet, as well as a bathroom with a freestanding marble tub, complete with scented candles, exclusive spa toiletries, and a walk-in shower. Business travellers will appreciate the roomy work desk and high-speed Internet access. State-of-the-art sound systems, DVD players and data ports are standard room features.

For those who love the idea of being pampered in total privacy, reserve a residential spa guestroom. These special rooms feature built-in treatment areas (including a full steam and shower room) for massages and beauty treatments from the award-winning therapists at the hotel's Amara Spa. Private terraces in the residential spa rooms offer Dubai Creek and park views.

Park Hyatt Dubai's suites are well worth indulging in. The Park Executive Suites offer a private terrace and separate living, work and wardrobe areas. The Park Terrace Suites have the benefit of a large terrace overlooking the Creek. Both offer more than 100 sq m (1,076 sq ft) of living space with the highest levels of comfort and service. The suites feature satellite TV, elegant décor, comfy sofa and chairs, and marble bath with separate tub and walk-in rain shower. Discreet and attentive service is a hallmark of Park Hyatt

THIS PAGE: *Park Hyatt Dubai's location makes it a top choice for golf enthusiasts.*
OPPOSITE (FROM LEFT): *All rooms and suites have private balconies; the bedrooms radiate warmth and comfort.*

Dubai, with butlers on request and 24-hour concierge available. An irresistible desire for champagne and strawberries at 3.00 am, therefore, will not be a problem.

Park Hyatt Dubai has an exceptional range of dining options for guests. Traiteur presents modern European cuisine in striking surroundings, featuring a dramatic staircase that connects the restaurant's two levels and overlooks the elevated show kitchen which features the chefs creating their culinary magic. Lovers of fine wine will find much to discover at Traiteur's exclusive Cave Privée, one of the best-stocked wine cellars in Dubai, with more than 4,000 bottles. The restaurant's Champagne Friday lunch is also very popular. Café Arabesque celebrates the culinary delights of the Middle East with mouthwatering fresh grills, buffets offering an outstanding mezze selection, and an à la carte menu. The Lounge serves breakfast all day (perfect if one has had a lie-in after a night out in one of Dubai's clubs), as well as light meals. For an authentic taste of Thailand in an opulent Oriental setting, visit The Thai Kitchen. For morning coffee or afternoon tea served with hand-made Arabic sweets and gourmet pastries, visit Pistache. For the best sundowners on the Creek, pop into The Terrace. This brilliantly designed bar, with floor-to-ceiling windows and an outside terrace, is a favourite Dubai watering hole. Delicious oysters at the raw bar, fresh caviar, Baltic salmon and a choice of more than 40 premium vodkas complete the picture.

Park Hyatt Dubai has an alluring array of activities to keep guests happy. There is the stunning 25-m (82-ft) pool fringed by palm trees, and a 24-hour gym with personal trainers and the latest TechnoGym equipment. The pleasures of golf can be had at the nearby renowned 18-hole, par-76 Dubai Creek Golf Course. There is also a par-3, 9-hole floodlit course and driving range, in addition to private sunset cruises, and sailing and fishing charters at the Dubai Creek Yacht Club, which sits next door to the hotel.

...a chic, sleek and secluded hotel with a boutique feel.

Spa connoisseurs have a treat in store when they visit Park Hyatt Dubai's award-winning Amara Spa. It features eight spacious luxury suites, three of which are couple's suites that allow guests to experience spa treatments with their loved ones. Each suite has its own private outdoor terrace, lounge area, and indoor and outdoor rain showers, all set within a pretty garden courtyard. The spa carries brands such as Shiffa, Carita, Aromatherapy Associates and Anne Semonin, four of the finest beauty product ranges in the world. The Shiffa Arabian Rose massage is a special indulgence, featuring lusciously scented oils made from the Middle East's favourite flower. The spa also offers healing treatments like Reiki and Hot Stone.

For those combining business with pleasure, Park Hyatt Dubai's meeting and event planning team can organise anything from a cocktail party for key clients to a sit-down dinner and event for up to 800 guests. With its subtle sophistication and impressive attention to details, Park Hyatt Dubai is an outstanding hotel that can certainly hold its own among the best in town.

rooms
225

food
Traiteur: modern European • Cafe Arabesque: Middle Eastern • The Thai Kitchen: Thai • Pistache: pastries • The Terrace: raw bar and international cuisine

drink
The Lounge • The Terrace Bar • Traiteur Bar

features
high-speed Internet access • 24-hour business centre • conference facilities • outdoor pool • fitness centre • spa • Dubai Creek views • private balconies

nearby
Dubai Creek • Dubai Creek Golf & Yacht Club • Deira City Centre • Burjuman • Wafi City • Gold and Spice Souks • Heritage Village • Dubai International Airport • Dubai International Convention and Exhibition Centre • Dubai International Financial Centre

contact
PO Box 2822, Dubai, UAE •
telephone: +971.4.602 1234 •
facsimile: +971.4.602 1235 •
email: dubai.park@hyatt.com •
website: dubai.park.hyatt.com

bateaux dubai

THIS PAGE: *Step onboard for exquisite cuisine and a memorable cruise.*

OPPOSITE (FROM LEFT): *A sunset cocktail reception is just one of the tailor-made cruise options; elegant seating while floating past sleek and glittering modern buildings.*

Cruising the Creek is one of the 'must do' attractions of Dubai for good reason. With the renaissance of this famous waterway has come spectacular new buildings and a restored shoreline featuring the traditional homes of early traders with their distinctive wind towers. The Creek defines Dubai much the same way as the Thames does London or the Seine does Paris.

Dubai Creek has played a major role in the city's economic development, ever since Dubai flourished as a pearl fishing and trading village. To take a cruise along the Creek is to see the real Dubai in action. Ancient dhows and the latest yachts ply the waterway, cementing the city's status as one of the world's greatest ports. There are a variety of Creek cruises on offer, but the undisputed leader of the pack is Bateaux Dubai. The vessel's glass-enclosed interior offers passengers unobstructed views of Dubai's most famous landmarks.

Constructed in 2003 by Seine Design, France, Bateaux Dubai seamlessly combines technology with the latest in luxury. There is nothing else like it in Dubai. Guests enjoy gourmet international cuisine prepared to the highest standard by chefs on board, thanks to the full-service kitchen rivalling any on land. This enables all meals to be freshly prepared onboard—a distinct advantage. Guests are treated to panoramic views from all seats, courtesy of the anti-reflective glass enclosure. A high-tech air-conditioning system ensures maximum comfort, while a state-of-the-art sound system makes the most of the music quality on board. Bateaux Dubai also incorporates a host of environmentally friendly features which ensure that the vessel produces no effluent, while simultaneously reducing noise and exhaust emissions.

The journey begins in the early evening, as the first stars come out to compete with the twinkling lights of the city. Passengers float past Bur Dubai's wind towers, Deira's gleaming skyscrapers and iconic architectural

...a marvellous way to see Dubai, free from the crowds, heat and hassle.

capacity
300

food
international

drink
extensive wine and beverage list

features
anti-reflective glass enclosure • full-service kitchen • air-conditioning • event planners • fully licensed

nearby
British Embassy

contact
Dubai Creek, Dubai, UAE •
telephone: +971.4.399 4994 •
facsimile: +971.4.399 4995 •
email: mail@bateauxdubai.com •
website: www.bateauxdubai.com

landmarks such as the National Bank and the Sheikh Saeed House. Attentive staff serve a four-course, à la carte meal that creatively combines Eastern and Western flavours, with entrées like pan-fried Hammour or glazed breast of duck. Fine wines, cocktails and a variety of non-alcoholic beverages are also available for passengers' enjoyment.

Along with daily scheduled cruises, Bateaux Dubai can be chartered for private events. Whether it is a special celebration like a 40th birthday bash, or a corporate party for key clients, the events team at Bateaux Dubai ensures the utmost in personalised, professional service. Tailor-made cruises can be booked at guests' preferred time of day, whether it be a breakfast, lunch, afternoon tea, sundowner or dinner cruise. Choose from any of the superb menus designed for a variety of events, or allow the Executive Chef to create a special meal for the occasion. The spacious 56-m- (184-ft-) long craft can easily accommodate up to 200 guests for a sit-down dinner and 300 for a cocktail reception. Every private charter cruise feature personalised décor, flexible seating and unique themes. Chocolate fountains, ice carvings, table dressings in corporate colours, unusual branding options—everything is possible on the elegant Bateaux Dubai.

A Bateaux Dubai cruise can be a romantic dinner à deux, or a fun evening among friends. It is a marvellous way to see Dubai, free from the crowds, heat and hassle.

dubai golf

If luxury is defined by the ability to enjoy what others cannot ordinarily imagine, then the world-class golfing facilities offered by Dubai Golf—incredibly lush green courses and professionally designed landscapes set in the middle of the desert—fit the bill with ease. In just two short decades, this government organisation has seen to it that the UAE's second-largest emirate is firmly on course to become one of the world's most exciting golfing destinations.

Key factors in achieving this goal are the three internationally-acclaimed courses owned and operated by Dubai Golf. Designed by some of the most respected professionals in the industry, each course at Emirates Golf Club and Dubai Creek Golf & Yacht Club offers a unique play experience to challenge everyone, from the seasoned veteran to the adventurous beginner. Away from the lawns, these two properties' beautiful clubhouses are oases of top-notch dining, practice facilities, and other recreational activities for the whole family.

When Emirates Golf Club opened its doors with the Gulf's first all-grass championship golf course in 1988, it was hailed as a landmark achievement and given an appropriate nickname: The Desert Miracle, for what was once an unthinkable prospect had become a reality. In the years since, the club created by His Highness General Sheikh Mohamed Bin Rashid Al Maktoum has enjoyed unflagging popularity

...incredibly lush green courses and professionally designed landscapes...

as scores of new visitors and returning guests alike travel from all over the world to test themselves on its fairways. The club hosts the PGA European Tour-sanctioned Dubai Desert Classic, and boasts 36 holes spread over two spectacular must-see courses. The Majlis is a 6,594-m (7,211-yd) par-72 course designed by Karl Litten that has won numerous accolades, including *Business Traveller's* 'Best Course in the Middle East' for four years running, as well as a place on *Golf Digest's* '100 Best Courses Outside the USA' list.

Also at the Emirates Golf Club is the redesigned Wadi by Faldo. Originally known as the Wadi Championship Course, it opened in 1995 based on a design by Jeremy Pern and Karl Litten and was hugely successful as a sister course to the Majlis. In 2006, the Wadi was closed for an intensive 18-month overhaul by Faldo Design, under the direction of European golfing legend Nick Faldo. The result is a golf course much better than the original in terms of looks, playability and design, one that is expected to draw top international players by the thousands. Incorporating fine details such as Sealsle Paspalum grass for a bolder and greener appearance, the 6,797-m (7,433-yd) course promises an invigorating ride across the naturally rolling desert terrain. Wadi by Faldo's revised layout defines it as a 'risk

THIS PAGE: Emirates Golf Club's unique clubhouse looks like a cluster of Bedouin tents amid verdant golf courses.
OPPOSITE: The majestic clubhouse of Dubai Creek Golf & Yacht Club was designed to resemble the sail of an Arabian dhow.

THIS PAGE: The Aquarium is famous for its floor-to-ceiling fish tank teeming with exotic fish and corals.

OPPOSITE: The Boardwalk is the place to be as dusk falls and lends a romantic glow to the Creek.

and reward' course, one that challenges golfers to think ahead, and step outside their comfort zones.

Over at Emirates Golf Club's distinctively shaped clubhouse, which takes the appearance of Bedouin tents, guests enjoy the use of squash and tennis courts, a gymnasium, pool and children's play area. Golfers may also put in valuable training time on floodlit driving ranges, enroll in a special Golf Academy dedicated to short-game coaching and make use of the well-stocked Golf Shop. There are also six superb bar and dining options with lovely views of the grounds. Choose from fine dining at Le Classique, international cuisine and cocktails at Spike Bar, pub fare and televised sporting events at the Sports Bar, al fresco dining on The Terrace, lounge-style meals at The Conservatory, and relaxing tropical drinks at the Pool Bar.

The second property in Dubai Golf's sparkling portfolio resides down by the shimmering blue waters of the city's inland creek. Far more than just a golf course, Dubai Creek Golf & Yacht Club is an expansive resort that combines a headlining 18-hole course with a smaller 9-hole, par 3 course, a 121-berth marina, the 225-bedroom Park Hyatt Dubai, 92 four-bedroom Executive Villas, and full recreational club facilities.

Situated between lush rows of date and coconut palms, the 6,270-m (6,857-yd), par-71 course's stately fairways and attractive water hazards promise a round of golf as beautiful as it is deceptively challenging. Sporting a front nine redesigned from 2004 to 2005 by Thomas Björn, in association with European Golf Design, it has been voted one of the 'Top 100 Must-Play Golf Courses' worldwide by *Golf World*.

The club also features a Golf Academy with programmes suited to all levels of skill, four full-time PGA qualified professionals on hand, a fully floodlit driving range, putting green and a high-tech digital swing analysis studio for that extra edge. For all occasions, the club has a range of venues that can accommodate up to 400 people. But for

...oases of top-notch dining, practice facilities, and other recreational activities.

smaller groups and intimate meals for two, the property offers a choice of six award-winning dining establishments.

The Boardwalk is an al fresco restaurant known for its relaxed atmosphere and superb international cuisine. Guests can dine indoors or outside on three wooden decks built directly over the creek. The Aquarium Seafood Restaurant and Vines Wine Bar is one of the city's best places to go for original ocean fare inspired by the countries of the Pacific Rim. Start with a pre-dinner drink and snack from the wine bar, and move on to greater things in the main dining hall with views of the open kitchen from all around. For uncomplicated, hearty fare, Legends Steakhouse serves the best cuts of meat and complementary dishes, accompanied by live piano music. In the center of the dining area, a beverage tower provides a popular conversation piece. Three bars—QD's, Lakeview, and The Academy Bar—are perfect for chilling out in style and comfort. Each offers sweeping views of the rippling waters of the Dubai Creek or the rolling greens of the golf course.

It is hard to believe that only 20 years ago, the mere thought of playing golf on a sand course was out of the question. But it is the spirit of Dubai to make the impossible happen out of sheer desire and strength of will, and the continuing efforts of Dubai Golf are testament to this tenacity, as well as the enduring allure of this great sport. Players may quickly feel right at home on Dubai Golf's three superb courses, but the experience will be like nothing they have ever encountered.

dubai creek golf + yacht club

food
The Boardwalk: international • The Aquarium: seafood • Legends Steakhouse: steak • Lakeview: international

drink
QD's • Lakeview • Golf Academy

features
golf academy • gym • pool • custom fitting centres • steam rooms • golf shops • boating marina • event facilities

nearby
Dubai International Airport • Dubai Museum • City Centre Mall • Four Seasons Golf Course

contact
PO Box 6302, Dubai, UAE •
telephone: +971.4.295 6000 •
facsimile: +971.4.295 6044 •
email: golfbooking@dubaigolf.com •
website: www.dubaigolf.com

emirates golf club

food
Le Classique: French • The Conservatory: international • Spike Bar: international

drink
Spike Bar • Sports Bar

features
golf academy • tennis courts • squash courts • gym • pools • golf shops • event facilities

nearby
American University in Dubai • Dubai Internet City • Dubai Media City • Dubai Marina

contact
PO Box 24040, Dubai, UAE •
telephone: +971.4.380 2222 •
facsimile: +971.4.380 1555 •
email: golfbooking@dubaigolf.com •
website: www.dubaigolf.com

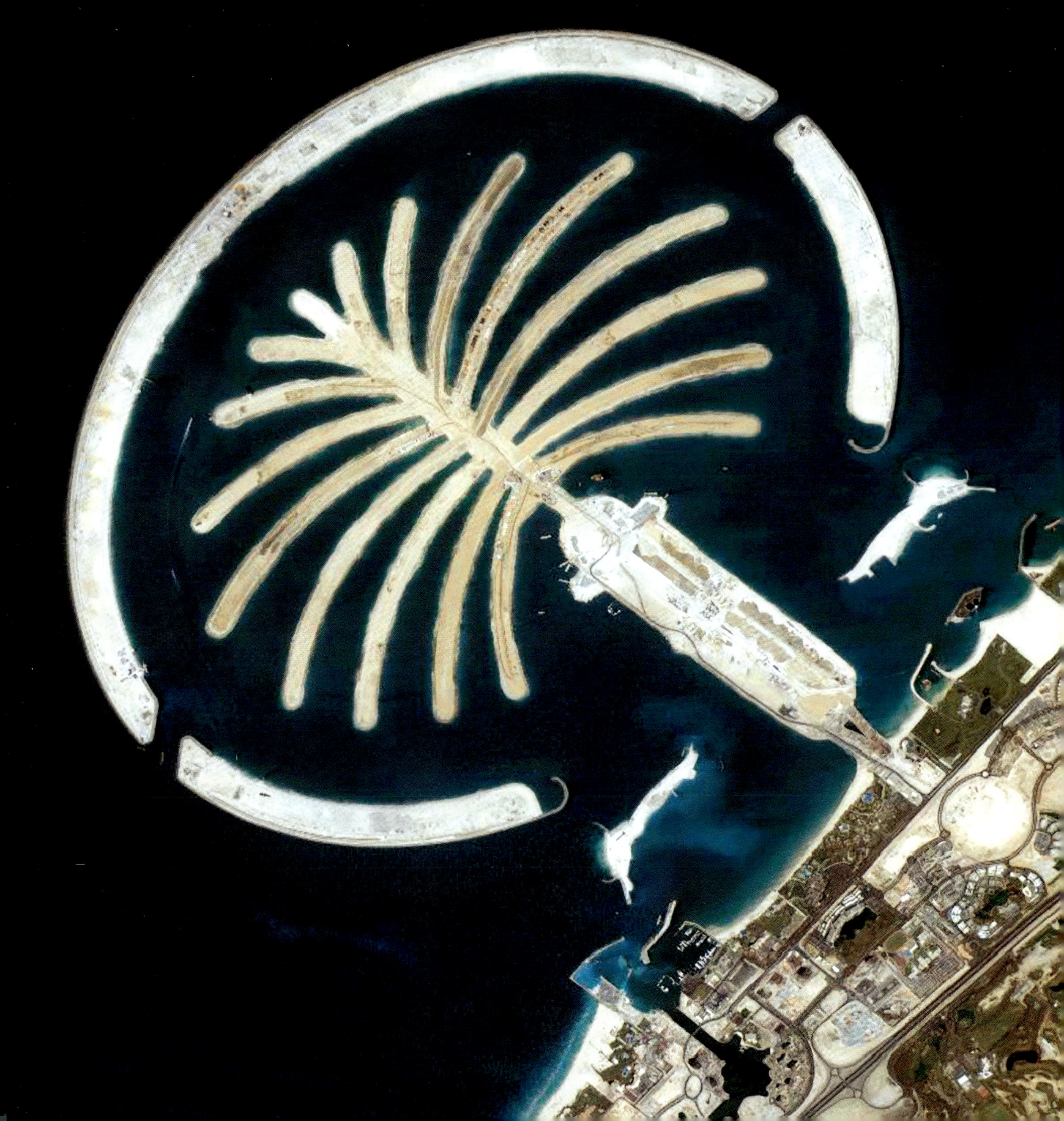

jumeirah

The Palm Jumeirah

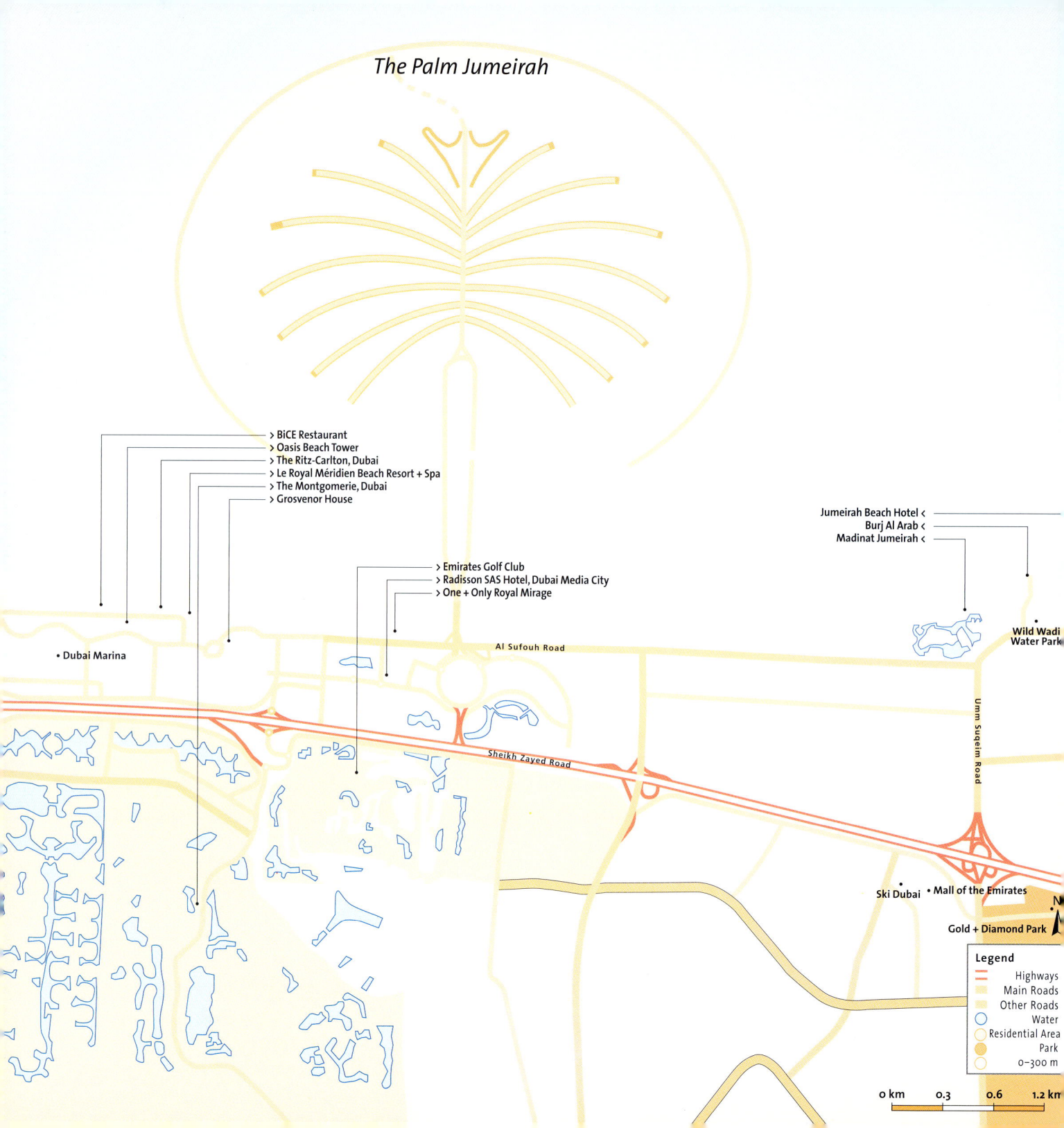

- BiCE Restaurant
- Oasis Beach Tower
- The Ritz-Carlton, Dubai
- Le Royal Méridien Beach Resort + Spa
- The Montgomerie, Dubai
- Grosvenor House

- Jumeirah Beach Hotel
- Burj Al Arab
- Madinat Jumeirah

- Emirates Golf Club
- Radisson SAS Hotel, Dubai Media City
- One + Only Royal Mirage

Al Sufouh Road

- Dubai Marina

Wild Wadi Water Park

Sheikh Zayed Road

Umm Suqeim Road

Ski Dubai · Mall of the Emirates

Gold + Diamond Park

Legend
- Highways
- Main Roads
- Other Roads
- Water
- Residential Area
- Park
- 0–300 m

0 km · 0.3 · 0.6 · 1.2 km

jumeirah

jumeirah bc (before chic)

Once upon a time (well about 60 years ago), Jumeirah was a quiet sandy stretch along the Dubai coast where palm frond shacks housed pearl divers, fishermen and their families. Donkeys brought fresh water in large clay pots, and camels brought just about everything else. There were no proper roads, no public transport, no shopping malls, hospitals, schools or electricity. Today, as a result of Dubai's economic miracle, Jumeirah is a fashionable area of five-star resorts, designer shopping malls, high-rise developments and expat villas that meander along the coast between Dubai Marina and Port Rashid. The main street of Jumeirah is Jumeirah Road, often referred to as Beach Road. Along its immaculate, palm-fringed route, you'll find such top attractions as Wild Wadi Water Park, one of the world's most creative and advanced water parks and the perfect place to cool off on a hot day, and the beautiful Jumeirah Mosque, a masterpiece of Islamic architecture open to visitors who book a guided tour through the Sheikh Mohammed Centre for Cultural Understanding. Within the area are the upscale neighbourhoods of Umm Suqeim and Al Sufouh, with their mega-million-dollar super villas, landscaped gardens, pools and 10-car garages, as well as new business enclaves such as Dubai Media City and Dubai Internet City.

life on the beach

Jumeirah is where the beach is, and that means where the action is. Its beachfront hotels are among the best in world, winning awards and rave reviews. The most famous is Burj Al Arab, which resides in solitary splendour on its own island. Designed to resemble the billowing sail of a dhow, the hotel soars to a height of 321 m (1,053 ft), dominating the coastline. This all-suite hotel recently won World's Best Hotel awards from the World Travel Awards and *Institutional Investor*. Also along this golden stretch of sand are the Jumeirah Beach Hotel, the recently refurbished Jumeirah Beach Club, The Ritz-Carlton, Dubai, the One&Only Royal Mirage and the Madinat Jumeirah resort. With so many top hotels in Jumeirah, the nightlife is so good you don't need to go anywhere else to drink, dine and dance in style. Venues such as Buddha Bar at Grosvenor House, Kasbah at One&Only Royal Mirage and Trilogy at Madinat Souk attract a party crowd until way after midnight. In Jumeirah, the beautiful people meet and mingle under starry skies and serene seas, enjoying the quintessential Dubai mix of sun, fun, shopping and relaxing in style.

THIS PAGE: *Tennis legends Andre Agassi and Roger Federer enjoy a quick rally on Burj Al Arab's helipad, an adrenaline-pumping 211 m (700 ft) above sea level.*

PAGE 104: *The Palm Jumeirah is one of the latest development extravaganzas off the Dubai coastline—a man-made island in the shape of a palm frond.*

The spectacular Arabian Gulf is warm and clear...

shopping superlatives

Jumeirah is home to some of Dubai's most popular shopping venues. The biggest is Mall of the Emirates, one of the world's great retail emporiums. Within its massive interior are literally hundreds of shops, from Accessorize to Zara, selling everything from top designer brands to teddy bears. There are also two excellent British department stores, upscale Harvey Nichols and the more practical Debenhams. But the Mall is much more than shopping. It's a social magnet that attracts every strata of Dubai society. People come to the Mall to have a pleasurable day out with friends and family. There are plenty of places to eat, whether you just want a quick bite or a lavish lunch. There is also entertainment, with a multi-screen cinema showing the latest blockbusters and Magic Planet, a huge games arcade. At the Mall there is also the glittering five-star Kempinski Hotel and Ski Dubai, the unmissable indoor mini ski resort that has become a Dubai institution. It is the world's largest indoor ski slope and has been a massive hit since it opened. Imagine burka-clad ski bunnies flying down the slopes—only in Dubai!

If the sheer scale of the superlative-inspiring Mall of the Emirates sounds a bit daunting, Mercato mall is a good alternative. It's friendly, accessible and small enough to get around in about an hour, yet full of desirable shops where you can indulge in a bit of retail therapy. The Magrudy Shopping Mall is also popular with Dubai's expat 'yummy mummies' who come to shop and meet friends at Gerard's coffee shop for their post-school-run cappuccinos. For Islamic art and textiles, the Miraj Islamic Arts Centre has everything from carpets to shawls.

Madinat Jumeirah is the retail and leisure complex that combines an Arabian 'super souk' with an array of restaurants, bars and entertainment centres. What makes it so special is the soaring Arabian architecture, with wind towers, roof terraces, courtyards and a scenic waterway complete with small abra boats to ferry people into the resort. Within the resort are three exceptional boutique hotels, Mina A' Salam, Al Qasr and Dar Al Masyaf, each with its own style. The concept works beautifully, making Madinat Jumeirah one of Dubai's favourite gathering places.

on the coastline

One of the great pleasures of Jumeirah is that of being on the water. The spectacular Arabian Gulf is warm and clear, a delight to swim in and perfect for every kind of watersport. Most hotels can easily arrange sailing, paragliding above the sea, jetskiing, windsurfing, powerboat cruising, fishing trips, snorkelling and diving.

THIS PAGE (FROM TOP): *Indoor hijinks on ice are part of a day well-spent at Ski Dubai—a winter wonderland in the desert; Dubai's economy is growing by leaps and bounds every day, as shown by the population's appetite for luxury items such as Louis Vuitton leather goods.*

OPPOSITE: *The crown jewels of Jumeirah's landscape dot the coastline, while vast tracts of empty land stretch into the distance, filled with promises of unbudgeted potential.*

The beaches along Jumeirah are tranquil and inviting. The Jumeirah Beach Park has a long stretch of golden sand, lifeguards on duty, a children's play area and a lawn with shady trees—ideal for an afternoon picnic. If your hotel doesn't have a big beach to play on, this is a great alternative to sitting at a crowded pool. Stroll along the shore early in the morning, while the air is still cool and the crowds still asleep, or sip a glass of perfectly chilled wine, while watching the sun set over the sea as the fishing dhows sail home through the twilight. At night, dine outside in the balmy air and enjoy freshly caught fish, such as Hammour—grilled to a fragrant crispness—under the stars. Hear the waves tumbling on to the beach and see the moon cast a silver sheen upon the water, as the lights of Burj Al Arab glow in the distance. Jumeirah is a romantic place to be, with the natural beauty of the coastline providing a suitably seductive background. No wonder it's such a popular honeymoon destination.

exciting new projects

Jumeirah's waterfront property is so sought after, they are creating miles more of it through offshore developments of man-made islands. The most famous of these is The Palm Jumeirah, an extravagant fantasy island in the shape of a palm frond stretching out into the Arabian Gulf's shimmering waters. The Palm has barely opened but already has attracted a celebrity following, with everyone from David Beckham to Brad Pitt buying their share of paradise. The eagerly awaited opening of Atlantis, The Palm will add a new dimension to Jumeirah's reputation as the fun zone of Dubai. The 46-hectare (113-acre) five-star resort will feature Dolphin Bay, a state-of-the-art dolphin encounter zone, Aquaventure, a water park with 30-m- (100-ft-) drop white-knuckle rides, and Ambassador Lagoon, a 11.3 million-litre (3 million gallon) marine habitat with 6,500 species of fish, including sharks and manta rays. Dubai Marina is a chic new development that is creating quite a stir. When complete, it will be the biggest man-made marina in the world, yet another notch on Dubai's belt of world records. Towering above the pretty yacht-speckled marina is Grosvenor House, one of the most sophisticated hotels in Dubai, along with luxury homes and a pedestrian area with fountains, waterfront walkways and a popular weekend market. Jumeirah has a laid-back, well-heeled ambience, with everything to make an idyllic beach holiday. Popular with locals, expats and tourists, it has a happy buzz and cosmopolitan atmosphere as pleasure-seekers from around the globe indulge in Dubai's version of the good life. Many visitors prefer to spend their entire stay on Jumeirah's beaches, far from the faster pace downtown.

THIS PAGE: *Attractions slated for top billing at Jumeirah include a dolphin encounter zone and a marine habitat that boasts a stunning 6,500 species of fish.*

OPPOSITE: *Work continues apace at The Palm Jumeirah, which like so much else in Dubai, will have the world gaping in wonder.*

...an extravagant fantasy island in the shape of a palm frond...

jumeirah beach hotel

THIS PAGE: *The glass façade of the hotel gleams like a beacon, beckoning to visitors.*

OPPOSITE (FROM TOP): *Rich colours lend warmth to all the rooms of Beit Al Bahar; the marble-clad bathroom within is a luxury in itself.*

For an idyllic, vibrant and luxurious destination, the five-star deluxe Jumeirah Beach Hotel is the place to visit. This multi-award winning luxury resort style hotel combines 19,600 sq m (211,000 sq ft) of pristine private beach and year-round sunshine with the Jumeirah Group's signature brand of outstanding service. Reinventing the hotel experience, Jumeirah Beach Hotel introduces a lifestyle that integrates excitement and exhilaration designed for couples, families and friends.

Jumeirah Beach Hotel's ingenious design provides a sense of endless space and light, ensuring that every one of the 598 luxury rooms and suites enjoys an unhindered view of the ocean through floor-to-ceiling windows. For those visitors searching for a truly personal, uniquely special holiday hideaway, Beit Al Bahar offers the ultimate luxurious home away from home. Every one of the 19 private villas has its own private terrace, plunge pool and outside dining area and embodies the essence of Arabic style

...an idyllic, vibrant and luxurious destination.

and hospitality. From ethnic charm and contemporary convenience to the extravagant use of space and sophistication, every feature is the hallmark of luxury. Private butlers assigned to each household address day to day needs, whatever the time, from bringing breakfast to pressing shirts. They can even draw a luxurious aromatherapy bath for complete relaxation.

For guests feeling more adventurous, the Pavilion Dive Centre, an accredited PADI 5 Star Gold IDC Resort and National Geographic Dive Centre offers a variety of diving trips. Whether one chooses to explore the Dive Centre's man-made reef and the wreckage of a sunken ship, or encounter rare marine species and remote islands in the Omani Peninsula, the opportunities are endless. The range of courses available cater for individuals as well as groups, and covers all levels of expertise from absolute beginners to seasoned professionals.

The Pavilion Marina and Sports Club also has a range of additional activities to spice up one's holiday, including water-skiing, wind surfing, hobie cat-sailing and deep-sea fishing. On land, there are tennis courts, squash courts and a fully equipped gym offering a wide range of exercise classes to keep those fitness levels up.

Grown-up fun is practically guaranteed here, but Jumeirah Beach Hotel ensures that younger guests are just as well looked after. With 30 state-of-the-art rides

jumeirah/hotels 113

THIS PAGE: *The stately living room provides more than enough space for entertaining.*

OPPOSITE (FROM LEFT): *Perched on the breakwater, Marina offers breathtaking views of the sea and guarantees a satisying seafood meal; the Beit Al Bahar villas ensure a stay in the lap of luxury.*

and attractions, Wild Wadi Water Park is conveniently located next to the hotel and is packed with thrills and spills for adults and children of all ages. Jumeirah Beach Hotel guests also receive complimentary access to Wild Wadi for the duration of their stay. Sinbad's Kids Club offers a varied programme of activities for children aged two to 12, under the supervision of highly trained and qualified staff, and teenagers are kept entertained at VIBES.

Dining choices at this landmark of luxury are extraordinary. Discover the world and its blissful delights, and go on a unique culinary journey through Jumeirah Beach Hotel's portfolio of over 20 restaurants and bars. After an activity-packed day, enjoy a gourmet meal by the sea at one of Dubai's best seafood restaurants, Marina. Situated along a scenic breakwater, this casually stylish restaurant offers fresh seafood and Dubai's most incredible views.

...one of the best ways to appreciate the wonders of Dubai.

For a piquant taste of Latin heat, La Parrilla is an acclaimed Argentinean restaurant with live tango dancers to accompany the succulent grilled meats, and Al Khayal allows guests to experience Lebanese hospitality in its purest essence with a grand à la carte menu and a live Lebanese band.

At night, there are plenty of glamorous bars to keep the party mood upbeat long after the sun sets. The glitzy Apartment Lounge Club is a popular venue which continues to shape the local music scene. For breathtaking views of Dubai's skyline and the Arabian Gulf, Uptown Bar on the 24th floor is the perfect place to unwind. Or, for the total Dubai experience, head to a chic outdoor roof deck at 360°. Enjoy the laid-back atmosphere from the comfort of the oversized sofas and be soothed by the soft sea breeze. A range of fruity shisha tobacco flavours is also on offer for those who wish to engage in this unique Middle Eastern social activity.

For that touch of authentic Middle Eastern culture to enhance the beach experience, arrange for trips to the Spice Souk and Gold Souk at the historic quarter of Bastakiya, as well as the Dubai Museum. Another landmark that should not be missed is the splendidly restored Grand Mosque at Jumeirah itself, which is one of the largest mosques in the entire UAE and boasts Dubai's tallest minaret. A stay at the sophisticatedly modern Jumeirah Beach Hotel, with its surrounding rich, colourful and vibrant Arabian heritage is one of the best ways to appreciate the wonders of Dubai.

rooms
598 rooms and suites • 19 villas

food
12 restaurants

drink
8 clubs and bars

features
business centre • pools • Sinbad's Kids Club • The Pavilion Marina and Sports Club • unlimited access to Wild Wadi Water Park • The Pavilion Dive Centre • Premium Leisure Club • Club Executive Lounge • VIBES teens club

nearby
Dubai International Airport • Madinat Jumeirah • Grand Mosque

contact
PO Box 11416, Dubai, UAE •
telephone: + 971.4.348 0000 •
facsimile: +971.4.301 6800 •
email: JBHinfo@jumeirah.com •
website: www.jumeirahbeachhotel.com

burj al arab

THIS PAGE: *The majestic Burj Al Arab dominates the Dubai coastline with its unique, billowing-sail design.*

OPPOSITE: *Feast on seafood with a contemporary twist in the aquarium environment of Al Mahara.*

Burj Al Arab is undeniably one of the world's most fabulous hotels. 'Nothing succeeds like excess', a wit once said; this is certainly true for the Burj Al Arab. It gleams across Dubai as a symbol of the creative spirit that has powered a tiny trading port into a global phenomenon. Other hotels may grab the limelight, other tall towers may grace the skyline, but Burj Al Arab will always reign supreme in its position as Dubai's original icon. Burj Al Arab is an Alice-in-Wonderland hotel. It stretches the limits of imagination (it is made from Teflon), it surprises (guests take a simulated submarine ride to the seafood restaurant) and it enchants (the lobby fountain is an aqueous ballet shooting jets of water 42 m, or 138 ft, high into the air). A stay at Burj Al Arab is unique. No matter how many luxury hotels in every corner of the world a traveller visits, he or she will never be able to say that the experience was akin to a stay at Burj Al Arab.

Burj Al Arab does not do anything by halves. This means guests are not just picked up from the airport. Rather, they are met by a hotel representative as they step off their flight, and whisked through immigration, past the envious eyes of those in the queue. They are then led to a gleaming white Rolls-Royce Phantom and driven to the hotel, where they are welcomed with rose water, refreshing cold towels, dates and Arabic coffee. At Burj Al Arab, there are no guests hanging about the lobby and waiting to check in. Each floor has a dedicated service desk, so visitors are taken directly to their suites for check-in.

Guests stay in duplex suites, which feature winding marble staircases separating the living area from the bed and bath upstairs. The suites look like a 1930s Hollywood film set, and ooze such sex appeal and star quality that one would half expect Rita Hayworth to descend the stairs in a satin negligée. The

...Dubai's original icon.

duplex suites are designed not only to make guests feel at home, but also to make them feel fantastic. It is the kind of place where James Bond would ask a woman up for a martini. Once inside, it is really hard to leave. A bucket of iced Bollinger, a bath sprinkled with rose buds, a masseuse to soothe away jet lag—whatever a guest's wish, Burj Al Arab does its best to fulfil.

Beneath the delightful fantasy element lies a superbly organised and managed hotel that takes its mission seriously—and rightfully so, because it serves some of the world's most demanding guests. No expense was spared to create the palatial 158-sq-m (1,700-sq-ft) suites, from the lavish use of silks and fine textiles to the pure gold leaf on the mirrors. There is a sumptuous living and dining area (with a proper dining table for candlelit suppers), a state-of-the-art DVD entertainment system and a private bar. In addition, each suite has an office area complete with a full-sized desk, laptop, Internet access, private fax, printer and copier. The only thing lacking is a secretary—but a guest can have that too with just a call. Touch-screen technology in each suite make a range of tasks a breeze for guests, from controlling the plasma-screen TV to closing the floor-to-ceiling curtains.

The huge, beautifully furnished bedroom features a Sultan-sized bed swathed in Versace linen. The bathroom is bigger than most hotel rooms. It offers extensive amenities that would make even Cleopatra feel right at home, including a whirlpool bath, full-size his and hers Hermes toiletries and decadent bath oils.

Travellers with children need not worry, as Burj Al Arab similarly treats its young guests like royalty. Children have their own special amenities, a dedicated kids' club, in-room gaming options, kid-friendly menus, and babysitting service.

Visually, the hotel is extraordinary, even surreal. It rejects the whole dull nothingness of minimalism and embraces colour, texture, warmth and creativity. This is particularly true of Burj Al Arab's restaurants, which are destinations in themselves. A Dubai favourite for special occasions is Al Mahara, an award-winning seafood restaurant that guests reach by way of a three-minute virtual submarine voyage. The floor-to-ceiling oval aquarium, teeming with exotic fish, creates the illusion of dining undersea. Al Muntaha, on the other hand, is a sophisticated restaurant hovering 200 m (656 ft) above the Arabian Gulf. It offers Mediterranean cuisine and bird's eye views of The Palm Jumeirah and The World islands. Next door is the Skyview Bar, where

THIS PAGE (FROM TOP): Relax at the Assawan Spa & Health Club; the Upper Lobby is a futuristic marvel and a wonderful sight to behold.

OPPOSITE (FROM TOP): Plush fabrics in red and blue lend a regal air to this Deluxe Suite bedroom; savour mouthwatering Asian dishes in a stylish setting at Junsui.

...the hotel is extraordinary, even surreal.

the drinks come with unrivalled views of Dubai. For a taste of Arabian cuisine, visit the dramatic gold, red and black Al Iwan restaurant, or dine al fresco at Majlis Al Bahar. For authentic Asian cuisine, head to Junsui, where 12 live cooking stations serve to enhance guests' dining experience. After a day of sightseeing, relax over afternoon tea at Sahn Eddar, or have a quiet moment with a favourite cigar at the Juna Lounge. For casual all-day dining, the convivial Bab Al Yam, with its sea views, is a popular choice.

Guests wanting to burn off some calories should head to the Assawan Spa & Health Club. Located on the 18th floor, the club offers the latest in fitness equipment. It has two exercise studios, classes ranging from yoga to aerobics, personal trainers, hydrotherapy baths, a solarium, sauna, steam room and jacuzzi, two infinity-edge pools and a squash court. The spa itself is one of the most lavish in the region, and features exclusive brands such as E'Spa, La Prairie and Aromatherapy Associates.

There is as much or as little to do at Burj Al Arab. Lounge at the lovely outdoor pool all day, gaze at the crystalline Gulf waters, hire a helicopter for a bit of airborne sightseeing, or charter a yacht—whatever a guest's idea of holiday bliss, nothing gets much better than a stay at Burj Al Arab.

rooms
202 suites

food
Al Mahara: seafood • Al Iwan: Arabic and international • Majlis Al Bahar: al fresco Mediterranean • Junsui: Asian • Bab Al Yam: international • Al Muntaha: modern European

drink
Sahn Eddar • Juna Lounge • Skyview Bar

features
in-suite check-in • 24-hour butler service • conference room • boardrooms • business centre • high-speed Internet access • spa • health club • infinity-edge pools • sauna • jacuzzi • squash court • access to the water sports facilities of Jumeirah Beach Hotel • unlimited complimentary access to Wild Wadi Water Park • yacht charters • limousine and helicopter transfers

nearby
Jumeirah Beach Hotel • Wild Wadi Water Park • The Montgomerie, Dubai • Emirates Golf Club

contact
PO Box 74147, Dubai, UAE •
telephone: +971.4.301 7777 •
facsimile: +971.4.301 7000 •
email: BAAreservations@jumeirah.com •
website: www.jumeirah.com

madinat jumeirah

Upon entering Madinat Jumeirah, be prepared for nothing less than royal treatment. This beach resort community is Middle Eastern renaissance at its finest, with palatial, award-winning boutique hotels, abras (traditional water taxis) gliding gently along the waterways in all their old-world charm, and a bustling souk (Arabian bazaar) filled with shops, restaurants and bars. All of these features are accompanied by a stretch of beautiful beach and that unmistakable touch of generous Arabian hospitality—the very dictionary definition of indulgence.

One has the choice of living the high life at any one of Madinat Jumeirah's regal hotels. The traditional Arabic-inspired Mina A' Salam stands nobly next to the harbour, so guests are treated to picturesque views of the Arabian Gulf from their balconies. Those who have always wondered about the decadent leisure living of the highest sheiks can satisfy their curiosity at Al Qasr, which is built to resemble a summer palace with large gardens and pools that are perfect for those delicious, do-nothing days. For a more intimate haven, opt for a breezy courtyard summerhouse at Dar Al Masyaf, which is just a stone's throw away from the beach and comes with a private pool and a personal butler at one's beck and call.

It is quite impossible to get bored at Madinat Jumeirah—just step into an abra to explore this vast holiday empire along its tapered man-made canals. First stop: Souk

...be prepared for nothing less than royal treatment.

Madinat Jumeirah, a colourful air-conditioned bazaar with over 100 boutique shops, cafés, bars and restaurants. The souk is a masterful blend of history and modernity, with its 21st-century retail and food outlets co-existing in harmony with the Moroccan architecture, traditional Arabian stalls and lively street performances. If looking for authentic crafts from Dubai, try shops like Persian Carpet House, Mirage Glass and Kenza Art Gallery. Haggling with street sellers, however, can be infinitely more entertaining, yielding up some good banter and a sharp, quick exchange of wits, not to mention a great bargain worth all the more for the experience had getting it. Many in fact come away from their first interaction with the locals in this unique Arabian market tradition slightly bruised in the pocket, but richer in ways beyond pecuniary measurement.

After an afternoon thus spent, a little retreat to Talise Spa will restore the body and mind into a state of blissful relaxation. This 26-room spa is designed into little island clusters so each guest has a private oasis. The two-hour Talise Absolution treatment is reputed to be the ultimate stress buster with two therapists providing head-to-toe pampering with a variety of massages and skin treatments. In the same path of wellness, Talise also offers a range of yoga classes, Ayurvedic treatments, foot reflexology, meditation sessions and Magnolia, an organic vegetarian restaurant.

THIS PAGE: *Sail in an abra—a traditional water taxi—for a different way to get around.*
OPPOSITE: *The vivid blue waters of the pool contrast pleasantly with the turquoise canals surrounding the resort.*

THIS PAGE: Intricate wooden carvings and fine fabrics enhance the luxurious atmosphere of the room.
OPPOSITE (FROM LEFT): Waterways connect and intersect at every turn in this opulent, self-contained community; this room provides stunning views of Burj Al Arab.

There are also plenty of opportunities to dabble in epicurean therapy with the wide range of restaurants at Madinat Jumeirah. Zheng He, located at Mina A' Salam hotel, has wowed diners with its modern Chinese fusion cuisine and stunning view of the iconic Burj Al Arab. Pisces is a popular seafood restaurant at the Souk, located on a breezy terrace that is ideal for partaking of fresh Pacific shellfish with a glass of crisp Chardonnay. Hop on a water taxi down to Dar Al Masyaf, where a taste of imperial dining awaits at PaiThai, a Thai restaurant that faces lush landscaped gardens and tranquil waterways.

At night, the energy and excitement at Madinat Jumeirah kicks up a notch. Drop by Trilogy, a club set in a three-storey, Moroccan-industrial hybrid-influenced building where top DJs from all over the world drop the latest beats and party tunes. Go up to the rooftop bar and chill out in the company of Dubai's cool crowd amid sparkling water views. For something with a little more traditional flavour, head down to Shoo Fee Ma Fee, where Arabic tapas and Moroccan snacks are served to guests snuggled comfortably on plush, colourful cushioned benches. The established 442-seater Madinat Theatre at the Souk caters to the highbrow culture mavens, bringing in top international entertainment ranging from opera to comedy acts.

Just a little further out of Madinat Jumeirah are even more exhilarating holiday activities. Walk along a connecting boardwalk

...a fantasy fulfilled for people of all ages.

rooms
Mina A' Salam: 292 rooms and suites • Al Qasr: 292 rooms and suites • Dar Al Masyaf: 283 rooms and suites in 29 summer houses • Malakiya Villas: 7 villas

food
42 restaurants and cafes

drink
12 bars and lounges

features
Souk Madinat Jumeirah • Madinat Theatre • Talise Spa • The Quay Healthclub • business centres • Madinat Arena • Madinat Conference Hall • Fort Island

nearby
Dubai International Airport • Dubai Media City • Jumeirah Beach Hotel • Dubai Internet City • Wild Wadi Water Park • Jumeirah Mosque • Burj al Arab

contact
PO Box 75157, Dubai, UAE •
telephone: +971.4.366 8888 •
facsimile: +971.4.366 7788 •
email: MJinfo@jumeirah.com •
website: www.madinatjumeirah.com

to Wild Wadi Water Park, a massive outdoor amusement park that promises non-stop entertainment with thrilling rides like Master Blaster, an uphill water roller coaster, and Jumeirah Sceirah, a speed slide that hurls visitors downhill at an explosive 80 km (50 miles) per hour. Those looking for something more adventurous may arrange to go on a desert safari, where one can try camel riding, dune bashing, sand skiing and, of course, taking in glorious views of the unforgettable sunset in the Dubai desert.

Madinat Jumeirah is a fantasy fulfilled for people of all ages, occupying the top end of the spectrum for accommodations and entertainment. While only a few in this world can become true royalty, staying at Madinat Jumeirah comes pretty close to the real deal.

one + only royal mirage

Just as images of wealth, grandeur and first-rate living come to mind upon the mention of Dubai, visitors often find the experience of sand, surf, and sun inseparable from vacations to the emirate's best resorts. These two perspectives meet on the exclusive stretch of beach known as Jumeirah, from which pearls and international trade once flowed into the city. These days, the district is home and playground to the world's wealthiest and most discerning travellers. And nowhere can this opulent lifestyle be better enjoyed than at the impressive One&Only Royal Mirage.

Composed of three separate and distinctive properties sharing a private beach and 26 hectares (65 acres) of lush, landscaped gardens, the self-contained resort offers unequalled privacy and calm in the heart of new Dubai. Overlooking the sea and in full view of the marvel that is Palm Island Bay, the three five-star hotels are full-fledged destinations in their own right. Brought together in one package, they invite superlatives.

Guests are assured of a stay in the lap of luxury at any of the three properties. Service standards are first-class, and the attentive

THIS PAGE (FROM TOP): *Traditional washbasins like this are usual features of Oriental hammams; find luxury and comfort at the Residence & Spa's opulent Garden Villa.*

OPPOSITE: *Arabian Court's exterior looks even more stunning at night, mirrored in the hotel's Reflection Pool.*

...a stay in the lap of luxury...

staff see themselves not as employees—the very word seems indelicate—but as hosts. The famed Arabian hospitality, the genuine care and concern, is evident in every move and gesture here. No wonder then, that One&Only Royal Mirage has won high praise from respected publications and organisations worldwide. It was named 'Best Leisure Resort Hotel in the Middle East' at the 2007 Business Traveller Awards and 'Middle East's Leading Resort' at the World Travel Awards (US and UK). The hotel also made *GQ's* '100 Best Things in the World' list.

The first of One&Only Royal Mirage's properties, The Palace, is worth every letter of its name. An an awe-inspiring structure of great romantic beauty, it houses 246 guestrooms and suites, as well as leisure and sporting facilities. The sprawling grounds are a wonderful backdrop for slow walks, generously planted with palms and ferns, and cooled by gently flowing waterfalls and other water features. By night, warm lamps light the way up to the regal arches of the main complex, as they might have done at a palace hundreds of years ago.

All rooms face the sea, and feature either private balconies or ground-floor terraces. The design scheme of The Palace is extended throughout in the form of ornamental arches, and they are lavishly fitted with custom-made furniture on exquisite terracotta tiled floors. In addition to special touches such as a welcome beverage and twice-daily

THIS PAGE: Look out onto the sea from The Palace's stylish Deluxe Rooms.
OPPOSITE: Lie down on a heated marble slab at the Oriental hammam and let an expert masseuse knead away the day's worries and stresses.

maid service, every room features satellite TV, voice and data lines, personal safes and outdoor furniture.

The 173 Deluxe Rooms at The Palace are spacious 45-sq-m (484-sq-ft) affairs, warmly decorated in the vivid colours of the Arabian Gulf, as befits the hotel's picturesque setting. They feature soft and comfortable king-sized beds, sitting areas, work desks, and en suite bathrooms with dark wood finishings and extra-large mirrors. An additional 53 Gold Club Rooms feature the same design as the Deluxe Rooms, but offer access to The Gold Club. An exclusive lounge and reception area, The Gold Club can be reached by a discreet members-only entrance and elevator for complete privacy. The lounge offers light continental breakfasts and a wide variety of drinks throughout the day.

A cut above the rest, the nine Executive Suites remove all barriers to rest and relaxation in 100 sq m (1,076 sq ft) of open-plan comfort. Fresh fruit is delivered daily, perfect for enjoying throughout the large rooms. Separate lounge areas have a traditional Arabic theme, with deep-pile carpets or terracotta tiling, and rare furnishings of wood, marble and fine fabrics. The bedrooms feature king-sized beds and have large en suite bathrooms. Throughout the space, surfaces are embellished with Moorish artefacts and contemporary artwork. As with the Gold Club Rooms, nine additional suites are available as Gold Club Suites with access to the private lounge.

Two Royal Suites are the pinnacle of The Palace's accommodation options. These two-bedroom luxury apartments offer 325-sq-m (3,498 sq ft) of space. Each bedroom is decorated in sumptuous colours and textures, from the four-poster canopy beds made with fine linens, to the charming recliners, coffee tables and artwork. Walk-in closets and luxurious en suite bathrooms increase the sense of freedom. There is a spacious living and dining area complete with kitchenette, and a large balcony from which Palm Island Bay can be seen just 50 m (164 ft) away.

...majestic fountains, grand walkways and picture-perfect green gardens...

Dining at The Palace knows no limits, with four restaurants offering a range of cuisines from the region and beyond. Olives is a casual all-day dining restaurant with a Mediterranean menu featuring cuisine from Italy, Spain, Greece and France. The sky-blue ceiling mingles with African slate floors, stained glass, and wrought iron chandeliers for a vibrant atmosphere. An outdoor terrace overlooking the pool gives the place a coastal café feel.

Tagine is a taste of Morocco in more ways than one. Open for dinner only, the food here is just as authentic as the decór, which was put together with artefacts from around the region to recreate a Marrakeshi home. Celebrities is a speciality restaurant serving international cuisine with a Middle Eastern twist, and is a romantic dining venue overlooking the gardens below. For those wanting to get away from it all, head for the Beach Bar & Grill out on the sand overlooking Palm Island. A relaxed terrace by day and a sensual candlelit outdoor restaurant by night, the grill serves lobster, tiger prawns, kebabs and prime steaks done to perfection.

The second property at One&Only Royal Mirage is named Arabian Court for its inspired Oriental design. The artfully lit structure gracefully combines a strict sense of symmetry with an opulent interpretation of paradise that reads like a passage straight from a legend. The surrounding landscape is formed by majestic fountains,

THIS PAGE: *The expansive patio of the Prince Suites at Arabian Court is an ideal place for entertaining.*

OPPOSITE: *The Roof Top is the perfect spot to watch the sky take on its evening hues.*

grand walkways and picture-perfect green gardens teeming with life. Walking up to the main entrance hall of the Grand Gallery, one realises that Arabian Court spreads out to wings on both sides offering a total of 162 rooms and 10 suites.

As it is with The Palace, every room at Arabian Court faces the sea, and comes with either a private balcony or garden patio and a full range of amenities. The Deluxe Rooms are more than comfortable at 50 sq m (538 sq ft), and are richly decorated with the use of wood, mosaics and distinctively Oriental patterns. The bathroom combines marble and slate with wood, and features a wet area with overhead and handheld shower, a granite bench, separate toilet and bidet, individual vanity with undershelf cupboards and a bath with handheld shower. Three configurations are available for each room: one king-sized bed, two queen-sized beds, or a king-sized bed and sofa bed.

Eight Executive Suites draw interior design inspiration from the desert, enclosing guests in the comfortable splendour of warm tones and rich natural fabrics. At 125 sq m (1,345 sq ft), they are perfect for relaxing and entertaining, and feature roomy living and sleeping quarters. The king-sized beds come with attractive decorative overhead canopies, and the lounge areas have an entrance foyer, a dining area, a separate guest toilet and 'majlis'-style seating areas, an Arabic term for a room in the house which is used to

...the comfortable splendour of warm tones and rich natural fabrics.

entertain guests. The suites either have a balcony or ground-floor patio, and are available in one or two-bedroom configurations.

For the very best that Arabian Court has to offer, there are the two Prince Suites. At 145 sq m (1,561 sq ft) each, they offer unparalleled space and comfort worthy of royal attention. Designed to capture the essence of Arabia in their fine details, they are revelatory experiences in themselves. Venture out onto the 25-sq-m (269 sq ft) terrace and one will find majlis-style seating—perfect for contemplating the view with friends while enjoying tea in the afternoon, or dinner in the evening. As with the Executive Suites, the Prince Suites come with everything that guests need and can be made to accommodate up to four people by opening a door to an adjoining room.

Visitors to Arabian Court should prepare themselves for rich feasts, as the hotel houses three restaurants of the highest quality. The Rotisserie is housed in a grand dining room with a show kitchen that allows patrons to participate in the excitement and energy of an expert chef at work. Alternatively, meals can be taken out to the open verandah, where the fresh air and sounds from the resort's gardens enrich the traditional European cuisine. Those with an adventurous side will want to make a reservation at Nina, a colourful new-wave Indo-European restaurant. Heady and spicy, the food brings sleeping palates to life every night. More

THIS PAGE: *Impressive pools can be found throughout One&Only Royal Mirage.*

OPPOSITE: *Enjoy afternoon high tea at The Library, which is for the exclusive enjoyment of Residence & Spa's guests.*

fusion cuisine awaits at Eauzone, which serves modern food with an Asian twist in an outdoor setting. The ambience here is casual by day and stylish at night.

The third and final component of the One&Only Royal Mirage experience is the Residence & Spa. A haven of healing and well-being, it offers a comprehensive array of spa treatments, massages and gastronomical pleasures that will rejuvenate any weary traveller. A dedicated Health & Beauty Institute shows others how to give guests the ultimate pampering experience. The Institute features a Givenchy Spa, a traditional Oriental hammam, a Zouari hair salon and a modern fitness centre, all housed within towering Arabian domes, carved arches and marble.

The authentic Oriental hammam has to be seen to be believed. The impenetrable bathhouse leads visitors through a series of winding corridors, tiled in classic white and blue, until finally they emerge in a sanctuary of relaxation. Heated massage tables, black soap, and the hands of a skilled tayeb, or masseur, is all that is required to leave you feeling renewed.

To provide the ultimate retreat, the Residence & Spa's restaurant and bar, The Dining Room and The Library, are reserved for the exclusive use of its guests. As with all the Spa's highly exclusive treatments, meals at The Dining Room are customised to suit the needs and desires of guests. With some of the finest fresh and seasonal ingredients at their disposal, the hotel's chefs are able to create masterpieces with exceptional creativity.

Reflecting the spirit of openness at the Residence & Spa, both in body and mind, the 32 Prestige Rooms offer 58 sq m (624 sq ft) of living space and tall glass doors that open out to scented gardens and expansive views of the Arabian Gulf. Inside, the tone is kept warm and inviting through the use of refined carved wood furnishings, flowing fabrics and soft cream colours whenever necessary. The en suite bathrooms are adorned with wood and slate, and feature a wet area with showers, marble benches, separate baths, toilets and bidets.

Twelve Junior Suites at 85 sq m (915 sq ft) offer an enhanced experience, and can even be joined with an adjacent Prestige Room to create a two-bedroom suite with a shared main entrance foyer. The Junior Suite has a light and airy lounge area with dining table, from which the Palm Island Bay is visible. For even more room and greater luxury, four Executive Suites offer all the comforts of the Residence & Spa in a deluxe 118-sq-m (1,270-sq-ft) mini-apartment. They feature dining areas, separate guest toilets and majlis-style seating for up to seven people.

However, if one desires to entertain guests or take loved ones away for an unforgettable holiday, only the Garden Villa will do. The property's crown jewel, this 300-sq-m (3,229-sq-ft) two-bedroom home

...a sensation that may have no other name than magic.

away from home is just a few steps away from the ocean and has a private stretch of beach all to itself. The Garden Villa features its own temperature-controlled pool, driveway and parking. The magnificently appointed sea-facing bedrooms, each with luxurious bathrooms are separated by an Arabesque-style living and dining area with kitchenette for preparing your own picnic baskets.

One&Only Royal Mirage's philosophy dictates that every element must contribute towards the creation of a resort stay without equal anywhere. In order to create the magic of Arabia, the hotel has infused every inch of its expansive property with traditional architecture and design, and hired only the best and most attentive of staff to serve every guest as if they were the hotel's only ones. A place becomes more than the sum of its parts when care of this degree is taken, and when walking through One&Only Royal Mirage's carefully manicured grounds, soaking up the sun on its pristine beaches, dining by candlelight beside a garden fountain, or relaxing at any of its spaciously elegant rooms, one is filled with a sensation that may have no other name than magic.

rooms
The Palace: 246 • Arabian Court: 172 • Residence & Spa: 48 rooms and suites • 1 villa

food
The Palace
Olives: Mediterranean • Tagine: Moroccan • Celebrities: international • Beach Bar & Grill: steak and seafood

Arabian Court
The Rotisserie: traditional European • Nina: Indo-European • Eauzone: modern Asian

The Residence & Spa
The Dining Room: private dining

drink
Kasbar • The Roof Top • The Samovar Lounge • The Library

features
Health & Beauty Institute • Givenchy Spa • Oriental hammam • hair salon • fitness centre • pools • water sports • tennis courts • putting green • meeting rooms • amphitheatre • business corner • childcare centre

nearby
Dubai Villa Moda • Mall of the Emirates • Dubai Museum • Palm Island Bay • Sheikh Saeed House • Bastakiya Cultural Walk • Jumeirah Mosque • Emirates Golf Club

contact
PO Box 37252, Dubai, UAE •
telephone: +971.4. 399 9999 •
facsimile: +971.4. 399 9998 •
email: info@oneandonlyroyalmirage.ae •
website: www.oneandonlyresorts.com

radisson SAS hotel, dubai media city

THIS PAGE (FROM TOP): *The Media Lounge is fashionable and inviting, ideal for gatherings; the Executive Suite comes with a separate office that can be used for meetings.*
OPPOSITE: *At Tamanya Terrace, guests can watch the sunset, have dinner, chat and mingle until late into the night.*

This cutting-edge newcomer has much more of a wow factor than one would expect from a conservative hotel group like Radisson. Perhaps it is the influence of Dubai, where even the most straight-laced society matron cannot resist an occasional burst of glitz. Or perhaps the fact that its location, in the deeply trendy Dubai Media City, demanded a bit more of the hip details young media whizzes expect. Even the most jaded editor of *Wallpaper* or the IT genius who has seen it all will be pleased with the hotel's attention to good design mingled with the latest in technology—all for a rate that is a steal compared with other hotels offering similar high style and standards. The Radisson SAS Hotel, Dubai Media City is indeed a gem.

The Radisson's central location makes it convenient for business in Dubai Media City and all the action of Jumeirah. Shopping is easy, with Dubai's favourite retail therapy centre, the Mall of the Emirates, close by. Golfers are spoilt for choice with both the Emirates Golf Club (a fixture on the PGA Tour) and The Montgomerie only a few minutes away. No need to hail a taxi, as the hotel's shuttle bus is ever ready to whisk guests off to the beach or the shops. With the opening of chic Dubai Marina and the Palm Jumeirah development, the area is blossoming and the Radisson is in the heart of it.

The hotel has 246 rooms, including special Business Class rooms for high-flying executives, and Executive Suites for more

...the handsome rooms reflect the best of contemporary chic.

space during longer stays. As befits a Media City hotel, all rooms have free wireless Internet access—no excuses for being offline—along with a host of advanced features. The Deluxe smart technology rooms have satellite TV, DVD systems, and touch screen controls to access everything from phones to room service. The handsome rooms reflect the best of contemporary chic, with high ceilings, picture windows with sweeping views, and stylish bathrooms stocked with toiletries. In Business Class there is more space, with a sofa and work area, and access to the popular Business Class Lounge where guests can use computers, printers and other executive facilities. Bonuses are the complimentary Super Breakfast Buffet and late checkout. Those upgrading to one of the five Executive Suites will have an expansive living and dining space ideal for meetings.

A good hotel is defined by a really good restaurant. Happily, the Radisson has Certo, a terrific modern Italian restaurant voted 'Best in Dubai' at the 2007 TimeOut Awards. Certo serves an innovative selection of antipasti, homemade pasta and gourmet pizza from a

THIS PAGE: *Order a healthy drink from the poolside bar and sip it on one of the sunloungers.*

OPPOSITE (FROM LEFT): *Certo is an acclaimed Italian restaurant that serves novel and tasty dishes; the pool beckons guests for a vigorous early-morning swim or a leisurely afternoon dip.*

traditional wood-fired oven. The show kitchen features the chefs in action, while the impressive 6-m (20-ft) wine tower holds 500 wines from Italy and around the world. The Italian Friday brunch is especially popular.

For casual dining, the Chef's House specialises in serving a delicious buffet from an imaginative setting that features an open kitchen and grill stations, where a tempting selection of Oriental and Middle Eastern dishes are prepared. The restaurant is perfect for business events or social gatherings, but guests can also request the intimate private dining room. A favourite watering hole for drinks after work is the hotel's Icon Bar, where the movers and shakers of the media world pop in for tapas, a glass of wine, the latest scoop, and a look at sports action on wide screen TV. The Media Lounge is another good place to meet or catch up on some work. With its glittering Swarovski crystals and sleek furnishings, the restaurant is as stylish as it is functional. Guests are served light lunches and all-day snacks. Techies will love the wireless Internet access so they can show off their laptops and stay on top of their work.

The Radisson pays special attention to the well-being of its guests. At the hotel's delightful Senso Spa, the senses are indulged with an exotic tour of massages, body treatments and facials from around the globe. There is everything from a 20-minute express back, neck and shoulder massage—perfect for getting rid of pre-presentation jitters—to a luxurious, hour-and-a-half Perle de Caviar facial that will leave skin glowing. The five treatment rooms each have a different Asian theme. Guests can pretend to be in Thailand for a Thai massage, or in India for an Ayurvedic treatment, complete with Indian music, incense and oils. It is a fun concept, all done with creativity and attention to detail. Next door is the Health Club, which has all the latest fitness equipment for keeping in shape.

...such great style and service...

There are separate steam rooms for men and women, a relaxation area, and an outdoor terrace with sunloungers and a lap pool.

Another relaxing place to take in the sunset over the Arabian Gulf is the Tamanya Terrace. This outdoor bar is an ideal spot to start or end an evening. Grab a quick shawarma before hitting the club, or pop in for a nightcap after partying in town. The bar serves drinks and nibbles until 2.00 am.

When business calls, the Radisson answers, with 12 conference rooms spread out over nearly 600 sq m (6,458 sq ft) of space, as well as smaller boardrooms. The rooms are cleverly designed, with natural daylight instead of the usual grim fluorescent lighting, and all the modern conveniences needed for a successful meeting or conference. Outdoor areas such as the Business Class Terrace are perfect for gatherings.

The hotel has a strong service ethic that really delivers. An example of the Radisson's empathetic ethos is its express laundry service, which guarantees clean shirts in under three hours. Minor repairs are also part of the service. It is a small detail, but it means a lot if a guest has just spilled coffee on his last clean shirt. Usually, service this good is only available in five-star hotels with butlers on hand. Indeed, the Radisson SAS Hotel, Dubai Media City has such great style and service that it just may end up a favourite.

rooms
246

food
Certo: Italian • Chef's House: Oriental and Middle Eastern

drink
Icon Bar • Media Lounge • Tamanya Terrace

features
outdoor pools • gym • poolside bar • spa • steam rooms • exclusive business class lounge • wireless Internet access • meeting rooms • business centre

nearby
Emirates Golf Club • The Montgomerie, Dubai • Mall of the Emirates • Ski Dubai • Jumeirah Beach

contact
PO Box 211723, Dubai, UAE •
telephone: +971.4.366 9111 •
facsimile: +971.4.361 1011 •
email: info.dubai@radissonsas.com •
website: dubai.radissonsas.com

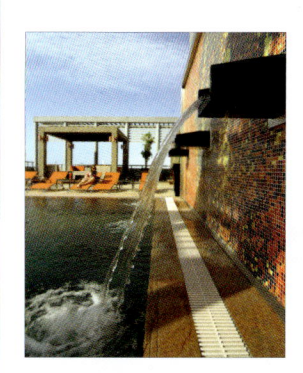

grosvenor house

THIS PAGE: *Lounge on these plush sofas and listen to mellow music while viewing the blazing hues of the Dubai skyline at night.*
OPPOSITE: *Bathed in the warm glow of lights, the reception area of Grosvenor House is elegant, inviting and impressive.*

Some hotels, despite being relatively new, become instant classics. Grosvenor House was an outsider that got on the inside track and never looked back. Its ascent from new kid on the block to one of Dubai's most sought-after hotels is a tribute to the creative flair and attention to detail that puts Grosvenor House in a class of its own. It towers majestically in neo-Art Deco splendour above the bright yachts and blue waters of the swanky new Dubai Marina. Perched on the ever-fashionable Jumeirah beachfront, Grosvenor House is fast becoming an enclave of chic in its own right.

It is a 1920s debutante—aristocratic and well brought up, but with a playful rebellious streak. Instead of a predictable five-star hotel, guests are treated to a lavish world where they are indulged and adored like favourite children. An atmosphere of style permeates every corner of hotel. It is no surprise then why *Condè Nast Traveller* voted Grosvenor House 'one of the coolest hotels in the world', the only hotel in the UAE to appear on the magazine's 2006 Hot List.

Typical of how Grosvenor House does things is the way it handles its spa, Retreat. The hotel has devoted an entire floor to the spa, so that guests need not traipse about in their robes and trainers. Even better, the gym and pool are for their exclusive use, so guests need not worry about half of Dubai popping in after work for a swim or a workout.

The spa's signature treatment is the Rasul, a traditional Turkish all-over mineral body pack that not only cleanses and tightens the skin, but also stimulates circulation and muscle tone. There are other treatments to choose from, all set within seven natural wood treatment rooms, including a double room. The tranquil atmosphere creates an

...an atmosphere of style permeates every corner...

immediate sense of well-being and balance. Retreat's jacuzzi, steam room, sauna and hydropool soothes away any aches and tension, leaving you refreshed, rejuvenated and ready to face the world.

The Retreat Terrace and Health Bar, a spa-cuisine café, complements Retreat's services. There is also the hip and trendy N Bar, a one-stop haven for the perfect make-up, manicure, pedicure, waxing and other beauty treatments for women. Just along the hall is retro-cool JetSet, the best place in town for an updo or a blow-dry inspired by 1960s airline style, when globetrotting stewardesses were the height of glamour. The gents will love 1847, a men's grooming zone with all the services needed to recharge the batteries of even the most jet-lagged executive.

Outside the spa, on an attractive deck in the terrace above the marina, the pool beckons. Relax in the sun on the comfortable sunloungers and order something cool from the bar. Overlooking the pool is a gym equipped with the latest cardiovascular and weights equipment. Professional instructors are on hand to advise and motivate guests in their eternal quest for the body beautiful.

Guests at Grosvenor House also benefit from the facilities that the hotel shares with Le Royal Méridien Beach Resort & Spa, which has a private beach and the clear blue waters of the Arabian Gulf on its doorstep. These shared facilities include beach access, water sports, pools and tennis courts.

THIS PAGE: *Rooms combine contemporary design and the very latest in technology.*

OPPOSITE (FROM TOP): *The soothing colours of this spacious bedroom ensure a blissful night of sleep; the sleek Rhodes Mezzanine is a good place to tuck into a sumptuous meal.*

Grosvenor House provides impeccable service on all levels, from the 24-hour butler, who is only too happy to run a bath, fix a torn hem or unpack bags, to the waiter at the Deli Café who considerately asks if a guest would like mayonnaise on his sandwich. This impeccable service is most impressively on display at the 12 bars and restaurants that make Grosvenor House a hot ticket when it comes to reserving a table. Celebrity and Michelin-starred chefs, combined with delectable food and imaginative and stunning restaurant interiors always make dining at Grosvenor House a treat.

The main dining establishment, Sloane's, is a bustling restaurant serving food as fresh as it comes. Without the restrictions of a menu or traditional buffet, Sloane's open kitchen showcases culinary art at its best, with food cooked to order. Located on the mezzanine level, guests can choose to dine inside or al fresco on the terrace while enjoying views of the evening sky.

Ottomans is an exotic and evocative tribute to the sophistication of Istanbul at the height of the famed Ottoman Empire. The stylish restaurant mixes influences of the old Turkish tradition with the flavour of the Mediterranean sea. It features two cosy bars, live entertainment and a shisha terrace overlooking Dubai Marina.

The bright and contemporary Rhodes Mezzanine, on the other hand, elegantly fuses baroque-style furniture with modern lighting elements. The place was voted 'TimeOut Best New Restaurant' in 2006 and has evolved into a culinary destination in itself with British star chef Gary Rhodes at the helm. The traditional and classical Anglo-modern dishes served at Rhodes Mezzanine is as seductive as the restaurant's interior, and a satisfying evening here is a highlight of any trip to Dubai.

...*impeccable service on all levels...*

Indego is Dubai's premier gourmet Indian restaurant. It is home to Chef Patron Vineet Bhatia, the world's only Indian Michelin-star winner and the man behind such famous and successful restaurants as Safran in Mauritius and Rasoi in London.

The Deli Café caters for gourmets on the go. Sip a frothy cappuccino at this buzzing meeting point. Relax with a just-baked pastry while reading the papers, or tuck into a savoury snack before checking out the boutiques. Other popular places to chill out are the Lobby Lounge and The Gallery, a discreet bar with a colonial ambience where a selection of fine whiskies, cognacs, sakes and grappas are served.

At teatime, the place to be is Leaves, a tranquil haven where you can choose from the world's finest teas. The place is perfect for an intimate rendezvous in an oriental setting.

As the sun sets and the lights of the hotel take on their evening hues, Dubai's social butterflies flit to Bar 44, an exclusive champagne and cocktail bar located on the 44th floor. True to its name, the bar offers 44 types of champagne and a wide array of

THIS PAGE: *Savour Indian delights in the Art Deco splendour that is Indego.*

OPPOSITE (FROM LEFT): *Guests will enjoy the ambience as much as the food at Buddha Bar; soak away the stresses of the day at the Retreat spa.*

exotic drinks, and is a great place to watch the Dubai elite mingle. Buddha Bar is another hot spot. The city's in-crowd flock to this bar-cum-restaurant for the Asian fusion cuisine and the activity. Staff mill about unobtrusively, serving cocktails and food.

With so much to delight and distract at Grosvenor House, guests barely have reason to stay in their rooms. However, this would mean missing a chance to enjoy the thoughtful comforts that make the place so special. The 217 guestrooms and suites are exceptionally spacious, with high ceilings and big windows that afford good views of the sea. The 205 apartment suites, on the other hand, offer outstanding Marina views. Interior décor is sophisticated, with hues of cream and chocolate brown complementing the extensive use of natural wood and marble. The beds are huge and come with buttery-soft linens and pillows. There are all sorts of signature touches, like a personalised 24-hour butler service, CD and DVD players, and plasma TV. The walk-in dressing area and closets have plenty of room. The bathrooms have everything guests could want—bath, separate toilet, separate shower, twin wash basins and Bvlgari toiletries.

The topmost 11 floors of the hotel are reserved for Grosvenor Club members, and offer premium executive accommodation with access to a dedicated lounge located on the 44th floor. The three-bedroom penthouse suite on the 45th floor offers the best in luxury living, with floor-to-ceiling windows that provide 360° views of Dubai. For longer stays, the hotel's apartment suites are an attractive option. However, no matter where guests stay, they can be assured that everything at Grosvenor House is first class, with flair.

...everything at Grosvenor House is first class, with flair.

rooms
217 rooms and suites • 205 apartment suites

food
Buddha Bar: Asian fusion • Indego: Indian • Ottomans: Turkish • Sloane's: international • Rhodes Mezzanine: Anglo-modern • Retreat Terrace: spa cuisine

drink
Bar 44 • The Gallery • Leaves • The Deli Café • The Lobby Lounge • Retreat Pool Bar

features
24-hour concierge • high-speed and wireless Internet access • outdoor pool • gym • spa • babysitting service • business centre • beauty salon • sauna • spa cuisine

nearby
Dubai Internet City • Dubai Media City • Emirates Golf Club • Mall of the Emirates • Gold & Diamond Park • Ibn Batuta Shopping Mall • Dubai Zoo • Dubai Museum

contact
Al Sufouh Road, PO Box 118500, Dubai, UAE • telephone: +971.4.399 8888 • facsimile: +971.4.399 8444 • email: reservations@lrm-gh-dubai.com • website: www.grosvenorhouse-dubai.com

le royal méridien beach resort + spa

THIS PAGE: *The sumptuous décor of the main reception makes guests feel as though they have stepped into a palace.*

OPPOSITE: *Le Royal Méridien boasts impressive pools, a pristine beach and a wide array of water sports for guests to indulge in.*

Enjoying a privileged position on the famed upmarket stretch of Jumeirah, along the coast of Dubai overlooking the Arabian Gulf, is the elegant and classy Le Royal Méridien Beach Resort & Spa. This luxurious, award-winning five-star property is set on a private stretch of white, sandy beach bordering clear blue waters, and is considered by many to be one of Dubai's premier resorts. That is no small praise in a city of extremes.

Enclosed on all sides by beautiful, idyllic gardens, it is a sublime get-away for those seeking real quality time with themselves or loved ones. Featuring a unique Roman-style spa renowned for exceptionally indulgent treatments, the hotel has received numerous awards for being an ideal all-in-one holiday destination. At the 2007 World Travel Awards, it swept three honors: 'Dubai's Leading Spa Resort', 'UAE's Leading Spa Resort', and 'Middle East's Leading Spa Resort'.

Boasting a total of 500 guest rooms and suites, with ample capacity for events with up to 1,500 guests, the hotel has two extension wings, each with their own special services and facilities. Regardless of whether you choose to stay in the Main Building, Club or Tower, a team of helpful staff ensures that guests' needs are attended to. After all, choice is what a stay at Le Royal Méridien is all about. The hotel strives to provide an experience as welcoming and as intimate as possible. This it does by offering guests an enticing range of options, coupled with a personalised service that always begins with a VIP welcome at the airport.

Rooms at the Club carry the Deluxe signifier. The Deluxe Rooms are the last word in understated luxury, with modern furniture in attractive finishings and colours. Soft throw cushions make the large king-sized beds even more inviting, and soft lighting completes the mood. As with all rooms, they come complete with all the conveniences one

...one of Dubai's premier resorts.

would expect from a top-notch hotel: high-speed Internet access, minibars, satellite TV, IDD, and in-room safes.

Rooms at the Club grant their residents the use of an exclusive Club lounge where breakfast and cocktails are served. The environment is conducive to business meetings, and encourages the combination of work and play. The stylish rooms are relaxed and inviting, featuring soft, neutral tones that create an airy ambience. Generous work desks with data ports allow guests to stay in touch at all times.

For travellers seeking the ultimate Le Royal Méridien experience, the hotel's Tower rooms and suites are not to be missed. They are the very finest, with lofty sea views. Each one is furnished to the highest standards, with luxury duvets and covers, carved wood furniture, and the thoughtfulness of three telephones each. For entertainment, the rooms and suites are equipped with large-screen TV, DVD players, and CD stereo systems with complimentary access to a music library.

The Tower Suites are extra spacious, with comfortable lounge areas connected to wide and very accommodating bedrooms complete with four-poster, king-sized beds. Throughout the room, a loving attention to detail is evident in the use of classically styled furniture, rich fabrics, and ornate designs. Another of the Tower Suites' surprises are the large, en suite bathrooms, fitted with deep bathtubs, separate showers, toilets, and

THIS PAGE: Watch the sun set while enjoying Mexican favourites at Maya.
OPPOSITE (FROM LEFT): Plush, soft fabrics in creamy hues at the Royal Suite Bedroom invite guests to relax; Le Royal Méridien offers a variety of choices for superb wining and dining.

bidets. Even the toiletries are top-notch—the finest offerings from Hermès, the prestigious Parisian house of high fashion.

For extended stays at the resort, or for very special occasions, Le Royal Méridien has a limited number of suites designed for the most discerning of visitors. The Royal Suites, Presidential Suite, Royal Apartment and Club Penthouse are veritable homes in themselves, leaving nothing to be desired and offering everything to satisfy the senses. However, no matter where guests choose to stay, all the rooms and suites at the hotel ensure utmost comfort and elegance, combined with the very best in business facilities. Butler service is available 24 hours a day, ensuring that guests' needs are catered for at all times.

An incredible wealth of dining options is on offer at Le Royal Méridien. There are 15 restaurants and bars ready to take guests to the far corners of the culinary world. Modern Mexican food is done to perfection at Maya, which was named 'Best Fine Dining Restaurant' at the MENA Travel Awards 2007. Prime Rib is sure to satisfy cravings for the most succulent of steaks. Ossigeno and Pizzeria bring a touch of Italy to Jumeirah Beach, while Fusion does the same for Southeast Asian cuisine. Mi Vida, on the other hand, recreates the magic of the Mediterranean. A range of fresh seafood makes any romantic evening under the stars a memorable one. Seabreeze is a relaxing setting where guests can enjoy a selection of bistro meals paired with a marvellous wine list. The Brasserie offers sumptuous buffets and à la carte meals daily, and Al Khaima focuses on the gastronomical experience of Arabia. After a satisfying meal at any of these restaurants, head to The Piano Bar, Maya Rooftop, Satchmo's, the Al Murjan tea lounge or the outdoor Pool Bar for some conversation over drinks.

Another winning feature of Le Royal Méridien is the Caracalla Spa and Health Club, situated over three floors. Inspired by ancient Rome, the spa offers tailor-made programmes to both relax and invigorate tired minds and

...refined accommodation, heavenly spa relaxation and exquisite dining...

bodies. Caracalla features five hammam pools, a sauna, steam room and a jacuzzi. It also offers soothing procedures such as facial and body exfoliation, firming and hydrating treatments and blissful massages by highly qualified and experienced spa therapists. One such pleasure is the Exotic Lime and Ginger Salt Glow, which involves a warm oil rub, followed by exfoliation with the rare salt. After a final application of an island-flower body balm, skin is deeply cleansed and positively glowing.

Once guests are sufficiently pampered, they will find that Le Royal Méridien is also equipped for every conceivable leisure activity. A large gym and fitness centre overlooks the landscaped gardens outside. An aerobics centre, four tennis courts, three pools and two squash courts are available. Guests can also choose to go parasailing, water skiing and windsurfing.

Before encountering Le Royal Méridien Beach Resort & Spa, one might find it difficult to conceive of a place that offers the holiday experience of three or more hotels. But this sprawling, self-contained cluster of refined accommodation, heavenly spa relaxation and exquisite dining on one of the region's best beaches has the uncanny power to change even the most jaded of minds.

rooms
500

food
Maya: Mexican • Prime Rib: steak • Ossigeno: Italian • Fusion: Southeast Asian • Mi Vida: seafood • Seabreeze: Mediterranean • Pizzeria: Italian • Brasserie: international • Al Khaima: Arabic

drink
The Piano Bar • Satchmo's • Al Murjan • The Pool Bar • Maya Rooftop

features
Caracalla Spa and Health Club • fitness centre • Penguin Kids Club • 24-hour concierge • car rental • water sports • tennis courts • heated pools • squash courts • business centre • hair salon • function rooms

nearby
Emirates Golf Club • Mall of the Emirates • Gold & Diamond Park

contact
Al Sufouh Road, PO Box 24970, Dubai, UAE • telephone: +971.4.399 5999 • facsimile: +971.4.317 6980 • email: reservations@lrm-gh-dubai.com • website: www.leroyalmeridien-dubai.com

the ritz-carlton, dubai

THIS PAGE: *Nestled in a tropical garden set on prime beach front, The Ritz-Carlton, Dubai is ideal for guests craving for some fun in the sun.*

OPPOSITE: *Listen to the sound of waves lapping the shore while dining in outdoor comfort at Amaseena.*

The Ritz-Carlton, Dubai is an oasis of calm and quiet luxury along the Jumeirah coast. Guests are enveloped in an atmosphere of relaxed refinement the minute they enter the hotel's elegant lobby. Rose petals float serenely in the marble fountain, bowls of white orchids add a graceful touch, and floor-to-ceiling picture windows afford a view of gardens stretching down to the white beach and sapphire sea.

The Ritz-Carlton, Dubai is in an enviable position. It has a lovely 350-m (1,148-ft) private beach on the most sought-after part of the Jumeirah coast, next to the shops, restaurants and nightlife of the fashionable new Dubai Marina. Just a few minutes away are the popular shopping and entertainment centre Madinat Jumeirah and the famous Wild Wadi Water Park, a fun zone for kids of all ages.

Guests are enveloped in an atmosphere of relaxed refinement...

Golfers will appreciate the resort's proximity to both Emirates Golf Club and The Montgomerie. The graceful Mediterranean style of the resort blends harmoniously with its environment, in one of the most attractive landscaped gardens in Dubai. The 35,000-sq-m (377,000-sq-ft) garden ramble throughout the resort, connecting the three swimming pools, children's area and spa. Guestrooms all overlook the gardens and have a private patio or balcony.

The Ritz-Carlton, Dubai is a classic hotel with a boutique feel. Business travellers will like the combination of first-rate executive services and leisure activities, while couples will love the romantic setting and sense of privacy. Guests with children do not have to compromise on luxury in order to keep the children amused.

The redecorated rooms are charming and traditional, yet with all the latest gadgets like flat-screen TV. The Club Level rooms have the added benefit of complimentary access to the Club Lounge, an exclusive retreat with stunning sea views, food and beverage presentations and business services, including wireless Internet access and a dedicated concierge.

The range of activities for a hotel this size is impressive. There is a full-service fitness centre complete with personal trainers, four floodlit tennis courts and two squash courts, a golf putting green, three outdoor pools which include a children's pool with a water

THIS PAGE: *The ornate windows high, corniced ceilings and marble fountain in the lobby are sure to impress guests.*
OPPOSITE (FROM LEFT): *Opulent rooms like this are hallmarks of The Ritz-Carlton, Dubai; indulge in Eastern therapies and treatments at the Balinese-inspired spa.*

slide, and a spa with eight treatment rooms. The Ritz-Carlton, Dubai is also happy to organise quintessential Dubai activities such as sand skiing, desert driving, paragliding, dhow cruises, sailing and falconry tours.

Families will love the award-winning Ritz Kids Club, one of the best resort children's programmes in town. The Ritz Kids Club offers supervised physical and creative activities designed especially for children ages four to 12. Offering full or half-day options, seven days a week, the club has something for every child, with games, beach explorations, storytelling sessions and lessons in magic and cookery, as well as a dedicated playground, shallow pool and indoor playroom. Parents can enjoy a relaxing, guilt-free break knowing their children are well looked after and having fun.

Within the heart of the splendid resort lies The Ritz-Carlton Spa. Inspired by the ancient healing treatments of the East and the beauty secrets of Europe, the spa has a range of stress-busting massages, cleansing and rejuvenating facials, and blissful body treatments. The soft lighting, scented candles and caring staff all create a serene atmosphere. Spa facilities include a dry sauna room, whirlpool bath and eucalyptus steam rooms, a relaxation area and a swimming pool. There are also two new ladies-only treatment rooms for complete privacy. Try the delicious Choco Heaven body treatment—an indulgent therapy that starts with a cocoa scrub, followed by a chocolate masque, and topped off with a nourishing coconut and chocolate massage that leaves the skin glowing. Men will enjoy the Gentlemen's Bath, an in-room spa bath that mixes essential oils of lavender, ylang-ylang and marjoram for total relaxation. The treatment is accompanied by a Ritz-Carlton Selection cigar and a glass of cognac.

...a world where good taste, good manners and good service prevail.

Dubai is famous for the quality and variety of its restaurants, and The Ritz-Carlton, Dubai provides guests with a superlative choice in dining. From the casual chic of the poolside Gulf Pavilion, to the gourmet dining of La Baie, guests are spoilt for choice. To sample a traditional Arabian feast, complete with shisha pipes and belly dancing, there is Amaseena. This restaurant of Bedouin tents is where guests can relax under the stars, while enjoying freshly grilled shish kebabs and mouthwatering mezzes. For morning coffee or afternoon tea with fresh pastries, try The Lobby Lounge. The Library Bar is a good option for guests wanting cigars and Scotch, leather armchairs and quiet appeal. The culinary delights of Italy are represented at Splendido. Dine al fresco in the terrace overlooking the Arabian Gulf while tucking into mozzarella salad with lobster medallions and a glass of chilled Prosecco. The famed Gulf seafood is given star treatment at the hotel's signature restaurant, La Baie, where Asian fusion flavours create a new taste sensation in a sleek modern setting.

The Ritz-Carlton, Dubai seamlessly blends all the best features of a luxury hotel with family-friendly amenities usually found in bigger resorts. Within its charmed circle, guests will find a world where good taste, good manners and good service prevail. Add to this a beautiful setting, removed from the bustle of town yet close to all that is happening in Jumeirah, and it is easy to see why The Ritz-Carlton, Dubai is a perennial favourite among travellers.

rooms
138

food
Splendido: Italian • Amaseena: Arabic • La Baie: seafood and sushi • Gulf Pavilion: poolside snacks

drink
The Library Bar • The Lobby Lounge

features
tennis courts • squash courts • private beach • pool • fitness centre • spa • Ritz Kids Club • miniature golf course • technology butler • high-speed Internet access • meeting rooms • banquet facilities

nearby
Dubai Internet City • Dubai Media City • Wild Wadi Water Park • Jumeirah Mosque • Dubai Museum • Dubai Zoo • Mall of the Emirates

contact
PO Box 26525, Dubai, UAE •
telephone: +971.4.399 4000 •
facsimile: +971.4.399 4001 •
email: rcdubai@emirates.net.ae •
website: www.ritzcarlton.com

oasis beach tower

THIS PAGE: *The bedrooms are simply but stylishly furnished, so that guests will feel right at home.*
OPPOSITE (FROM LEFT): *The living room offers floor-to-ceiling views of the outside; the iconic Oasis Beach Tower is one of the most prominent towers in Dubai Marina.*

Created to meet the needs of a discerning luxury stay, the Oasis Beach Tower offers an enclave of space and luxury for extended stays within easy reach of Dubai's exciting new developments. Located in the Dubai Marina area on Jumeirah Beach, this dynamic, modern structure stretches 245 m (804 ft) upwards, holding 180 apartments across 49 storeys which provide excellent views of the Arabian Gulf. It features fully serviced luxury accommodation with all the exclusive benefits of a hotel, coupled with the extra space and expansive comforts that only these apartments—the largest serviced hotel apartments in Dubai—can offer. Elegant, warm, inviting, spacious and sophisticated—Oasis Beach Tower provides guests with an unparalleled living experience, regardless of the duration of their stay.

The tower is separated into four distinct bands: Deluxe Floors 4–14, Superior Floors 15–32, Premium Floors 33–41 and Superior Floors 42–49. Each is served by six high-speed elevators, four of which offer incredible panoramic views. Deluxe Floors 4–14 feature spacious apartments with balconies and furnished with contemporary high-quality interiors. They are well-suited for vacationing families, business travellers and long-term residents. The Superior Floors 15–32 are similarly appointed, but offer further-elevated views of the tower's surroundings.

Premium Floors 33–41 and Superior Floors 42–49 deliver on their promise of the high life. Premium floor guests are free to enjoy the rarefied air throughout the deluxe interiors, or out on their balconies, while a butler service takes care of everything else. Occupants of these floors may also make use of the VIP Premium Lounge on the 33rd floor, where breakfast, light lunches, evening canapés and refreshments are served. Each level has a mix of stylish two-bedroom, three-bedroom and four-bedroom apartments offering 190–340 sq m (2,045–3,360 sq ft) of premium real estate, ensuring that guests can relax in spacious comfort.

...an enclave of space and luxury for extended stays...

The exclusivity of a stay at the Oasis Beach Tower becomes clear when one realises the complete flexibility that a stay here offers. While guests have the freedom of arranging their very own meals in a fully equipped kitchen with modern appliances, 24-hour in-apartment catering means that a visit to the kitchen is not essential to enjoy a delicious meal.

Easy access to one of Dubai's premier dining destinations can also be enjoyed by making a reservation at Frankie's Italian Bar & Grill on the ground floor. This contemporary restaurant was created by horse racing legend Frankie Dettori and the flamboyant celebrity chef Marco Pierre White. Guests are spoilt for choice with an array of Italian favourites like traditional lasagne and exotic homemade ravioli filled with shredded duck meat, thyme sauce and smoked ricotta.

A stay at Dubai's most spacious and luxurious serviced apartments by the sea is guaranteed to tempt anyone into making a permanent home of this city. As the Dubai Marina project nears its completion and cements it status as the world's largest man-made marina, experiencing a slice of the luxurious Oasis Beach Tower is certainly an attractive proposition. At the very least, a short-term stay here is in order.

rooms
180 apartments

food
Frankie's Italian Bar & Grill: Italian • Wagamama: Far Eastern

features
beach access • shopping service • in-apartment catering • 24-hour concierge • business services • pool • premium butler service

nearby
Emirates Golf Club • The Montgomerie, Dubai • Jebel Ali Golf Resort & Spa • Mall of the Emirates • Ibn Battuta Mall • Dubai Internet City • Dubai Media City

contact
PO Box 26500, Dubai, UAE •
telephone: +971.4.399 4444 •
facsimile: +971.4.399 4200 •
email: obt@jaihotels.com •
website: www.oasisbeachtower.com

bice dubai

THIS PAGE: *BiCE Restaurant serves mouthwatering Italian cuisine in a light, breezy and sophisticated environment.*
OPPOSITE (FROM TOP): *BiCE Skybar is the perfect spot to enjoy a few drinks and amazing views of the twinkling lights of Dubai; the restaurant is a favourite among the rich and famous.*

When in Dubai, lovers of Italian cuisine need look no further than Hilton Dubai Jumeirah for the most authentic meal in town. Since the hotel's opening in 2000, one restaurant tucked away in a corner of the ground floor has been satisfying the palates of both guests and residents of the emirate alike. This restaurant shares a proud heritage of fine food and excellent service with a global family of 22 locations worldwide, each one dedicated to bringing the real taste of Italy to the world under the famed name of BiCE.

The restaurant was named after founder Beatrice Ruggeri, who was called Bice (pronounced bee-cheh) by family and friends. Opened in Milan in 1926, the little trattoria was known for its warm hospitality and love of good food that showed in the dishes it served on its small tables. As Milan's popularity as a fashion and business hub exploded in the 1970s, Ruggeri's restaurant flourished and earned a following of loyal international customers who had fallen for the Tuscan-style food and charming service. Before long, more outlets were opened in Italy, with the landmark BiCE New York opening its doors in 1987 to great fanfare.

Every BiCE restaurant worldwide extends that remarkable history with a simple goal: to serve the true taste of Italy. BiCE Dubai has won *What's On* magazine's 'Best Restaurant in Dubai' title for several years running, under the expert leadership of Executive Chef Andrea Mugavero and Manager Roberto Rella.

Hailing from the small town of Catania, near Sicily, Chef Mugavero has had a lifetime of cooking experience since learning from his restaurateur mother at the age of 12. His experience includes working at the Grand Hotel Bagioni in Parma under two-star Michelin chef Jean Franco Vissani, and serving at four BiCE kitchens worldwide since 1990.

...bringing the real taste of Italy to the world...

Rella has over two decades of experience working in top dining establishments the world over, rubbing shoulders with a who's who list of celebrities from Michael Jordan to Elton John. In addition to being in charge of BiCE Dubai, he also directs the company's operations in the Middle East and Asia.

To dine at BiCE Dubai is to experience a medley of unforgettable tastes in an unforgettable setting. The restaurant is lit with natural light by day, with views of the inviting pool and lush gardens beyond its timber blinds. Black and white photos of celebrities such as Marcello Mastroianni and Sophia Loren adorn the walls, adding flair to the décor. In the evening, BiCE is the picture of warmth and sophistication, complete with live piano music. No wonder, then, that the dining room is often packed with famous faces. The restaurant is often solidly booked, serving over 150 guests in the evening.

The menu features 47 dishes of traditional Italian fare and a selection of the latest dining trends straight from Italy. All meals begin with freshly baked breads accompanied by a black olive tapenade, sun-dried tomato paste, and the finest extra virgin olive oil. Everything on the menu is divine, but the warm lobster carpaccio with crispy artichokes and caviar dressing is considered the signature starter. The classic thin-slice beef carpaccio, BiCE style, with Venetian sauce is another must-try, along with the home-made ricotta and spinach tortelli with a creamy white truffle sauce and black truffle brunoise, and the Rigatoni Sicilian with eggplant, tomato, basil and aged ricotta cheese. The signature main course is the Milanese-style veal chop, which is served with potato salad, arugula and cherry tomato salad. For those who like a taste of everything, all main dishes are available in half-sized portions upon request. The kitchen features the largest balsamic vinegar and olive oil collection in Dubai, and the cellar boasts an international list of more than 200 wines to complement every meal.

For the perfect after-dinner drink, head to BiCE Skybar on the hotel's 10th floor. Converted from a penthouse suite, the bar offers fantastic views to go with the live music and cocktails. Be warned though, the sight of Dubai's magnificent skyline after a wholly satisfying Italian meal may cause some slight but pleasant disorientation.

seats
BiCE Restaurant: 132 • BiCE Skybar: 60

food
classic and contemporary Italian

drink
extensive wine list

features
authentic Italian cuisine • cheese trolley • balsamic vinegar and olive oil collection • live piano music • private rooms

nearby
Gold Souk • Heritage Village • Wild Wadi Water Park • Nad Al Sheba Racecourse • Emirates Golf Club • Dubai Museum

contact
Hilton Dubai Jumeirah, Dubai Marina
PO Box 2431, Dubai, UAE •
telephone: +971.4.318 2520 •
facsimile: +971.4.318 2503 •
email: bicerest.jumeirah@hilton.com •
website: www.bice.ws

the montgomerie, dubai

THIS PAGE: *Dubbed Dubai's 'best kept secret', the luxurious hotel is as magnificent as the golf course surrounding it.*
OPPOSITE: *The guestrooms are classy, sleek and chic.*

As a sport that regularly transports fans and enthusiasts to some of the most beautiful places on Earth, golf has truly outdone itself with a recent breakthrough into the Middle East. In the midst of the most unlikely conditions, Dubai's wealth and penchant for uncompromising luxury has created a conducive atmosphere for some of the most amazing golfing developments of the last quarter century. One such establishment, in particular, stands out for being a superbly engineered confluence of great course design, tasteful opulence, elegantly superior accommodation and first-class dining.

Bringing all of those elements together seems like a natural choice, but few have done it with the passion and panache that radiates from The Montgomerie, Dubai. This establishment offers best-of-class quality and service in every aspect of its operation. From the championship course, to the US$21 million clubhouse and boutique hotel with spa, everything is assuredly perfect for a golfing getaway that serves the mind, body and senses. From Troon Golf's portfolio of 185 facilities, The Montgomerie, Dubai was recognised as 'Facility of the Year' in 2006, while also securing the award for 'Dubai's Leading Golf Resort' in the 2006 World Travel Awards.

Designed by and named after the pre-eminent Colin Montgomerie, eight-time European Order of Merit winner and Ryder Cup champion, the course is impeccable and satisfyingly complex. Since debuting in 2002, the 6,763-m (7,396-yd), links-style design has drawn players from all the world over, with annual rounds increasing year over year. One look at the grounds and it is easy to see why. Covering 107 hectares (265 acres) of incredible natural beauty, of which 20 hectares (49 acres) are calm lakes and 38 hectares (94 acres) are beautiful landscaped gardens, the 18-hole championship course elicits awe and anticipation. Only the finest Tifway 419 and Floradwarf ultradwarf grass will do here. Designed in association with Desmond Muirhead, fairways lead to generous landing areas between undulating

...a golfing getaway that serves the mind, body and senses.

slopes. Large sand bunkers, of which there are 81, keep players of all levels on the alert. Deliciously misleading are the course's greens, which hide gentle features for a touch of the unpredictable. Packed with shape and consistently rolling above 3 m (9.5 ft), they make putting an even larger part of the game.

To give members and guests ever more time to indulge in their favorite sport, The Montgomerie, Dubai has established five-star accommodation on its premises. A very exclusive collection of 21 guestrooms has been created, each one spaciously laid out and decorated with the utmost care in order to appeal to modern sensibilities. Dark woods mingle with glass and smooth metallic surfaces. Designer lighting brings out the best in carefully curated pieces of contemporary artwork, and minimalist patterning produces a sophisticated look and feel throughout each room.

Available in five configurations, guests can choose to stay in Superior Rooms with either a view of the golf course or courtyard. Other options are The Skyline Suite, which offers a courtyard view; The Montgomerie Suite, which provides views of the golf course; and The Executive Suite, which has a separate bedroom, lounge and dining area, as well as a private office. Completing these intimate retreats is a full complement of amenities. Each room has an LCD TV with CD and DVD support, complimentary high-speed Internet access, minibars, and access to an in-house movie and music library. Guests can also avail themselves of a personalised butler service, as well as discounts on green fees and spa treatments.

For those who say that a round of golf is the ultimate form of relaxation, The Montgomerie, Dubai introduces the Angsana Spa as due argument. All spa therapists undergo training at the Banyan Tree Spa Academy in Phuket, learning the secrets of

THIS PAGE: *Enjoy an after-dinner cognac at Monty Cristo's.*

OPPOSITE (FROM LEFT): *After an intense day of golf, take a cooling dip in the plunge pool; The Montgomerie, Dubai's championship golf course attracts enthusiasts from all over the world.*

natural ingredients, aromatherapy and a fusion of techniques from the East and West. Treat yourself to a menu of soothing therapies in the spa's six treatment rooms and prepare to reconsider your idea of satisfaction.

Dining at The Montgomerie, Dubai's restaurant, Nineteen, is a similarly powerful experience for the senses. The winner of *What's On* and *TimeOut Dubai*'s 'Best New Restaurant' awards in 2007, Nineteen serves sophisticated fusion food that is a guaranteed crowd-pleaser. Dining here is made even more enjoyable by the chic decór. Dark wood panels and tables contrast with brown marble flooring and a white ceiling gently lit to a warm gauzy glow. Dashes of red

...one of Dubai's most exclusive golf clubs.

liven up the interior as unexpectedly as the food surprises the palate. A show kitchen lets indoor guests enjoy a visual feast, while an outdoor terrace entertains the eye with a view of the 18th hole.

Bunkers Restaurant also offers sweeping views of the 18th hole and putting green, with traditional pub fare in a casual setting just off the course. The Academy is a sports-themed bar and restaurant serving light refreshments and pub-style fare. Watch sporting events on the four large plasma-screen TV, or dine al fresco in view of the Dubai Marina skyline. After a satisfying meal, visit Monty Cristo's and choose from a selection of fine cigars and distinguished single malt whiskies. It is the perfect way to end an evening at one of Dubai's most exclusive golf clubs.

With its promise to deliver a quality of game equal to that of the greatest clubs in the world, The Montgomerie, Dubai certainly has its heart in the right place. And if its loyal following of golfers far and wide is any indication, The Montgomerie, Dubai's star will only shine brighter. With its new leisure facilities, it is hard to imagine this golf club as anything less than an essential destination.

rooms
21

food
Nineteen: fusion • Bunkers: pub fare • The Academy: pub fare

drink
Monty Cristo's • Nineteen Lounge

features
butler service • business centre • gym • plunge pool • steam room • outdoor pool • Angsana Spa • meeting room • Golf Academy • practice facilities • golf pro shops

nearby
Safa Park • Ibn Battuta Mall • Mall of the Emirates

contact
PO Box 36700, Dubai, UAE •
telephone: +971.4. 390 5600 •
facsimile: +971.4. 360 8981 •
email: info@themontgomerie.ae •
website: www.themontgomerie.com

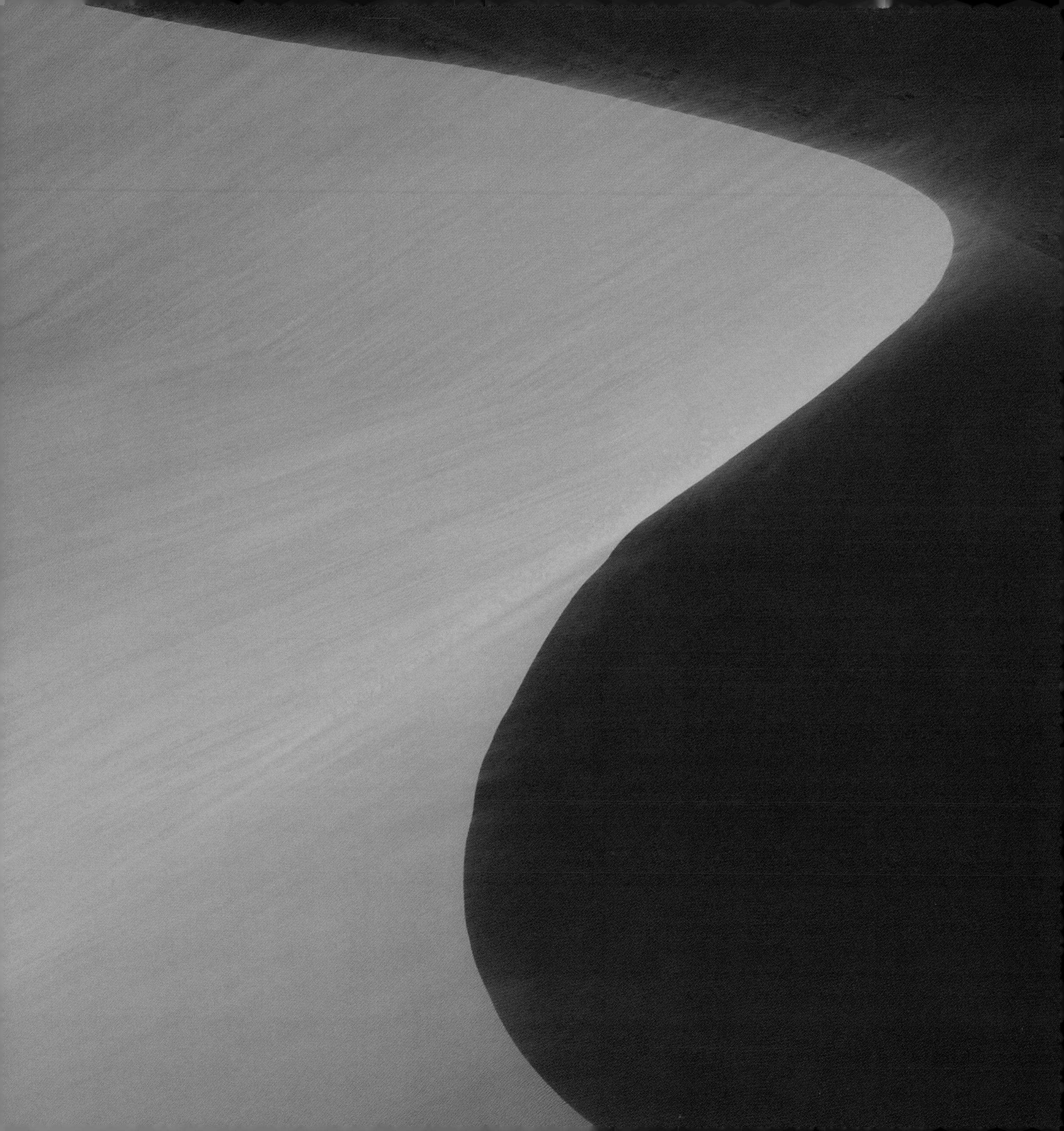

desert+outskirts

Jebel Ali Harbour

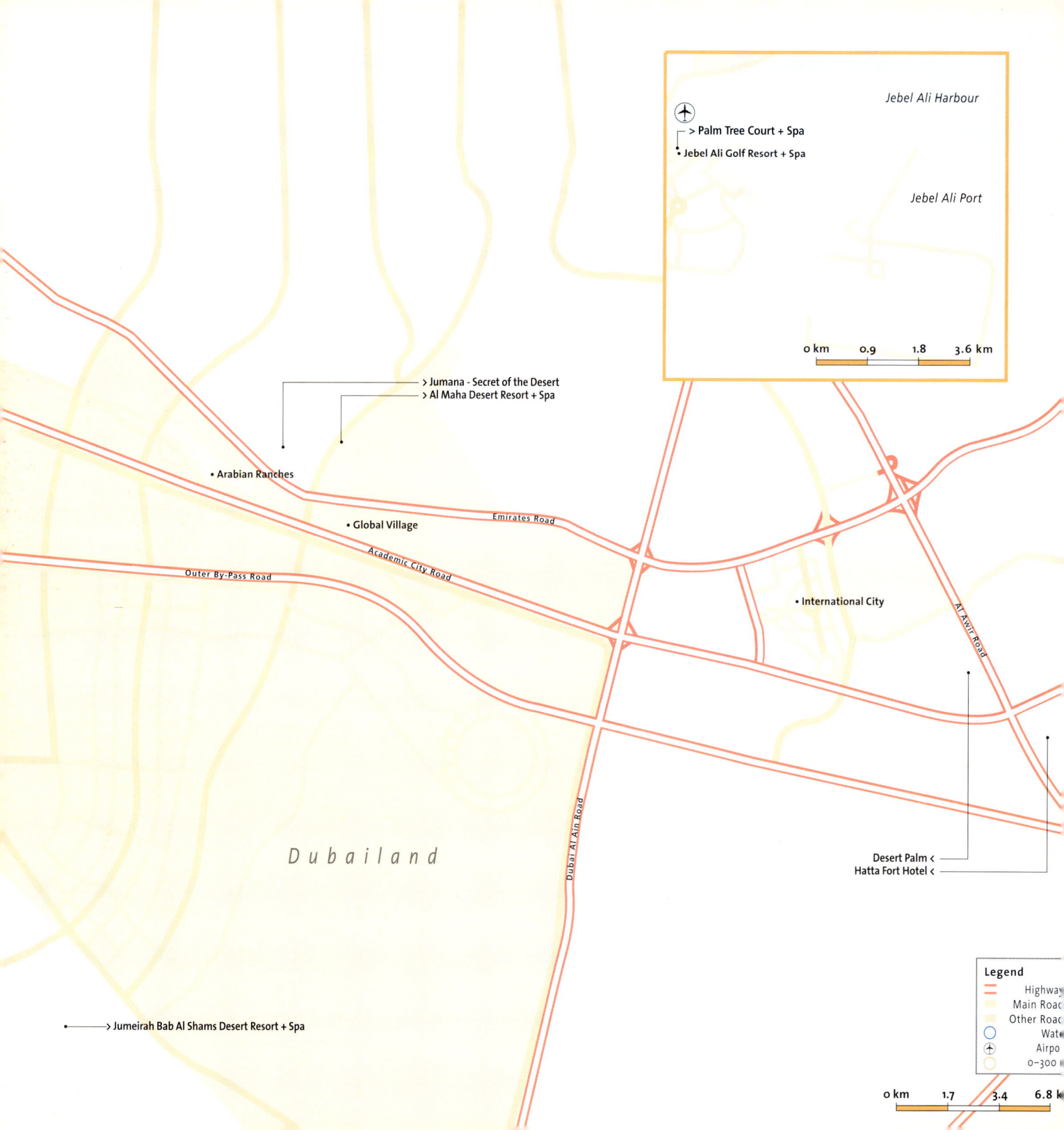

✈
> Palm Tree Court + Spa
• Jebel Ali Golf Resort + Spa

Jebel Ali Port

0 km   0.9   1.8   3.6 km

> Jumana - Secret of the Desert
> Al Maha Desert Resort + Spa

• Arabian Ranches

• Global Village

Emirates Road

Outer By-Pass Road

Academic City Road

• International City

Dubai Al Ain Road

Al Awir Road

Dubailand

Desert Palm <
Hatta Fort Hotel <

> Jumeirah Bab Al Shams Desert Resort + Spa

Legend
— Highway
— Main Road
— Other Road
○ Water
✈ Airport
○ 0–300

0 km   1.7   3.4   6.8 k

desert + outskirts

the sand sea

The eternal allure of the Arabian desert has captivated romantics as diverse as Freya Stark, the explorer Wilfed Thesiger and TE Lawrence. Out among the soaring dunes, with just the wind whispering by, one feels a sense of oneness with nature. The desert is so uncompromisingly itself, it demands your respect. It has been there way before you were born and it will be there long after you are gone. The Bedouin were the trading nomads of the desert who traversed the sandy domains of Arabia for thousands of years along ancient camel routes. Although their way of life has all but disappeared, you can experience something of their culture on a desert safari. There are many options to choose from but it's best to go with an established safari company like Arabian Adventures, Gulf Ventures or Desert Rangers. Dubai's timeless desert landscape provides a total contrast to its ever-changing urban cityscape. Don't miss the chance to explore this other Dubai, a world away from 21st century urban life.

a day among the dunes

Your journey begins in late afternoon with the thrill of four-wheel-drive 'dune-bashing' when jeeps tackle the shifting sands of the big dunes. Driving the dunes is great fun and a real roller coaster ride. Other activities can include sand-boarding (just like snowboarding but a lot warmer), camel rides, falconry demonstrations and wildlife spotting. At first, the desert seems completely uninhabited, but the closer you look, the more you will discover. Graceful oryx peek out from a crop of date palms and an Arabian red fox scampers past in search of a tasty desert hare. Above a peregrine falcon dives like lightning towards the earth, while a comical group of camels shambles across the dune. The ever-changing light and colour of the desert provides the backdrop to a wide variety of wildlife.

Back at camp, enjoy the Technicolor beauty of a desert sunset as a campfire beckons. Evening meals are usually barbecues with mouthwatering freshly grilled kebabs and warm pitta bread or Arabic mezzes. You might be asked to try a puff of a shisha—the traditional Arabic hookah (water pipe) or 'hubble-bubble'. It is hugely popular in the UAE and a traditional Arabic way of socialising. The aromatic, often fruit-flavoured, tobacco is mild. Evening entertainment might be storytelling around a fire, with legends from the *Arabian Nights*, or an exotic belly dancer twirling before you—although chances are she is probably Lebanese and not a Bedouin desert flower!

THIS PAGE (FROM TOP): *Four-wheel-drives are a popular option for exploring the shifting sands—best for the adrenaline-raising activity of desert dune bashing; the traditional Arab pastime of shisha smoking is a highly popular social activity.*
PAGE 158: *The sinuous curve of a dune ridge is highlighted in a play of light and shadow.*

If you want a real adventure, stay overnight. Sleeping out under the millions of stars that glide above the desert is an unforgettable experience. In the morning, the gentle rose-tinted dawn slowly wakens the desert. Enjoy a bracing cup of Arabic coffee and feel part of a Bedouin tradition stretching back over the centuries.

variety of activities

Despite what you might think, there are various desert places to visit. A favourite with Dubai dune-bashers is 'Big Red', an enormous sand dune about an hour's drive from the city. The bright reddish-orange colour of the sand provides a dramatic landmark as it rises in undulating curves to a height of 100 m (328 ft) against a bright blue sky. Along with jeep drives along the dunes, there are also quad bikes available for hire. You can also take an afternoon out to learn the art of dune driving from the experts. Companies like Desert Rangers, Off-Road Adventures and Emirate Driving Institute have popular one-day courses that will have you flying over the ridges in a four-wheel-drive in true Dubai desert warrior style.

Along with the desert are wilderness areas like Hatta. This hidden gem is the oldest village in the emirate of Dubai. It has a lovely 200-year-old mosque and the oldest fort in the emirate, built in 1896. There is also the Hatta Heritage Village, a recreation of a traditional mountain trading post. The small town nestles up against the dramatic backdrop of the Hajar Mountains. Its deep gorges and wadis are perfect for action-packed jeep safaris. Swim in the famous Hatta rock pools and laze in the shade of a date palm and have an Arabic picnic, or enjoy lunch at the pretty Hatta Fort Hotel, whose lush garden grounds attract a bevy of tropical birds.

conservation in the desert

Dubai's rapid expansion has caused concern about the fragile desert ecosystem. In order to conserve and protect Dubai's unique environment, the Dubai Desert Conservation Reserve was created. The 225 sq km (87 sq miles) of the reserve are the largest protected land area under conservation management in the Gulf and the only one of its kind in the Middle East. The Reserve operates as a National Park, providing a location where visitors can see free-roaming wildlife in a totally natural environment. A maximum daily limit has been placed on visitor numbers and just four selected Safari Operators have been granted concessions to enter. They are Arabian Adventures, Alpha Tours, Travco and Lama Desert Tours. You can stay overnight in the Reserve at Al Maha, a luxurious eco-resort that provides desert safaris by horse, camel or jeep, as well as falconry demonstrations and lectures on desert wildlife. A visit to Dubai's desert, whether just for an afternoon, or for a few days, is an unmissable adventure.

THIS PAGE: An exotic belly dancer draped with gossamer scarves twirls in the desert, echoing the undulating curves of the surrounding sand dunes.
OPPOSITE: A herd of Arabian oryx canters across the sands—the desert is teeming with wildlife.

A visit to Dubai's desert...is an unmissable adventure.

palm tree court + spa

As the most luxurious hotel at the Jebel Ali Golf Resort & Spa, known as Dubai's only true resort, the Palm Tree Court & Spa offers guests a secluded leisure destination right by the beach. Not only has the resort won the World Travel Award as 'Middle East's Leading Golf Resort', the Palm Tree Court & Spa is also a member of The Leading Hotels of the World—a testament to the level of luxury that can be experienced at this exemplary hotel.

Positioned at the very foot of Dubai's most significant new developments—The Palm Jebel Ali and the Dubai Waterfront—the Palm Tree Court & Spa provides easy access to major attractions, yet one senses nothing of the outside world when relaxing within its gates. The property is surrounded by a lovely stretch of private beach overlooking the Arabian Gulf and acres upon acres of landscaped gardens, streams, and unspoilt greenery. Complete with its own restaurants, shops and bars, this five-star collection of exquisite suites contains all the ingredients for a stay of transcendental opulence.

Spread across six low-rise villas, the property's 134 suites and junior suites create the perfect tropical atmosphere. The elegant Junior Suites feature either private terraces or balconies, perfect for dining in peace or enjoying the cool evening breeze. The bedrooms are spacious at 54 sq m (581 sq ft),

THIS PAGE (FROM TOP): Start an evening at the White Orchid Lounge & Terrace; get the perfect tan or read a riveting book by the pool.
OPPOSITE (FROM TOP): Each Junior Suite features a private balcony that provides a view of the landscaped gardens; the spa is an ideal place to unwind and rejuvenate.

...a secluded leisure destination right by the beach.

with large en suite bathrooms. The Palm Tree Court Suites also feature terraces and balconies, and add a seating area to their list of pleasures. They have the luxury of two separate bathrooms for extra convenience.

The Royal Jasmine Suites and Junior Suites come with a full range of special privileges that make up the complete Palm Tree Court & Spa experience. A Host Service handles all requests and takes care of needs such as packing and unpacking, while a Signature Bath Experience provides a great start to any visit. A superb selection of sports and recreation facilities can be enjoyed by guests, including a private horse riding paddock, an 80-berth marina and a nine-hole championship-standard golf course.

All that time on the beach is sure to build an appetite, so it is fortunate that the hotel has three fine restaurants, with another four available in the rest of the resort. Signatures is a fine dining French restaurant, while White Orchid invites guests to discover a fusion of Chinese, Japanese and Thai specialities. For breakfast buffets, international cuisine and themed dinners, La Fontana is the place to go.

Set in a little corner of paradise, the Palm Tree Court & Spa is a joy from the moment a chauffeured caddy brings guests from the reception to their suites. Walking around the hotel and taking in the wonder of its waterfalls, ponds and gardens, it is not unusual to discover that there is nowhere else one would rather be.

rooms
134

food
Signatures: French • White Orchid Lounge & Terrace: Asian fusion • La Fontana: international and Mediterranean • La Traviata: Italian • Ibn Majid Restaurant: international • Shooters: steak • Sports Café: fusion and traditional pub fare

drink
Clipper Bar • The Anchor • Captain's Bar • Plantation Bar & Terrace • White Orchid Lounge & Terrace

features
high-speed Internet access • pools • gym • sauna • tennis courts • billiard room • spa • landscaped gardens • private beach • golf course • golf academy • horse riding • shooting club • meeting rooms • water sports • marina • fishing trips

nearby
Jebel Ali Free Zone • Mall of the Emirates • Ibn Battuta Mall • Dubai Media City • Dubai Internet City • Dubai Investment Park

contact
PO Box 9255, Dubai, UAE •
telephone: +971.4.883 6000 •
facsimile: +971.4.883 5543 •
email: jagrs@jaihotels.com •
website: www.jebelali-international.com

jumeirah bab al shams desert resort + spa

THIS PAGE: *Bab Al Shams is an elegant desert resort in a traditional Arabic fort setting.*
OPPOSITE: *The beautifully appointed rooms and suites are stylish and comfortable.*

It would be a shame to go to Dubai and miss the beauty, romance and Arabian culture of the desert. It was only a generation ago when Bedouin traders rode out of the dunes on their camels to trade with dhows bringing precious cargo across the sea. The legacy of these intrepid nomads, with their ancient customs based on honour, hospitality and self-reliance, lives on in legends that have been passed down over the years. A stay at Jumeirah Bab Al Shams Desert Resort & Spa enables guests to experience the thrill of the desert in a style fit for a sheikh.

The resort is less than an hour's drive from Dubai, far from the madding crowds of town, in a secluded spot amid the honey-coloured sands of the desert. Built in the style of an oasis fortress, Bab Al Shams blends seamlessly with the environment. The Gateway to the Sun (as the resort's name translates in English) certainly has plenty of sun-filled days and cool, starry desert nights. Voted 'Favourite Weekend Getaway Hotel in the UAE' at the 2006 and 2007 What's On Awards, Bab Al Shams is a haven of relaxation and peace, yet with all the amenities one would expect from a top resort.

Bab Al Shams has 113 rooms, including 10 suites featuring traditional Gulf décor using natural stone, dark wood, Arabian glasswork and textiles. The rooms are exceptionally well-designed and have genuine character. Guests can choose from spacious Royal Suites, Executive Suites, Superior King Rooms, Superior Twin Rooms, Deluxe Twin Rooms and Deluxe King Rooms. Interconnecting rooms, cots and extra rollaway beds are available for families with children. In-room features include a minibar, satellite TV and radio, high-speed Internet connection, coffee and tea making facilities, 24-hour room service and large, beautifully appointed bathrooms with rain showers, separate oversized bathtubs,

...experience the thrill of the desert in a style fit for a sheikh.

robes, slippers and exclusive toiletries. The Royal Suites and Executive Suites offer a separate majlis-style sitting area.

The hotel features a variety of bars and restaurants, including Al Hadheerah, the region's first authentic open-air, Arabic-desert restaurant. At the heart of the resort, Al Forsan has a warm and family-friendly atmosphere. The restaurant features indoor and outdoor seating, international cuisine, children's menus and à la carte and buffet meal options. When the sun goes down, head to the Al Sarab Rooftop Bar for stunning sunset views across the desert. The bar serves a variety of beverages, cocktails and mocktails, as well as a selection of shishas and cigars. Guests can even watch a thrilling falconry exhibition as these desert hunters catch their prey.

For casual dining, an ideal place to cool off during the day is the resort's Pool Bar. Indulge in a wide variety of snacks, cocktails, salads and beverages while looking out over the rolling desert dunes. Children will love the ice-cream section and the fresh-fruit smoothies. The pool area at Bab Al Shams is one of the highlights of the resort. It covers an area of 1,400 sq m (15,069 sq ft) and offers panoramic desert views. Aside from an infinity-edge pool, there is also a lap pool, leisure pool, shaded children's pool, temperature-controlled continuous waterfall, jacuzzi, a swim-up pool bar, beach sand on the deck and plenty of sunloungers.

The Ya Hala lounge in the attractive lobby is a quiet enclave away from poolside action. The lounge creates a traditional ambience of comfort and hospitality, with its Arabian antiques and works of art. Try a cup of aromatic Arabic coffee with dates, mint tea or a snack from the à la carte menu. Relax in the courtyard, an intimate terrace that overlooks the water well, while sipping Ya Hala's signature Desert Classic drink.

For the ultimate Arabian dining experience, spend a magical evening at Al Hadheerah. This award-winning restaurant offers diners a unique chance to enjoy scenes straight out of an Arabian legend. Guests can delight in whirling belly dancers, live music and entertainment. There is a small souk as well, with henna painters, falcons and stalls selling local crafts. It is fairytale bliss for children, who play Lawrence of Arabia while their parents enjoy the show. The restaurant is made to look like a Bedouin camp—although much more upmarket than the average camel stop—and serves a remarkable variety of ethnic cuisine from open cooking stations featuring wood-fired ovens, charcoal grills, spit roasts and Arabic bread ovens.

Bab Al Shams offers a wide range of activities for its young guests. Sinbad's Kids Club runs a creative programme from 9.00 am to 8.00 pm for children aged 5–12. Kids can play with remote-controlled cars, have fun on the trampoline, go on camel rides and desert explorations, or participate in swimming games. Tiny tots can play safely in a sand pit with specially-developed silica sand. There is a dedicated activity room, with everything from art supplies to the latest Playstation games, as well as an indoor and outdoor playground, a shaded children's pool, children's menus and more. If a trip into town sounds fun, the resort provides free shuttle-bus service to and from Dubai and

THIS PAGE: *This bedroom evokes rustic Arabian charm.*
OPPOSITE (FROM LEFT): *Al Hadheerah features live cooking stations and a souk area; indulge in an aromatherapy bath at the Satori Spa.*

...everything for a unique holiday in the desert...

Wild Wadi Water Park. In-room entertainment options for children include videos, games and satellite TV. The resort's babysitting service gives busy parents the chance to have a well-deserved night off.

A great selection of desert adventures is also available at Bab Al Shams. Four-wheel-drive jeep excursions in the dunes, horse riding with trained guides and camel safaris give guests a chance to experience the remarkable eco-system of the desert up close.

A good place to unwind after a day of sightseeing is the Satori Spa, a haven of tranquillity with a pampering range of massage and beauty treatments. There are four indoor treatment rooms and a single outdoor treatment room. The word 'satori' refers to the joy, peace and inner harmony of enlightenment, and this is the very atmosphere that the spa creates for its guests, who leave the premises relaxed and refreshed.

Bab Al Shams has everything for a unique holiday in the desert, including special services for business executives. Three state-of-the-art meeting rooms make the hotel an ideal venue for high-level conferences in an atmosphere of complete privacy. The resort has been privileged to host top government officials, royalty, celebrities and leading figures in the business world. In a place like Dubai, where five-star resorts can seem very much alike, Bab Al Shams is a true original.

rooms
113

food
Al Hadheerah: traditional Arabic • Masala: Indian • Al Forsan: international • Pizzeria Le Dune: Italian • Ya Hala Lobby Lounge: light fare

drink
Al Sarab Rooftop Bar & Lounge • Pool Bar

features
meeting rooms • business centre • high-speed and wireless Internet access • horse riding • falconers • camel rides • E-Gate card service • infinity-edge pool • spa • gym

nearby
Endurance Village • Wild Wadi Water Park • Madinat Souk

contact
PO Box 8168, Dubai, UAE •
telephone: +971.4.832 6699 •
facsimile: +971.4.832 6698 •
email: JBASreservations@jumeirah.com •
website: www.jumeirahbabalshams.com

al maha desert resort + spa

THIS PAGE: *The stunning main pool at Al Maha Desert Resort & Spa is a desert traveller's dream come true.*

OPPOSITE (FROM LEFT): *The Timeless Spa beckons guests to enjoy its wide array of pampering and rejuvenating treatments; watch the sun set from the Royal Suite's wooden deck.*

Rising from the champagne-coloured dunes of the Dubai desert, Al Maha Desert Resort & Spa offers a unique chance to experience the beauty and peace of this timeless landscape in an atmosphere of refined luxury. There is no other hotel like it, and Al Maha's many awards and accolades are a fitting tribute to the originality of its concept. It is Dubai's premier eco-tourism resort; a success story that proves five-star facilities can live in harmony with their surroundings. Al Maha is located in Dubai's largest desert preservation area, amid 225 sq km (87 sq miles) of utterly unspoilt, stunning scenery. The hotel feels like a world away, even though the city is just 45 minutes down the road. It transports its guests into a different state of mind—one much more in tune with the timeless rhythms of the desert than the artificial pressures of urban life.

Only 42 suites ramble along the low dunes, attractively blending in with their desert surroundings. The suites are homes in themselves, complete with private infinity-edge pools and outside terraces. There are also thoughtful touches such as field binoculars, an easel and pastels, a detailed guide to the desert wildlife and Bulgari toiletries, along with wireless Internet access and the usual amenities that one would expect from a first-rate hotel.

The suites feature artwork and antiques reflecting the Arabian heritage of the location, while the super-soft linens and goose down pillows epitomise European chic. Along with the 75-sq-m (807 sq ft) one-bedroom Bedouin Suites, there are two-bedroom Royal Suites offering 175 sq m (1,883 sq ft) of space, two-bedroom Emirates suites with 375 sq m (4,036 sq ft) of space, and a palatial three-bedroom Presidential Suite. All the bigger suites benefit from larger pools.

Those who can bear to leave their suites will find a delightful array of diversions. Two complimentary on-site activities per stay are offered, so guests can explore the desert's quiet wonders. Go on a camel trek to catch a spectacular sunset, or board a four-wheel drive vehicle for a ride up and down the sand dunes. Falconry, archery, horse riding and guided nature walks are also offered.

One can also opt for a massage at the excellent Timeless Spa, which boasts a sauna, steam room, jacuzzi and plunge pool. The peace and serenity at Al Maha make the place a welcome retreat from the clamour and crowds found at bigger resorts. Children are not allowed, which helps create an ambience suited to romance and relaxation.

Al Maha has won prestigious awards, including *National Geographic Traveler's* World Legacy Award, for its commitment to conservation and environment-friendly tourism. Indeed, guests will not find a theme park version of Arabia at Al Maha. The resort offers the real thing—the essence of the Arabian desert in a boutique setting with every imaginable comfort.

...the essence of the Arabian desert in a boutique setting.

rooms
42 suites

food
Al Diwaan: Middle Eastern and international

drink
bar deck • lounge

features
infinity-edge pool • high-speed and wireless Internet access • majlis • conference facilities • business centre • gym • spa • in-room private check-in and personal check-out • camel treks • archery • dune driving • sand skiing

nearby
Hajar Mountains • Hatta Village • Fossil Rock • Camel Rock

contact
Al Maha Head Office, 3rd Floor Emirates Holidays Building, Sheikh Zayed Road
PO Box 7631, Dubai, UAE
telephone: +971.4.303 4222 •
facsimile: +971.4.343 9696 •
email: almaha@emirates.com •
website: www.al-maha.com

desert palm

THIS PAGE: *Paintings in the Palm Suite help to brighten up the simple, elegant décor.*

OPPOSITE: *Afternoon tea is best enjoyed outdoors, on Desert Palm's manicured gardens; take a walk through the hotel grounds, sheltered by lush, colourful bougainvillea.*

South of Dubai's opulence, grandeur and silver skyscrapers, on the city's outskirts, lies a holiday destination of stirring contrasts. Where there should be nothing but sand, there are 61 hectares (150 acres) of greenery on a polo estate. When the cares of the world seem a lifetime away, an international airport is reachable in just 12 minutes; a major metropolis, in 15 minutes. In a city where opulence can reach the limits of taste, it is sometimes difficult to conceive that there exists an oasis of calm, minimalist style. Yet, Desert Palm is proof that there is such a place.

Desert Palm is the first boutique hotel in the UAE to be granted membership on the Small Luxury Hotels of the World list. Perhaps, the most important contrast at this place involves how guests spend their time. Days

...an oasis of calm, minimalist style.

can be filled with excitement a hundred ways, and they can also be very long on relaxation. An infinity-edge pool and six spa treatment suites are only the beginning.

The 24 suites and villas are designed to deliver a unique experience. Each of the 13 top-floor Palm Suites offers a view of the resort's polo fields, and the Dubai skyline in the distance. Four impressive Pool Villas each feature a private pool, as well as large living areas both inside and out. For large families and groups, the six Pool Residences are complete homes in their own right, down to their fully equipped kitchens. Each residence has a pool, sunbathing deck, outdoor dining area, and charming gardens enclosed by 3-m (9-ft) walls for privacy. The beautiful Villa Layali, on the other hand, is an exclusive two-bedroom, walled sanctuary surrounded by vegetation and palm trees. Each bedroom has its own bathroom, private courtyard garden, business centre and entertainment system.

Fine dining is taken to new heights at Desert Palm. Enjoy the world's best cuts of steak and game at Rare. Epicure is a gourmet market with fresh breads, beverages and imported delicacies, while Red Bar & Lounge offers an exceptional range of wine and beer.

The fine line of harmony between nature and modernity is pitch-perfect at Desert Palm. Summery sunshine permeates every inch of the resort, giving it—and your holiday—a sense of lightness that seems worth all the money in the world.

rooms
13 suites • 11 villas

food
Rare: steak and game • Epicure: deli café and gourmet market

drink
Red Bar & Lounge

features
Lime Spa • infinity-edge pool • art studio • saddlery • in-room personal business centres • wireless Internet access

nearby
city centre • Dubai International Airport • Dubai World Trade Centre • Dubai Festival City • Ras Al Khor Wildlife Sanctuary • Mall of Arabia • Global Village • Al Badia Golf Course • Nad Al Sheba Racecourse

contact
Al Awir Road, PO Box 103635, Dubai, UAE •
telephone: +971.4. 323 8888 •
facsimile: +971.4. 323 8053 •
email: reservations@desertpalm.ae •
website: www.desertpalm.ae

hatta fort hotel

THIS PAGE: *Hatta Fort Hotel is an exclusive retreat nestled in the majestic Hajar Mountains.*

OPPOSITE (FROM TOP): *The fantastic Rock Pool is one of the best features of the hotel; the deluxe chalet-style rooms offer either a balcony or terrace that offers good views of the surrounding mountains.*

There is more to Dubai than the experience of shopping high fashion one minute and traditional souks the next. Likewise, there is a variety to the landscape that goes beyond the bustling energy of downtown developments. Located a comfortable hour's drive away from Dubai City, and just 10 minutes from the Oman border, is Hatta Fort Hotel.

Surrounded by the Hajar Mountains and untamed natural landscape, this relaxed retreat is 32 hectares (80 acres) of manicured gardens, leisure facilities and world-class accommodation. Its reputation as an escape destination has made it a favourite among families, businessmen and residents of neighbouring emirates. In fact, Hatta Fort Hotel was voted by *What's On* as the UAE's 'Favourite Weekend Getaway Hotel' in 2005.

For accommodation, guests can choose between deluxe chalet-style rooms and suites in either the East or West wing, or alternatively opt for one of the secluded villas. Deluxe chalet-style rooms are spacious enough to accommodate two adults and two children each, and feature minibars, satellite TV and large en suite bathrooms with quality toiletries. Warm tones of ochre, sienna, teak and bronze create a harmonious setting for spending some quality time with loved ones.

From every corner of the grounds, guests enjoy magnificent views of the Hajar Mountains. Two great places to start are the temperature-controlled Gazebo Pool and Rock Pool. The latter features a tranquil rock garden enclosure that encourages lazing away for hours on end. Golf enthusiasts will enjoy

...a completely self-contained mountain resort...

rooms
50

food
Jeema: international • Café Gazebo: light fare

drink
Roumoul Cocktail Bar • Pool Bar

features
outdoor pools • clay shooting range • archery lessons • golf driving range • practice green • four-wheel-drive tours • gym • tennis courts • billiards • Senses Beauty Salon • meeting suites • cross-country fun golf course • Abami Activity Centre

nearby
Oman • Hatta Heritage Village

contact
PO Box 9277, Dubai, UAE •
telephone: +971.4.852 3211 •
facsimile: +971.4.852 3561 •
email: hfh@jaihotels.com •
website: www.hattaforthotel.com

the driving range and practice green, while everyone else can play a round on the cross-country fun golf course or complete the mini-golf circuit.

Those looking for an outdoor adventure will want to try archery, with instructors on hand to give an introduction to this 'sport of kings'. The hotel also offers guided four-wheel-drive excursions into the desert and mountain areas. After a long day of activity, or a good workout at the gym, head to Senses Beauty Salon for a massage or body treatment.

Dining at the hotel guarantees the satisfaction of both the palate and the eyes. Jeema offers a well-rounded international gourmet menu against postcard views of distant summits and landscaped gardens, which are particularly memorable at sunrise and sunset. Café Gazebo serves light meals in a glass-enclosed space overlooking one of the pools. Open from 6.00 pm until midnight is Roumoul Cocktail Bar, an ideal place to start an evening. Its vintage leather seats are a luxurious pleasure in themselves.

As its name subtly suggests, Hatta Fort Hotel offers a completely self-contained mountain resort from which the beauty and majesty of Dubai's outer limits, along with examples of that legendary Arabian hospitality, can be enjoyed in comfort.

jumana – secret of the desert

THIS PAGE: Al Sahra Desert Resort, an eco-tourism destination that is part of the Dubailand complex, hosts the spectacular Jumana – Secret of the Desert imagistics theatre show.

OPPOSITE (FROM TOP): Stunning water-projected images, animation, fireworks and laser are all part of the show; the amphitheatre can seat up to 1,400 spectators.

One of the most unique and exciting things to do in Dubai also serves to give visitors a glimpse into the future of entertainment in the emirate. Performed at 9.00 pm from Tuesday to Saturday at Al Sahra Desert Resort's amphitheatre, Jumana – Secret of the Desert is a multi-sensory, imagistics theatre extravaganza of high technology, music, dance, sound, amazing pyrotechnics and incredible water effects. As part of the Dubailand development, which is on track to become the world's largest leisure and entertainment complex and certainly one of Dubai's most talked-about tourist attractions, the headlining outdoor stage show is every bit as epic as its grand location.

Set in the middle of a natural desert dunescape approximately 40 minutes from Dubai International Airport, Jumana takes place on a world-class event stage built over a man-made body of water. A cast of over 60 dancers and acrobats, accompanied by camels and horses, tells the classic tale of two princes and one beautiful princess.

...a multi-sensory, imagistics theatre extravaganza...

food
Lahab Restaurant: international

drink
Jumana Lounge • King Othman Lounge

features
open air light, laser, sound and pyrotechnics show • fully licensed venue • event planners • arts and craft souk • silversmith workshop • pottery workshop • spice market • carpet weaving • henna painting studio • falconry display • camel treks • horse rides • donkey cart rides • petting zoo • date picking • archery • nature walks • belly dancing

nearby
Global Village • Arabian Ranches

contact
Al Sahra Desert Resort
PO Box 233, Dubai, UAE •
telephone: +971.4.367 9500 •
facsimile: +971.4.367 9501 •
email: reservations@alsahra.com •
website: www.alsahra.com

Narrated by acclaimed Hollywood actor Omar Sharif, the performance incorporates fables and themes from across the Gulf region, Yemen, Oman and Persia with the very latest in special effects engineering.

As the story of King Othman, Prince Omar and the princess unfolds on stage, images and 3D animation are projected on three towering 35 m by 15 m (115 ft by 49 ft) walls of water that hang in midair, high above the audience. Larger than life animals and characters come to life and interact with the cast as illuminated sprays of mist and smoke work together to create an atmosphere of wonder and mystery. Of particular interest are the dazzling dance routines and original collection of songs delivered over state-of-the-art surround sound speakers, punctuated by lasers, bursts of flame and fireworks that light up the night sky to great effect.

Make it a point to come early because there is plenty to do before and after the 65-minute show. There are restaurants and lounges, an arts and crafts souk, silversmith and pottery workshops, camel treks, horse rides and nature walks. Jumana is a complete evening experience that encapsulates the magic of the Middle East. Its carefully crafted setting, wealth of complementary activities, and meticulously designed sequences will transport you to another time and place.

index

Numbers in *italics* denote pages where both pictures and text are found. Numbers in **bold** denote property profiles.

A
abras (water taxis) 45, 76, 120, 121
Academy Bar, The 103
Agency, The 24, 27, 53
Ajmal Perfumes 29
Al Ain Mall 29
Al Burj 46
Al Bustan Rotana Hotel 22
Al Fahidi Fort 75
Al Fahidi Street 21, 76
Al Forsan 167
Al Hadheerah 20, 167, *168*
Al Iwan Bahar 119
Al Khaima 144
Al Khayal 115
Al Maha Desert Resort & Spa 17, *36*, 162, **170-171**
Al Mahara 22, *117*, 118
Al Maktoum Bridge 77
Al Manzil Hotel **64-67**
Al Moorj Rotana Hotel 23
Al Muntaha 118
Al Murjan tea lounge 144
Al Nafoorah 20
Al Nakheel Lounge 87, 91
Al Nasr Leisureland 21, 42
Al Qasr 20, 23, 109, 120
Al Sahra Desert Resort 176
Al Sarab 167
Al Sufouh 107
Al Sufouh Tram 47
Al-Ahmadiya School 80
Al-Boom Diving 38
Almaz 21
Alpha Tours 162
Amara Spa 18, *37*, 95, 97
Amaseena *146*, 149
Ambassador Lagoon 110
Amrita Spa 37
Amwaj 60
Andalusia Court 27
Andiamo! 90
Angsana Spa 155
Apartment, The 24, 25
Aquarium Seafood Restaurant, The 103
Aquaventure 110
Arabian Adventures 45, 161, 162
Arabian Court *124*, 127
Arabian Oud 29
Arabian Red Fox 161
Arabian Sea 58
Arabian Treasures 29
Arabic mezzes 161
Arabica 53
architecture 51, 54, 66, 75, 77, 98, 107, 109
Armani (Giorgio) boutiques 27, 28
Armani Caffe 23

Armani Hotel 17, 54
art galleries 34-35, 75 *also see* under gallery names
arts scene 18
Asado, The 63
Ashiana 21
Asia-Asia 46
Asiana 84
Assawan Spa & Health Club 18, *118*, 119
Atlantis 110
Autodrome 38, *39*, 44
Automatic 53

B
B21 34
Bab Al Yam 119
Balcony Bar 60
Baniyas Grand Ballroom 89
Bar 44 24, *139*
Barasti 24
BarZar 24
Basta Art Café 75
Bastakiah Nights 20, 75
Bastakiya 21, 34, 75, 115
Bateaux Dubai 23, 77, **98-99**
Bateel 29
Bawadi Project 46
Beach & Bar Grill 127
Bedouin, The 161, 166
Beyond the Beach 28
BiCE Dubai **152-153**
BiCE Restaurant 21, *152*
BiCE Skybar 153, *152*
Big Bus Company, The 41
Big Red 162
Blue Elephant, The 22
Boardwalk, The 103
Bond Street 18
Boom & Mellow 28
Boudoir 25
Boulevard, The 27, 53, 54
Brasserie, The 144
Buddha Bar 18, 25, 107, 110, *140*
Bulgari 27, *170*
Bur Dubai 75, 76
Bur Dubai Abra Station 77
Burj Al Arab 18, *20, 22*, 107, 110, **116-119**
Burj Dubai 17, 22, 46, *51*, 54, 57, 62, 64, 67, 68
Burj Dubai Boulevard 64, 71
Burj Dubai Interchange 51
Burj Dubai Lake Park 64, 71
Burj Durbai Mall 54
BurJuman Centre 26

C
Café Arabesque 96
Café Ceramique 43
Café Gazebo 175
Café Sushi 22
camels *12, 17, 20*, 44, *55*, 76, 161, 166, *170, 176*, 177
Caracalla Spa and Health Club 144
Cartier Jewellers 27, 28

Cave Privee 96
Caviar House & Prunier 23
Celebrities (restaurant) 127
Certo 22, *134*
Champagne Brunch, The 23
Chef's House 134
Chi 25, *37*, *61*
Children's City 43, 77
Chillout 53
China Club 22
China Court 27
China Moon Champagne Bar 84
Cirque Du Soleil 35
Cleopatra's Spa 37
CompuMe 29
Conservatory, The 66, 102
Cooz 90
Courtyard 66, *67*
Courtyard Al Quoz, The 34
Creek Art Fair, The 34
Creekside Park 77
Crossroads 24, 84
Crowne Plaza 53

D
D&G boutique 27
Damas 28
Dar Al Masyaf 109, 120, 122
Debenhams 109
Deepak 31
Deira 21, 75, 77, *78, 79*, 80
Deira City Centre 29, 42
Deli Café 138, *139*
desert 158-177
Desert Bedouins *13*, 54
Desert Palm **172-173**
Desert Rangers 45, 161, 162
Dhow Boatyards 44
Dhow Palace Hotel 25
DKNY boutique 27
Dolphin Encounter Zone 110
downtown Dubai 48-71
Dream Girl 31
Dubai Art Fair 34
Dubai Chamber of Commerce & Industry 77
Dubai Community Theatre and Arts Centre 45
Dubai Country Club 39
Dubai Creek *14-15*, 75, 77, 79, 80, *81*, 86, 98, 103
Dubai Creek Golf & Yacht Club 22, 39, 79, 92, 94, 96, 100, 102
Dubai Desert Conservation Reserve 162
Dubai Desert Classic *19*
Dubai Festival City 28, 80, 93
Dubai Golf 39, **100-103**
Dubai Healthcare City 47
Dubai International Convention Centre 57
Dubai International Financial Centre (DIFC) 51
Dubai Internet City 107

Dubai Kartdrome 44, *45*
Dubai Mall 46, 54, 63, 64, 67, 71
Dubai Marina 43, 47, 107, 136, 146, 150, 151
Dubai Marine Beach Resort 20
Dubai Media City 22, 107, 132
Dubai Metro 47
Dubai Museum 35, 44, 75, 77, 93, 115
Dubai Outlet Mall 28
Dubai Tennis Championship 38, *39*
Dubai Waterfront 164
Dubai World Central International Airport 47, 176
Dubai World Cup *18*, 39
Dubai World Trade Centre 57
Dubailand 17, 28, 47, 176
DubaiSat-1 47
Dunes, The 39
Dunes Café, The 57

E
Eauzone 130
Egypt Court 27
Emad Carpets 33
Emirate Driving Institute 162
Emirate Towers 18
Emirates Golf Club *19*, 92, 100, 101, 132, 147
Emirates Riding Centre 38
Encounter Zone 42
Epicure 173
Esca 70
Escada 26
Etoile 26
Ewaan Restaurant 54, 63
Exchange Grill, The 22
Eye Art Gallery 75

F
Fab India 28
FAE boutique 75
Falcon City of Wonders 47
Fairmont Hotel, The 17, 22, 23, 53
Fibber Magee's 53
Fiesta Café 28
Fifth Avenue 18
50°C 33
Fire & Ice 22, 23
Five Green 28
Four Seasons Golf Club 39, 80
Frankie's Italian Bar & Grill 151
Fudo 23
Fun City 27, 42
Fusion (restaurant) 144

G
Galactica 42
Galleria Ice Rink 44
Gallery, The 139
Garden Pavilion 85
Gate, The 51
Gazebo Pool 174
Gift Tent 32
Ginger & Lace 26, 28

Giorgio Armani boutiques 27, 28
Global Village 29
Gold & Diamond Park 29
Gold Souk, The 32, 79, 93, 115
Graff 28
Grand Cinema Megaplex 27, 42
Grand Club Lounge 88
Grand Hyatt Business Centre, The 89
Grand Hyatt Dubai 22, **86-93**
Grand Mosque 75, 115
Grand Spa 37
Great Dubai Wheel, The *46*, 47
Green Art Gallery 34
Grosvenor House 18, 21, 23, 24, 43, 107, 110, **136-141**
Gucci boutique 27
Guggenheim 35
Gulf Pavilion 149
Gulf Ventures 45, 161

H
H_2O 18, 37
Habtoor Grand Hotel 25
Hajar Mountains 174
Handi 21
Harvey Nichols 21, 26, 109
Hatta 162
Hatta Fort Hotel 162, **174-175**
Hatta Heritage Village 162
Health & Beauty Institute 36
Health Club & Spa, The 61
Heritage and Diving Village 35, 44, 77, 93
Heritage House 80
Hermes boutique 27, 118
Hilton Dubai Jumeirah 21, 23, 152
Hindu Shri Nathje Jayate Temple 75
Hoi An 60
Horizon Club 58
hotels 17, 53, 80, 107
Hyatt Regency Dubai 22, 44
Hydropolis 47
Hymenocallis flower 54

I
Ibn Battuta Mall 27, 42
Icon Bar 134
Indego 21, *139*, *140*
India Court 27
India House 21
Interchange One 51
InterContinental Dubai 24, 80
International Rugby Sevens *39*
iZ 90

J
Jam Base 24
Jam Jar, The 43
Japengo 23
Jebel Ali Equestrian Club 38
Jebel Ali Golf Resort & Spa 164
Jeema 175
JetSet 137
Jimmy Choo boutique 27

178 dubaichic

index

Johnny Rockets (restaurant) 43
Jumana – Secret of the Desert 176-177
Jumeirah 79, 104-157
Jumeirah Bab Al Shams Desert & Resort Spa 20, 166-169
Jumeirah Beach Club 107
Jumeirah Beach Hotel, The 17, 22, 24, 25, 38, 107, 112-115
Jumeirah Beach Park 110
Jumeirah Emirates Towers 20, 22, 27, 36, 51, 53
Jumeirah Mosque 107
Jumeirah Road 107
Juna Lounge 119
Just Cavalli 27

K

Kachins Tailors 31
Kahn Murjan 33
Karama Complex 21, 31
Kasbar 25
kebabs 161
Kempinski Hotel 26, 109
Kenza Art Gallery 121
Khazana 21
Knightsbridge 18

L

La Baie 23, 149
La Fontana 166
La Parrilla 22, 115
Lakeview 103
Lama Desert Tours 162
Le Classique 102
Le Royal Méridien Beach Resort & Spa 22, 24, 137, 142-145
Leaves (teahouse) 139
Lebanese shawarma wraps 53
Left Bank 24
Legends Steakhouse 22, 103
Library Bar, The 149
Lime Tree Café, The 23
Lobby Lounge, The 149
Lobo Tailors 31
Local House 21, 75
Loft, The 53
Lotus One 25, 53
Louis Vuitton 27
Lounge Bar 63
Louvre museum 35
LunarLand 42

M

Madinat Jumeirah 22, 23, 32, 107, 109, 120-123, 146
Madinat Souk 20-21, 23, 24, 32, 33, 107, 120
Madinat Theatre, The 24, 45, 122
Magic Planet 26, 42, 109
Magnolia (restaurant) 22
Magrudy's 29
Magrudy Shopping Mall 109
Majlis 34, 75, 101
Majlis Al Junsui 119

Mall of Arabia 46
Mall of the Emirates 23, 26, 27, 28, 42, 109, 132
Manabu Ozawaand 28
Manhattan Grill 22, 90
Marina 114
Marina Market 43
Market Café, The 90
Marrakech 20, 21, 60
Maya 144
Media Lounge, The 134
Meem Gallery 34
Meena Bazaar 31
Mercato Mall 23, 28, 43, 109
Mi Vida 144
Mina A' Salam 22, 109
Mirage Glass 121
Miraj Islamic Art Gallery 29, 109
MIX 90
Miyako 22
Mokaroma 66
Montgomerie, The 22, 39, 132, 147, 154-157
Monty Cristo's 156, 157
More 23
Morgan Stanley 51

N

Nad Al Sheba Club 23, 38, 39
National Bank of Dubai 77, 99
National Geographic Dive Centre 113
National Iranian Carpet 33
Nature Centre 43
Nezesaussi 66
nightlife 24-25 also see under specific drinking holes
Nina 129
Nineteen 22, 156
Noble House, The 85
Noodle House, The 22

O

Oasis Beach Tower 150-151
Off-Road Adventures 162
Old Town Island 22, 54, 62, 64, 68
Old Town Souk 71
One&Only Royal Mirage 17, 18, 24, 25, 107, 124-131
Orient (restaurant) 90
Oriental Spa 63
Oryx 161, 163
Ossigeno 144
Ostra Gallery 75
Ottomans 138
oud (Arabian incense) 31
Oud Metha 21

P

PADI 5 Star Gold IDC Resort 113
PaiThai 122
Palm Island Bay 124, 127, 130
Palm Jebel Ali, The 164
Palm Jumeirah, The 46, 132, 110, 111
Palm Tree Court and Spa 164-165

Panini 90
Paris Gallery 37
Park Hyatt Dubai 18, 24, 94-97
PAUL 28
Pavilion Dive Centre 38, 113
Pavilion Marina and Sports Club 113
Peppermint Club 25
Persia Court 27
Persian Carpet House 121
Perfume Souk, The 31, 79
PGA Tour Dubai Desert Classic 39, 101
Piano Bar, The 144
Pierchic 22
Pink Sushi 28
Pisces 122
Pistache 96
Planetarium 43
Plug-Ins 29
Polo Annual 39
Pool Bars 90, 102, 167
Port Rashid 107
Prada boutique 27
Pride of Kashmir 28, 33
Prime Rib 144

Q

Qamardeen Hotel 68-71
QD's 103

R

Racecourse 23
Radisson SAS Hotel, Dubai Media City 22, 132-135
Raffles Botanical Garden 84
Raffles Dubai 22, 23, 26, 82-85
Raffles Inc Lounge 83
RafflesAmrita Spa 85
Ralph Lauren boutique 27
Rampworks Skatepark 44
Rare 173
Rasul Suite 18
Red Bar & Lounge 173
Regent Hotel 25
Rent-A-Crib 40
Residence & Spa, The 36, 130
restaurants 20-23 also see under specific restaurants
Restless Planet 47
Retreat 37, 136
Retreat Terrace and Health Bar, The 137
Rhodes Mezzanine 21, 23, 138
Ritz-Carlton, Dubai, The 17, 107, 146-149
Ritz-Carlton Spa 36, 148
Rivoli (fabric boutique) 31
Roccobarocco 33
Rock Bottom Café 25
Rock Pool 174
Rooftop Lounge 24
Rotisserie 129
Roumoul Cocktail Bar 175
Rue de La Paix 18

S

Saadia Zahid boutique 28

Sahn Eddar 119
Saj Express 25, 53
Sakonis 21
Saks 5th Avenue 26-27
Satchmo's 144
Satori Spa 37, 169
Scarlett's 53
Seabreeze 144
Second Cup 23
SensAsia 37
Senses Beauty Salon 175
Senso Spa 134
Shakespeare & Co 53
Shang Palace 22, 60
Shangri-La Hotel 20, 22, 23, 24, 53, 56-61
shawarma wraps (Lebanese) 53
Sheikh Maktoum bin Butti 13
Sheikh Maktoum bin Rashid 15
Sheikh Mohammed bin Rashid 15, 18, 22, 80, 100
Sheikh Mohammed Centre for Cultural Understanding 107
Sheikh Rashid bin Saeed 14, 15
Sheikh Rashid Road 82
Sheikh Saeed Al Maktoum House 35, 77, 99
Sheikh Zayed Road 26, 27, 29, 51, 52, 53, 86
Sheraton Dubai Creek 21
Shindagha Road 77
Shirtaholics Anonymous 28
Shisha 66, 161, 115, 149
Sho Cho 25
Shoo Fee Ma Fee 20, 24, 122
shopping 26-29 also see under specific shops and chains
Signatures (restaurant) 165
Sikh Gurudaba 75
Sinbad's Kids Club 114
Ski Dubai 26, 42, 43, 109
skyscrapers 18, 51, 77, 98, 172
Skyview Bar 24, 118
Sloane's 138
souks (traditional market) 30-33
Souk Al Bahar 33, 54
Souk Al Manzil 67
spa 18, 36-37 also see under individual listing
Spectrum on One 23, 53
Spice Souk, The 30, 79, 93, 115
Spike Bar 23, 102
Splendido 149
sports championship 38-39 also see under individual listing
Sports City 38
Submarine Bar 25
Sukothai 22
Sumo Sushi 22

T

Tagine 127
Taj Palace Hotel Spa 18, 21, 37

Talise Spa 18, 36, 121
Tamanya Terrace 132, 135
Terrace, The 96, 102
Terrace Bar 24
Textile Souk, The 31, 77
Thai Kitchen, The 96
The Palace – The Old Town 23, 54, 62-63, 125
Thiptara 22, 23, 63
Third Line, The 34
360° 17, 24, 115
Tiffany's 28
Tiger Lily 26
Timeless Spa 37, 170
Times Square Centre 53
Tokyo (restaurant) 22
Topshop boutique 26, 28
Total Arts 34
Trade Centre 53
Trader Vic's 24
trading, maritime 13, 75, 77, 98
Traffic (gallery) 34
Travco 162
Trilogy 18, 24, 107
Tunisia Court 27

U

Umm Suqiem 107

V

Verre 23
Versace 26, 117
Via Rodeo 26, 28
VIBES 114
Victory 38
Vines Wine Bar 103
Vinoteca 90
Virgin Megastore 28
Vista 90
Vu's 21, 22, 24, 53

W

Wafi City Mall 26, 33, 43, 85, 86, 93
Wafi Gourmet 29
Warm Pitta Bread 161
Watersport 109
White Orchid 166
Wild Wadi Water Park 17, 41, 107, 114, 123, 146, 156
Willow Stream Spa 37
Wonder Bus Tours 41
Wonderland 42
World, The 46, 47, 118
Wox 90

X

XVA 34, 75

Y

Ya Hala Lounge 168
Yves Saint Laurent 27

Z

Zheng He's 22, 122
Zinc 25, 53
Zyara 53

picture credits

AFP/Getty Images 18 (bottom), 35 (top right), 39 (middle), 54 (bottom), 78, 111
Al Maha Desert Resort & Spa 170–171
Al Manzil Hotel 64–67
Amy Guip/Getty Images 110
Arabian Adventures 44, 45 (top left)
Aurora/Getty Images 41 (middle)
Bateaux Dubai 98–99
BiCE Restaurant front cover (dining table), 152–153
Burj Al Arab 2, 116–119
Celia Peterson/Getty Images 28 (middle), 43 (right),
Cristian Scutaru 53
Desert Palm 172–173
Desert Rangers 20 (top)
DreamPictures/Getty Images 162
Dubai Autodrome 39 (bottom), 45 (bottom)

Dubai Golf 100–103
epa/Corbis 107
Five Green 6, 27 (bottom)
Gallo Images/Getty Images 28 (bottom), 31 (top)
Gavin Hellier/JAI/Corbis 31 (bottom left)
Georgina Bowater/Corbis 46 (bottom)
Getty Images 13, 16, 18 (top), 19, 51, 109 (bottom), 161 (bottom)
Grand Hyatt Dubai 86–93
Grosvenor House 4, 21 (bottom), 25, 136–141
Hashim/Gulfimages/Getty Images 72
Hatta Fort Hotel 174–175
Jörg Sundermann 1, 5, 8–9, 36,
Jorge Ferrari/epa/Corbis 47
Jumana – Secret of the Desert 176–177
Jumeirah Bab Al Shams Desert Resort & Spa 166–169

Jumeirah Beach Hotel 17, 24 (bottom), 112–115
Jumeirah Emirates Towers 21 (top right), 37 (bottom), 54 (top)
Kirsten Holst 39 (top), 45 (top right)
Le Royal Méridien Beach Resort & Spa 142–145
Madinat Jumeirah 22, 33, 120–123
Martha Camarillo/Getty Images 28 (top)
Oasis Beach Tower 150–151
One&Only Royal Mirage 124–131
Palm Tree Court & Spa 164–165
Pankaj & Insy Shah/Getty Images 48
Park Hyatt Dubai 24 (top), 94–97
Patrick Frilet/Hemis/Corbis 20 (bottom)
Pete Turner/Getty Images 161 (top)
Photodisc/Getty Images 12
Photolibrary 14–15, 26, 28 (top), 30, 31 (bottom right), 32, 34, 38, 40, 41 (top and bottom), 42, 43

Qamardeen Hotel 68–71
Radisson SAS Hotel, Dubai Media City 132–135
Raffles Dubai 23 (top), 82–85
Richard Du Toit/Getty Images 163
Sajid Shafique/Getty Images 46 (top)
Sam Robinson/Getty Images 55
Shangri-La Hotel, Dubai 21 (top left), 56–61
Stephanie Kuykendal/Corbis 29 (bottom), 109 (top)
The Montgomerie, Dubai 154–157
The Palace – The Old Town 23 (bottom), 62–63
The Ritz-Carlton, Dubai 37 (bottom), 146–149
Toby Adamson/Getty Images 29 (top)
Traffic Gallery 35 (top left)
Walter Bibikow/Getty Images 77 (bottom)
XVA Gallery 35 (bottom)

(top left and bottom left), 52, 72, 75–76, 77 (top), 79–81, 104, 108, 158

directory

HOTELS

Al Maha Desert Resort & Spa (page 170)
Al Maha Head Office
3rd Floor Emirates Holidays Building
Sheikh Zayed Road, PO Box 7631, Dubai, UAE
telephone : +971.4.303 4222
facsimile : +971.4.343 9696
almaha@emirates.com
www.al-maha.com

Al Manzil Hotel (page 64)
PO Box 114822, Burj Dubai Boulevard
The Old Town, Dubai, UAE
telephone : +971.4.428 5888
facsimile : +971.4.428 5999
reservationsalmanzil@southernsun.ae
www.almanzilhotel.com

Burj Al Arab (page 116)
PO Box 74147, Dubai, UAE
telephone : +971.4.301 7777
facsimile : +971.4.301 7000
BAAreservations@jumeirah.com
www.jumeirah.com

Desert Palm (page 172)
Al Awir Road, PO Box 103635, Dubai, UAE
telephone : +971.4.323 8888
facsimile : +971.4.323 8053
reservations@desertpalm.ae
www.desertpalm.ae

Grand Hyatt Dubai (page 86)
PO Box 7978, Dubai, UAE
telephone : +971.4.317 1234
facsimile : +971.4.317 1235
dubai.grand@hyattintl.com
dubai.grand.hyatt.com

Grosvenor House (page 136)
Al Sufouh Road, PO Box 118500, Dubai, UAE
telephone : +971.4.399 8888
facsimile : +971.4.399 8444
reservations@lrm-gh-dubai.com
www.grosvenorhouse-dubai.com

Hatta Fort Hotel (page 174)
PO Box 9277, Dubai, UAE
telephone : +971.4.852 3211
facsimile : +971.4.852 3561
hfh@jaihotels.com
www.hattaforthotel.com

Jumeirah Bab Al Shams Desert Resort & Spa (page 166)
PO Box 8168, Dubai, UAE
telephone : +971.4.832 6699
facsimile : +971.4.399 9998
JBASreservations@jumeirah.com
www.jumeirahbabalshams.com

Jumeirah Beach Hotel (page 112)
PO Box 11416, Dubai, UAE
telephone : +971.4.348 0000
facsimile : +971.4.301 6800
JBHinfo@jumeirah.com
www.jumeirahbeachhotel.com

Le Royal Méridien Beach Resort & Spa (page 142)
Al Sufouh Road, PO Box 24970, Dubai, UAE
telephone : +971.4.399 5999
facsimile : +971.4.317 6980
reservations@lrm-gh-dubai.com
www.leroyalmeridien-dubai.com

Madinat Jumeirah (page 120)
PO Box 75157, Dubai, UAE
telephone : +971.4.366 8888
facsimile : +971.4.366 7788
MJinfo@jumeirah.com
www.madinatjumeirah.com

Oasis Beach Tower (page 150)
PO Box 26500, Dubai, UAE
telephone : +971.4.399 4444
facsimile : +971.4.399 4200
obt@jaihotels.com
www.oasisbeachtower.com

One&Only Royal Mirage (page 124)
PO Box 37252, Dubai, UAE
telephone : +971.4.399 9999
facsimile : +971.4.399 9998
info@oneandonlyroyalmirage.ae
www.oneandonlyresorts.com

Palm Tree Court & Spa (page 164)
PO Box 9255, Dubai, UAE
telephone : +971.4.883 6000
facsimile : +971.4.883 5543
jagrs@jaihotels.com
www.jebelali-international.com

Park Hyatt Dubai (page 94)
PO Box 2822, Dubai, UAE
telephone : +971.4.602 1234
facsimile : +971.4.602 1235
dubai.park@hyatt.com
dubai.park.hyatt.com

Qamardeen Hotel (page 68)
PO Box 11788, Burj Dubai Boulevard
The Old Town, Dubai, UAE
telephone : +971.4.428 6888
facsimile : +971.4.428 6999
reservationsqamardeen@southernsun.ae
www.qamardeenhotel.com

Radisson SAS Hotel, Dubai Media City (page 132)
PO Box 211723, Dubai, UAE
telephone : +971.4.366 9111
facsimile : +971.4.361 1011
info.dubai@radissonsas.com
dubai.radissonsas.com

Raffles Dubai (page 82)
Sheikh Rashid Road, Wafi City
PO Box 121800, Dubai, UAE
telephone : +971.4.324 8888
facsimile : +971.4.324 6000
dubai@raffles.com
dubai.raffles.com

Shangri-La Hotel, Dubai (page 56)
Sheikh Zayed Road
PO Box 75880, Dubai, UAE
telephone : +971.4.343 8888
facsimile : +971.4.343 8886
sldb@shangri-la.com
www.shangri-la.com

The Palace – The Old Town (page 62)
The Old Town Island, Downtown Burj Dubai
PO Box 9770, Dubai, UAE
telephone : +971.4.428 7888
facsimile : +971.4.428 7999
h6230-re@accor.com
www.sofitel.com

The Ritz-Carlton, Dubai (page 146)
PO Box 26525, Dubai, UAE
telephone : +971.4.399 4000
facsimile : +971.4.399 4001
rcdubai@emirates.net.ae
www.ritzcarlton.com

RESTAURANTS

Bateaux Dubai (page 98)
Dubai Creek, Dubai, UAE
telephone : +971.4.399 4994
facsimile : +971.4.399 4995
mail@bateauxdubai.com
www.bateauxdubai.com

BiCE Restaurant (page 152)
Hilton Dubai Jumeirah
Dubai Marina, PO Box 2431, Dubai, UAE
telephone : +971.4.318 2520
facsimile : +971.4.318 2503
bicerest.jumeirah@hilton.com
www.bice.ws

GOLF COURSES

Dubai Golf (page 100)

Dubai Creek Golf & Yacht Club
PO Box 6302, Dubai, UAE
telephone : +971.4.295 6000
facsimile : +971.4.295 6044
golfbooking@dubaigolf.com
www.dubaigolf.com

directory

Emirates Golf Club
PO Box 24040, Dubai, UAE
telephone : +971.4.380 2222
facsimile : +971.4.380 1555
golfbooking@dubaigolf.com
www.dubaigolf.com

The Montgomerie, Dubai (page 154)
PO Box 36700, Dubai, UAE
telephone : +971.4.390 5600
facsimile : +971.4.360 8981
info@themontgomerie.ae
www.themontgomerie.com

THEATRE

Jumana – Secret of the Desert (page 176)
Al Sahra Desert Resort
PO Box 233, Dubai, UAE
telephone : +971.4.367 9500
facsimile : +971.4.367 9501
reservations@alsahra.com
www.alsahra.com

GOURMET SAFARI

Al Hadheerah
Jumeirah Bab Al Shams Desert Resort & Spa
PO Box 8168, Dubai, UAE
telephone : +971.4.832 6699
facsimile : +971.4.832 6698
JBASrestaurants@jumeirah.com
www.jumeirahbabalshams.com

Al Mahara
Burj Al Arab
PO Box 74147, Dubai, UAE
telephone : +971.4.301 7600
facsimile : +971.4.301 6076
BAArestaurants@jumeirah.com
www.burj-al-arab.com

Al Nafoorah
Jumeirah Emirates Towers
PO Box 72127, Dubai, UAE
telephone : +971.4.319 8088
facsimile : +971.4.319 8079
JETrestaurants@jumeirah.com
www.jumeirahemiratestowers.com

Al Qasr
Dubai Marine Beach Resort & Spa
PO Box 5182, Dubai, UAE
telephone : +971.4.346 1111
facsimile : +971.4.346 0234
dxbmarin@emirates.net.ae
www.dxbmarine.com

Al Qasr
Madinat Jumeirah
PO Box 75157, Dubai, UAE
telephone : +971.4.366 8888
facsimile : +971.4.366 7788
MJrestaurants@jumeirah.com
www.madinatjumeirah.com

Almaz by Momo
Harvey Nichols, Mall of the Emirates
Sheikh Zayed Road
PO Box 72999, Dubai, UAE
telephone : +971.4.409 8877
www.malloftheemirates.com

Armani Caffe
Mall of the Emirates
Sheikh Zayed Road
PO Box 72999, Dubai, UAE
telephone : +971.4.341 0591
www.malloftheemirates.com

Ashiana
Sheraton Dubai Creek Hotel & Towers
Baniyas Street/Creek Road
PO Box 4250, Dubai, UAE
telephone : +971.4.228 1111
facsimile : +971.4.221 3468
www.starwoodhotels.com

Bastakiah Nights
Bur Dubai, Dubai, UAE
telephone : +971.4.353 7772
facsimile : +971.4.353 8376

Café Sushi
Fairmont Dubai
Sheikh Zayed Road
PO Box 97555, Dubai, UAE
telephone : +971.4.332 5555
facsimile : +971.4.332 4555
dubai@fairmont.com
www.fairmont.com/dubai

Caviar House
Souk Madinat Jumeirah, Madinat Jumeirah
PO Box 75157, Dubai, UAE
telephone : +971.4.366 6730
facsimile : +971.4.366 6649
MJrestaurants@jumeirah.com
www.madinatjumeirah.com

Certo
Radisson SAS Hotel, Dubai Media City
PO Box 211723, Dubai, UAE
telephone : +971.4.366 9111
facsimile : +971.4.361 1011
info.mediacity.dubai@radissonsas.com
dubai.radissonsas.com

China Club
Radisson SAS Hotel, Dubai Deira Creek
Bani Yas Road, 476 Dubai, UAE
telephone : +971.4.205 7333
facsimile : +971.4.228 4777
info.deiracreek.dubai@radissonsas.com
dubai.radissonsas.com

Fire & Ice – Raffles Grill
Raffles Dubai
Sheikh Rashid Road, Wafi City
PO Box 121800, Dubai, UAE
telephone : +971.4.324 8888
facsimile : +971.4.324 6000
dubai@raffles.com
dubai.raffles.com

Fudo
Jumeirah Beach Road, Dubai, UAE
telephone : +971.4.349 8586

Handi
The Taj Palace Hotel, Dubai
PO Box 42211, Dubai, UAE
telephone : +971.4.223 2222
facsimile : +971.4.227 8222
tphreservations.dxb@tajhotels.com
www.tajhotels.com

Indego
Grosvenor House
Al Sufouh Road, PO Box 118500, Dubai, UAE
telephone : +971.4.399 8888
facsimile : +971.4.399 8444
reservations@lrm-gh-dubai.com
www.grosvenorhouse-dubai.com

India House
Al Fahidi Street, Bur Dubai, Dubai, UAE
telephone: +971.4.352 6006

Japengo
Mall of the Emirates
Sheikh Zayed Road
PO Box 72999, Dubai, UAE
telephone : +971.4.341 1671
www.malloftheemirates.com

Khazana
Al Nasr Leisureland
PO Box 2652, Dubai, UAE
telephone : +971.4.337 1234
facsimile : +971.4.337 4952
alnasrll@elm.ae
www.alnasrll.com

Kiku
Le Méridien Dubai
Airport Road, PO Box 10001, Dubai, UAE
telephone : +971.4.217 0000
facsimile : +971.4.282 1650
reservation@lmdubai.com
www.starwoodhotels.com

La Baie
The Ritz-Carlton, Dubai
PO Box 26525, Dubai, UAE
telephone : +971.4.399 4000
facsimile : +971.4.399 4001
rcdubai@emirates.net.ae
www.ritzcarlton.com

La Parrilla
Jumeirah Beach Hotel
telephone : +971.4.406 8999
laparrilla@jumeirah.com
www.jumeirahbeachhotel.com

Legends Steakhouse
Dubai Creek Golf & Yacht Club
PO Box 6302, Dubai, UAE
telephone : +971.4.295 6000
facsimile : +971.4.295 6044
www.dubaigolf.com

Magnolia
Madinat Jumeirah
PO Box 75157, Dubai, UAE
telephone : +971.4.366 6730
facsimile : +971.4.366 6649
MJrestaurants@jumeirah.com
www.madinatjumeirah.com

Manhattan Grill
Grand Hyatt Dubai
PO Box 7978, Dubai, UAE
telephone : +971.4.317 1234
facsimile : +971.4.317 1235
reservations.grandhyattdubai@hyattintl.com
dubai.grand.hyatt.com

Marrakech
Shangri-La Hotel, Dubai
Sheikh Zayed Road, PO Box 75880, Dubai, UAE
telephone : +971.4.343 8888
facsimile : +971.4.343 8886
sldb@shangri-la.com
www.shangri-la.com

Miyako
Hyatt Regency Dubai
Deira, PO Box 5588, Dubai, UAE
telephone : +971.4.209 1234
facsimile : +971.4.209 1000
reservations.hyattregencydubai@hyattintl.com
dubai.regency.hyatt.com

More
Al Murooj Rotana Hotel & Suites, Dubai
Al Saffa Street, off Sheikh Zayed Road
PO Box 117546, Dubai, UAE
telephone : +971.4.321 1111
facsimile : +971.4.321 5555
almurooj.hotel@rotana.com
www.rotana.com

Nineteen
The Montgomerie, Dubai
PO Box 36700, Dubai, UAE
telephone : +971.4.363 1265/75
facsimile : +971.4.360 8971
nineteen@themontgomerie.ae
www.themontgomerie.com

Pierchic
Madinat Jumeirah
PO Box 75157, Dubai, UAE
telephone : +971.4.366 8888
facsimile : 1971.4.366 7788
MJinfo@madinatjumeirah.com
www.madinatjumeirah.com

Rhodes Mezzanine
Grosvenor House
Al Sufouh Road, PO Box 118500, Dubai, UAE
telephone : +971.4.399 8888
facsimile : +971.4.399 8444
reservations@lrm-gh-dubai.com
www.grosvenorhouse-dubai.com

Sakonis
PO Box 18873, Dubai, UAE
telephone : +971.4.396 6369

Second Cup
PO Box 1038, Dubai, UAE
telephone : +971.4.343 5314

Shang Palace
Shangri-La Hotel, Dubai
Sheikh Zayed Road
PO Box 75880, Dubai, UAE
telephone : +971.4.343 8888
facsimile : +971.4.343 8886
sldb@shangri-la.com
www.shangri-la.com

Shoo Fee Ma Fee
Madinat Jumeirah
PO Box 75157, Dubai, UAE
telephone : +971.4.366 6730
facsimile : +971.4.366 6649
MJrestaurants@jumeirah.com
www.madinatjumeirah.com

Spectrum on One
Fairmont Dubai
Sheikh Zayed Road
PO Box 97555, Dubai, UAE
telephone : +971.4.332 5555
facsimile : +971.4.332 4555
dubai@fairmont.com
www.fairmont.com/dubai

Sukothai
Le Royal Méridien Dubai
Airport Road, PO Box 10001, Dubai, UAE
telephone : +971.4.217 0000
facsimile : +971.4.282 1650
reservation@lmdubai.com
www.starwoodhotels.com

Sumo Sushi
Ground Floor, Jumeirah Town Centre,
Dubai, UAE
telephone : +971.4.800 7866
www.sumosushi.net

Ground Floor, Phase 3, Building 10
Dubai Media City, Dubai, UAE
telephone : +971.4.391 1041
www.sumosushi.net

The Blue Elephant
Al Bustan Rotana Hotel
Casablanca Road, Al Garhoud
PO Box 30880, Dubai, UAE
telephone : +971.4.282 0000
facsimile : +971.4.282 8100
albustan.hotel@rotana.com
www.rotana.com

The Exchange Grill
Fairmont Dubai
Sheikh Zayed Road
PO Box 97555, Dubai, UAE
telephone : +971.4.332 5555
facsimile : +971.4.332 4555
dubai@fairmont.com
www.fairmont.com

The Lime Tree Café
PO Box 1714, Jumeirah, Dubai, UAE
telephone : +971.4.349 8498
facsimile : +971.4.349 8477
limetree@emirates.net.ae
www.thelimetreecafe.com

The Noodle House
Dubai International Financial Centre
The Gate, Level 14
PO Box 74777, Dubai, UAE
telephone : +971.4.363 7093
info@thenoodlehouse.com
www.thenoodlehouse.com

Thiptara
The Palace – The Old Town
The Old Town Island, Downtown Burj Dubai
PO Box 9770, Dubai, UAE
telephone : +971.4.428 7888
facsimile : +971.4.428 7999
h6230-re@accor.com
www.sofitel.com

Tokyo
Jumeirah Emirates Towers
PO Box 72127, Dubai, UAE
telephone : +971.4.319 8088
facsimile : +971.4.319 8079
JETrestaurants@jumeirah.com
www.jumeirahemiratestowers.com

Verre
Hilton Dubai Creek
Baniyas Road, PO Box 33398, Dubai, UAE
telephone : +971.4.227 1111
facsimile : +971.4.227 1131
info.creek@hilton.com
www.hilton.com

directory

Vu's
Jumeirah Emirates Towers
PO Box 72127, Dubai, UAE
telephone : +971.4.319 8088
facsimile : +971.4.319 8079
JETrestaurants@jumeirah.com
www.jumeirahemiratestowers.com

Zheng He's
Mina A' Salam, Madinat Jumeirah
PO Box 75157, Dubai, UAE
telephone : +971.4.366 6730
facsimile : +971.4.366 6649
MJrestaurants@jumeirah.com
www.madinatjumeirah.com

ARABIAN NIGHTS

360°
Jumeirah Beach Hotel
PO Box 11416, Dubai, UAE
telephone : +971.4.406 8769
360degrees@jumeirah.com
www.jumeirahbeachhotel.com/dining/360_degrees

Bar 44
Grosvenor House
Al Sufouh Road, PO Box 118500, Dubai, UAE
telephone : +971.4.399 8888
facsimile : +971.4.399 8444
reservations@lrm-gh-dubai.com
www.grosvenorhouse-dubai.com

BarZar
Souk Madinat Jumeirah, Madinat Jumeirah
PO Box 75157, Dubai, UAE
telephone : +971.4.366 8888
facsimile : +971.4.366 7788
MJinfo@jumeirah.com
www.madinatjumeirah.com

Barasti Bar
Le Royal Méridien Mina Seyahi
Beach Resort & Marina
Al Sufouh Road, PO Box 24883, Dubai, UAE
telephone : +971.4.399 3333
facsimile : +971.4.399 3111
guestservices@lemeridien-minaseyahi.com
www.starwoodhotels.com

Boudoir
Dubai Marine Beach Resort & Spa
PO Box 5182, Dubai, UAE
telephone : +971.4.346 1111
facsimile : +971.4.346 0234
dxbmarin@emirates.net.ae
www.dxbmarine.com

Buddha Bar
Grosvenor House
Al Sufouh Road, PO Box 118500, Dubai, UAE
telephone : +971.4.399 8888
facsimile : +971.4.399 8444
reservations@lrm-gh-dubai.com
www.grosvenorhouse-dubai.com

Chi at The Lodge
Al Nasr Leisureland
PO Box 9332, Dubai, UAE
telephone : +971.4.337 9470
facsimile : +971.4.337 9471
contact@lodgedubai.com
www.lodgedubai.com

Crossroads
Raffles Dubai
Sheikh Rashid Road, Wafi City
PO Box 121800, Dubai, UAE
telephone : +971.4.324 8888
facsimile : +971.4.324 6000
dubai@raffles.com
dubai.raffles.com

Jambase
Souk Madinat Jumeirah, Madinat Jumeirah
PO Box 75157, Dubai, UAE
telephone : +971.4.366 6730
facsimile : +971.4.366 6649
MJrestaurants@jumeirah.com
www.madinatjumeirah.com

Kasbar
One&Only Royal Mirage
PO Box 37252, Dubai, UAE
telephone : +971.4.399 9999
facsimile : +971.4.399 9998
info@oneandonlyroyalmirage.ae
www.oneandonlyresorts.com

Lotus One
World Trade Convention Centre
Sheikh Zayed Road, Dubai, UAE
telephone : +971.4.329 3200

Peppermint Club
Habtoor Grand Hotel
PO Box 24454, Dubai, UAE
telephone : +971.4.399 5000
facsimile : +971.4.399 4547
grandjumeirah@habtoorhotels.com
grandjumeirah.habtoorhotels.com

Rock Bottom Café
Regent Palace Hotel
PO Box 26816, Dubai, UAE
telephone : +971.4.396 3888
facsimile : +971.4.396 4080
rameedxb@emirates.net.ae
www.ramee-group.com

Rooftop Lounge
One&Only Royal Mirage
PO Box 37252, Dubai, UAE
telephone : +971.4.399 9999
facsimile : +971.4.399 9998
info@oneandonlyroyalmirage.ae
www.oneandonlyresorts.com

Saj Express
Sheikh Zayed Road
PO Box 13975, Dubai, UAE
telephone : +971.4.321 1191

Sho Cho
Dubai Marine Beach Club
Dubai Marine Beach Resort & Spa
PO Box 5182, Dubai, UAE
telephone : +971.4.346 1111
facsimile : +971.4.346 0234
dxbmarin@emirates.net.ae
www.dxbmarine.com

Skyview Bar
Burj Al Arab
PO Box 74147, Dubai, UAE
telephone : +971.4.301 7600
facsimile : +971.4.301 6076
BAArestaurants@jumeirah.com
www.burj-al-arab.com

Submarine Bar
Dhow Palace Hotel
PO Box 121545, Dubai, UAE
telephone : +971.4.359 9992
facsimile : +971.4.359 9292
www.dhowpalacedubai.com

Terrace Bar
Park Hyatt Dubai
PO Box 2822, Dubai, UAE
telephone : +971.4.602 1234
facsimile : +971.4.602 1235
dubai.park@hyatt.com
dubai.park.hyatt.com

The Agency
Souk Madinat Jumeirah, Madinat Jumeirah
PO Box 75157, Dubai, UAE
telephone : +971.4.366 6730
facsimile : +971.4.366 6649
MJrestaurants@jumeirah.com
www.madinatjumeirah.com

The Apartment
Jumeirah Beach Hotel
PO Box 11416, Dubai, UAE
telephone : +971.4.406 8000
TheApartment@jumeirah.com
www.jumeirahbeachhotel.com

The Madinat Theatre
Souk Madinat Jumeirah, Madinat Jumeirah
PO Box 75157, Dubai, UAE
telephone : +971.4.366 8888
facsimile : +971.4.366 7788
MJinfo@jumeirah.com
www.madinattheatre.com

Trader Vic's
Crowne Plaza Hotel
Sheikh Zayed Al Nahyan Road
PO Box 23215, Dubai, UAE
telephone : +971.4.331 1111
facsimile : +971.4.331 5555
www.ichotelsgroup.com

Vista
InterContinental Dubai Festival City
PO Box 45777, Dubai, UAE
telephone : +971.4.701 1111
facsimile : +971.4.232 9098
www.ichotelsgroup.com

Zinc
Crowne Plaza Hotel
Sheikh Zayed Al Nahyan Road
PO Box 23215, Dubai, UAE
telephone : +971.4.331 1111
facsimile : +971.4.331 5555
www.ichotelsgroup.com

SHOPPING MECCA

Ajmal Perfumes
Ajmal International Trading Company
Hamarain Centre, Gate 8, 2nd Floor
PO Box 8809, Dubai, UAE
telephone : +971.4.269 0102
facsimile : +971.4.262 9747
info@ajmalperfume.com
www.ajmalperfume.com

Al Ain Mall
PO Box 1818, Al Ain, Dubai, UAE
telephone : +971.3.766 0333
facsimile : +971.3.766 3444
www.alainmall.org

Arabian Oud
Deira City Centre Office, Level 5
PO Box 86884, Dubai, UAE
telephone : +971.4.295 2585
facsimile : +971.4.295 2584
info@adgroup.ae
www.arabianoud.com

Bateel
PO Box 7634, Dubai, UAE
telephone : +971.4.228 9770
facsimile : +971.4.228 9771
bateelsa@emirates.net.ae
www.bateel.ae

Beyond the Beach
Mercato Shopping Mall
Jumeirah Beach Road
PO Box 755, Dubai, UAE
telephone : +971.4.349 0105

Boom & Mellow
Mall of the Emirates
Sheikh Zayed Road
PO Box 72999, Dubai, UAE
telephone : +971.4.409 9000

Bulgari
The Boulevard, Jumeirah Emirates Towers
PO Box 72127, Dubai, UAE
telephone : +971.4.330 0000
facsimile : +971.4.330 3030
www.bulgari.com

BurJuman Centre
PO Box 8022, Dubai, UAE
telephone : +971.4.352 0222
facsimile : +971.4.351 0824
www.burjuman.com

Cartier
The Boulevard, Jumeirah Emirates Towers
PO Box 72127, Dubai, UAE
telephone : +971.4.330 0000
facsimile : +971.4.330 3030
www.cartier.com

Chanel
Wafi City
Al Wasl Road, PO Box 721, Dubai, UAE
telephone : +971.4.324 0464
www.chanel.com

CompuMe
Garhoud Road, Zalfa Building
PO Box 27008, Dubai, UAE
telephone : +971.4.282 8555
facsimile : +971.4.282 8666
www.compume.com

DeBeers
Mall of the Emirates
Sheikh Zayed Road
PO Box 72999, Dubai, UAE
telephone : +971.4.341 2121
debeers@salam.ae
www.debeers.com/en/page/store/33

DKNY
BurJuman Centre
PO Box 8022, Dubai, UAE
telephone : +971.4.351 3788
www.dkny.com

Dubai Festival City
PO Box 49776, Garhoud, Dubai, UAE
telephone : +971.4.213 6135
info@dubaifestivalcity.com
www.dubaifestivalcity.com

Dubai Outlet Mall
Al Ain Road, Dubailand, Dubai, UAE
telephone : +971.4.367 9600
facsimile : +971.4.367 9009
info@dubaioutletmall.com
www.dubaioutletmall.com

Escada
Wafi City
Al Wasl Road, PO Box 721, Dubai, UAE
telephone : +971.4.324 4555
www.escada.com

Etoile
PO Box 20164, Dubai, UAE
telephone : +971.4.324 0465
facsimile : +971.4.324 0297

Fab India
Shop 7, Nashwan Building
Al Mankhool Road, Dubai, UAE
telephone : +971.4.398 9633/35
facsimile : +971.4.398.9634
fabindia@emirates.net.ae
www.fabindia.com

Five Green
Oud Metha, PO Box 73617, Dubai, UAE
telephone : +971.4.336 4100
facsimile : +971.4.336 4010
high@fivegreen.com
www.fivegreen.com

Ginger & Lace
Wafi City
Al Wasl Road, PO Box 721, Dubai, UAE
telephone : +971.4.324 5699
www.gingerandlace.com

Global Village
PO Box 117777, Dubai, UAE
telephone : +971.4.362 4114
facsimile : +971.4.362 4022
www.globalvillage.ae

Gold & Diamond Park
Sheikh Zayed Road, Dubai, UAE
telephone : +971.4.347 7788
facsimile : +971.4.347 3206
GDP@emaar.ae
www.goldanddiamondpark.com

Graff
Wafi City
Al Wasl Road, PO Box 721, Dubai, UAE
telephone : +971.4.324 4221
www.graffdiamonds.com

Gucci
The Boulevard, Jumeirah Emirates Towers
PO Box 72127, Dubai, UAE
telephone : +971.4.330 0000
facsimile : +971.4.330 3030
www.bulgari.com

Giorgio Armani
The Boulevard, Jumeirah Emirates Towers
PO Box 72127, Dubai, UAE
telephone : +971.4.330 0000
facsimile : +971.4.330 3030
www.giorgioarmani.com

directory

Hermes
BurJuman Centre, Level 2
PO Box 8022, Dubai, UAE
telephone : +971.4.351 1190
facsimile : +971.4.351 1192

Ibn Battuta Mall
Sheikh Zayed Road, PO Box 261177, Dubai, UAE
telephone : +971.4.362 1900
facsimile : +971.4.368 5140
info@ibnbattutamall.com
www.ibnbattutamall.com

Jimmy Choo
The Boulevard, Jumeirah Emirates Towers
PO Box 72127, Dubai, UAE
telephone : +971.4.330 0404
www.jimmychoo.com

Louis Vuitton
BurJuman Centre
PO Box 29948, Dubai, UAE
telephone : +971.4.359 2535
facsimile : +971.4.359 2506
www.louisvuitton.com

Luxecouture
PO Box 54235, Dubai, UAE
telephone : +971.4.344 7933
facsimile : +971.4.342 0405
info@shopluxecouture.com
www.shopluxecouture.com

Magrudy's
Beach Road, Jumeriah 2, Dubai, UAE
telephone : +971.4.344 4193
facsimile : +971.4.349 7819
shopjbs@magrudy.com
www.magrudy.com

Mall of the Emirates
Sheikh Zayed Road
PO Box 72999, Dubai, UAE
telephone : +971.4.409 9000
facsimile : +971.4.409 9888
info@malloftheemirates.com
www.malloftheemirates.com

Mercato Shopping Mall
Jumeirah Beach Road,
PO Box 755, Dubai, UAE
telephone : +971.4.344 4161
facsimile : +971.4.349 0066
information.mercato@mercatotowncentre.com
www.mercatoshoppingmall.com

Miraj Islamic Art Gallery
Jumeirah, Dubai, UAE
telephone : +971.4.394 1084

Monsoon
Wafi City
Al Wasl Road, PO Box 721, Dubai, UAE
telephone : +971.4.327 9001
monsoon.wafi@jawad.com
www.monsoon.co.uk

PAUL
BurJuman Centre
PO Box 8022, Dubai, UAE
telephone : +971.4.351 7009

Prada
Saks Fifth Avenue, 2nd Floor
BurJuman Centre, Dubai, UAE
telephone : +971.4.3515 5551
www.prada.com

Plug-Ins
Dubai Festival City, Dubai, UAE
Telephone : +971.4.206 6777
www.pluginselectronix.com

Pride of Kashmir
G-44, 1st Level, Mall of the Emirates
Sheikh Zayed Road
PO Box 72999, Dubai, UAE
telephone : +971.4.341 4477
www.prideofkashmir.com

Ralph Lauren
BurJuman Centre
PO Box 8022, Dubai, UAE
telephone : +971.4.352 5311
www.ralphlauren.com

Saks Fifth Avenue
BurJuman Centre
PO Box 8022, Dubai, UAE
telephone : +971.4.352 0222
facsimile : +971.4.351 0824
www.saksfifthavenue.com

S*uce
The Village Mall, Shop 29
Jumeirah Beach Road
PO Box 74015, Dubai, UAE
telephone : +971.4.344 7270
facsimile : +971.4.343 4940
ask@shopatsauce.com
www.shopatsauce.com

The Boulevard
Jumeirah Emirates Towers
PO Box 72127, Dubai, UAE
telephone : +971.4.330 0000
facsimile : +971.4.330 3030
JETinfo@jumeirah.com
www.jumeirahemiratestowers.com/lifestyle

Tiffany & Co
Wafi City
Al Wasl Road, PO Box 721, Dubai, UAE
telephone : +971.4.324 4959
tiffdxb@emirates.net.ae
www.tiffany.com

Topshop
Wafi City
Al Wasl Road, PO Box 721, Dubai, UAE
telephone : +971.4.327 9929
www.topshop.com

Virgin Megastore
Mercato Shopping Mall
Jumeirah Beach Road
PO Box 755, Dubai, UAE
telephone : +971.4.344 6971
www.vmeganews.com

Wafi City
Al Wasl Road, PO Box 721, Dubai, UAE
telephone : +971.4.324 4555
facsimile : +971.4.324 1212
customerservice@wafi.com
www.waficity.com

Wafi Gourmet
Wafi City
Al Wasl Road, PO Box 721, Dubai, UAE
telephone : +971.4.324 4433

Yves Saint Laurent
The Boulevard, Jumeirah Emirates Towers
PO Box 72127, Dubai, UAE
telephone : +971.4.330 0000
facsimile : +971.4.330 3030
www.ysl.com

OASIS OF CULTURE

B21
Al Quoz 3, PO Box 58182, Dubai, UAE
telephone : +971.4.340 3965
b21gallery@yahoo.com

Dubai Museum
Al Fahidi Fort, Dubai, UAE
telephone : +971.4.353 1862/393 7151

Green Art Gallery
PO Box 25711, Dubai, UAE
telephone : +971.4.344 9888
facsimile : +971.4.344 7449
greenart@emirates.net.ae
www.gagallery.com

Guggenheim
Saadiyat Island, Abu Dhabi, UAE
www.guggenheim.org

Louvre
Saadiyat Island, Abu Dhabi, UAE
www.louvre.fr

Majlis
Bastakiya Roundabout, Bur Dubai
PO Box 42885, Dubai, UAE
telephone : +971.4.353 6233
facsimile : +971.4.353 5550
majlisga@emirates.net.ae
www.majlisgallery.com

Meem Gallery
Umm Suqeim, Dubai, UAE
telephone : +971.4.347 7883
www.meem.ae

Sheikh Saeed Al Maktoum House
Al Shindagha Road, Dubai, UAE
telephone : +971.4.393 7139

The Courtyard Al Quoz
PO Box 14847, Dubai, UAE
telephone : +971.4.347 5050
facsimile : +971.4.347 0909
totalart@emirates.net.ae
www.courtyard-uae.com

The Third Line
Al Quoz 3, PO Box 72036, Dubai, UAE
telephone : +971.4.341 1367
facsimile : +971.4.341 1369
art@thethirdline.com
www.thethirdline.com

Total Arts
Sheikh Zayed Road E11
Al Quoz Industrial Area Courtyard Building
PO Box 14214, Dubai, UAE
telephone : +971.4.347 5050
facsimile : +971.4.347 0909
www.courtyard-uae.com
totalart@eim.ae

Traffic Design Gallery
Saratoga Building, Al Barsha,
PO Box 6716, Dubai, UAE
telephone : +971.4.341 8494
facsimile : +971.4.341 8566
info@viatraffic.org
www.viatraffic.org

XVA
Bastakiya, Bur Dubai
PO Box 37304, Dubai, UAE
telephone : +971.4.353 5383
facsimile : +971.4.353 5988
xva@xvagallery.com
www.xvagallery.com

SPA SANCTUARY

Amara Spa
Park Hyatt Dubai
PO Box 2822, Dubai, UAE
telephone : +971.4.602 1234
facsimile : +971.4.602 1235
dubai.park@hyatt.com
dubai.park.hyatt.com

Amrita Spa
Raffles Dubai
Sheikh Rashid Road, Wafi City
PO Box 121800, Dubai, UAE
telephone : +971.4.324 8888
facsimile : +971.4.324 6000
dubai@raffles.com
dubai.raffles.com

Cleopatra's Spa
Wafi City
Al Wasl Road, PO Box 721, Dubai, UAE
telephone : +971.4.324 0000
www.waficity.com

Grand Spa
Grand Hyatt Dubai
PO Box 7978, Dubai, UAE
telephone : +971.4.317 1234
facsimile : +971.4.317 1235
dubai.grand@hyattintl.com
dubai.grand.hyatt.com

H_2o
Jumeirah Emirates Towers
PO Box 72127, Dubai, UAE
telephone : +971.4.319 8181
facsimile : +971.4.319 8080
JETh2o@jumeirah.com
www.jumeirahemiratestowers.com

Health & Beauty Institute
One&Only Royal Mirage
PO Box 37252, Dubai, UAE
telephone : +971.4.399 9999
facsimile : +971.4.399 9998
info@oneandonlyroyalmirage.ae
www.oneandonlyresorts.com

Paris Gallery
3rd Floor, Deira City CentreDeira, UAE
telephone : +971.4.294 4000
parisgal@emirates.net.ae
www.uae-parisgallery.com

Retreat
Grosvenor House
Al Sufouh, PO Box 118500, Dubai, UAE
telephone : +971.4.399 8888
facsimile : +971.4.399 8444
reservations@lrm-gh-dubai.com
www.grosvenorhouse-dubai.com

Ritz-Carlton Spa
The Ritz-Carlton, Dubai
PO Box 26525, Dubai, UAE
telephone : +971.4.399 4000
facsimile : +971.4.399 4001
rcdubai@emirates.net.ae
www.ritzcarlton.com

Satori Spa
Jumeirah Bab Al Shams Desert Resort & Spa
PO Box 8168, Dubai, UAE
telephone : +971.4.832 6699
facsimile : +971.4.832 6698
JBASfeedback@jumeirah.com
www.jumeirahbabalshams.com/satori_spa

SensAsia
The Village, Jumeirah Beach Road
PO Box 71393, Dubai, UAE
telephone : +971.4.349 8850

Talise Spa
PO Box 75157, Dubai, UAE
telephone : +971.4.366 8888
facsimile : +971.4.366 7788
MJinfo@jumeirah.com
www.madinatjumeirah.com

The Residence & Spa
One&Only Royal Mirage
PO Box 37252, Dubai, UAE
telephone : +971.4.399 9999
facsimile : +971.4.399 9998
info@oneandonlyroyalmirage.ae
www.oneandonlyresorts.com

The Taj Palace Hotel Spa
The Taj Palace Hotel, Dubai
P O Box 42211, Dubai, UAE
telephone : +971.4.223 2222
facsimile : +971.4.227 8222
tphreservations.dxb@tajhotels.com
www.tajhotels.com

Timeless Spa
Al Maha Desert Resort & Spa
Sheikh Zayed Road,
PO Box 7631, Dubai, UAE
telephone : +971.4.303 4222
facsimile : +971.4.343 9696
almaha@emirates.com
www.al-maha.com

Willow Stream Spa
Fairmont Dubai
Sheikh Zayed Road
PO Box 97555, Dubai, UAE
telephone : +971.4.332 5555
facsimile : +971.4.332 4555
dubai@fairmont.com
www.fairmont.com/dubai

CHAMPIONSHIP DUBAI

Al-Boom Diving
Al Wasl Road, Dubai, UAE
telephone : +971.4.342 2993
facsimile : +971.4.342 2995
abdiving@emirates.net.ae
www.alboomdiving.com

Dubai Autodrome
POBox 24649, Dubai, UAE
telephone : +971.4.367 8700
facsimile : +971.4.367 8750
info@dubaiautodrome.com
www.dubaiautodrome.com

directory

Dubai Country Club
PO Box 5103, Dubai, UAE
telephone : +971.4.333 1155
facsimile : +971.4.333 1409
www.dubaicountryclub.com

Dubai Tennis Championships
Dubai Duty Free Tournament Owners & Organisers, PO Box 831, Dubai, UAE
telephone : +971.4.216 6444
facsimile : +971.4.224 4455
www.dubaitennischampionships.com

Dubai Polo & Equestrian Club
PO Box 7477, Dubai, UAE
telephone : +971.4.361 8111
facsimile : +971.4.361 7111
info@poloclubdubai.com
www.poloclubdubai.com

Dubai World Cup
Dubai Racing Club
Nad Al Sheba Racecourse
P O Box 9305, Dubai, UAE
telephone : +971.4.327 0077
facsimile : +971.4.327 0049
info@dubairacingclub.com
www.dubairacingclub.com/dubaiworldcup

Emirates Riding Centre
PO Box 292, Dubai, UAE
telephone : +971.4.336 1394
facsimile : +971.4.336 3934
emrc@emirates.net.ae

Four Seasons Golf Club
Dubai Festival City, Al Badia, Dubai, UAE
telephone : +971.4.601 0101
www.fourseasons.com/dubaigolf

Jebel Ali Equestrian Club
Jebel Ali Village, Dubai, UAE
telephone : +971.4.884 5245

Nad Al Sheba Club
PO Box 52872, Dubai, UAE
telephone : +971.4.336 3666
facsimile : +971.4.336 3717
www.nadalshebaclub.com

Pavilion Dive Centre
Jumeirah Beach Hotel
PO Box 11416, Dubai, UAE
telephone : +971.4.406 8828
divecentre@jumeirah.com
www.jumeirahbeachhotel.com/dive_centre

PGA Tour Dubai Desert Classic
PO Box 119813, Dubai, UAE
telephone : +971.4.380 1777
facsimile : +971.4.380 1818
www.dubaidesertclassic.com

Sports City
PO Box 111123, Dubai, UAE
telephone : +971.4.425 1111
facsimile : +971.4.425 1100
info@sc.ae
www.dubaisportscity.ae

The Dunes
Victory Heights
PO Box 117349, Dubai, UAE
telephone : +971.4.420 3553
facsimile : +971.4.420 3552
www.vh.ae

FAMILY AFFAIR

Al Nasr Leisureland
PO Box 2652, Dubai, UAE
telephone : +971.4.337 1234
facsimile : +971.4.337 4952
alnasrll@eim.ae
www.alnasrll.com

Arabian Adventures
1st Floor, Emirates Holidays Building
Sheikh Zayed Road
PO Box 7631, Dubai, UAE
telephone : +971.4.343 9966/303 4888
facsimile : +971.4.343 9977
arabian.adventures@emirates.com
www.arabian-adventures.com

Café Céramique
Jumeirah, Dubai, UAE
telephone : +971.4.344 7331
facsimile : +971.4.344 7881
events.marketing@cafe-ceramique.com
www.cafe-ceramique.com

Children's City
PO Box 67, Dubai, UAE
telephone : +971.4.334 0808
facsimile : +971.4.334 1122
childcity@dm.gov.ae
www.childrencity.ae

Desert Rangers
Dubai Garden Centre Building
Sheikh Zayed Road, Dubai, UAE
telephone : +971.4.340 2408
www.desertrangers.com

Dubai Community Theatre & Arts Centre
2nd Level, Mall of the Emirates, Ski Dubai Car Park
PO Box 117748, Dubai, UAE
telephone : +971.4.341 4777
facsimile : +971.4.341 4443/45
artsreception@ductac.org
box.office@ductac.org
www.ductac.org

Dubai Kartdrome
PO Box 24649, Dubai, UAE
telephone : +971.4.367 8700
facsimile : +971.4.367 8750
info@dubaiautodrome.com
www.dubaiautodrome.com

Dubai Museum
Old Al Fahidi Fort, Bur Dubai, Dubai, UAE
telephone : +971.4.353 1862

Encounter Zone
3rd Floor, Wafi City, Al Wasl Road
PO Box 721, Dubai, UAE
telephone : +971.4.324 7747
facsimile : +971.4.324 9977
www.waficity.com

Galleria Ice Rink
Hyatt Regency Dubai
Deira, PO Box 5588, Dubai, UAE
telephone : +971.4.209 1234
facsimile : +971.4.209 1000
reservations.hyattregencydubai@hyattintl.com
dubai.regency.hyatt.com

Grand Cinema Megaplex
Ibn Battuta Mall
Sheikh Zayed Road
PO Box 261177, Dubai, UAE
telephone : +971.4.366 9898
www.ibnbattutamall.com

Gulf Ventures
Al Awir Road, Dubai, UAE
telephone : +971.50 640 2058
facsimile : +971 4 885 0870

Heritage & Diving Village
Shindagha, Dubai, UAE
telephone : +971.4.393 7151

Ibn Battuta Mall
Sheikh Zayed Road
PO Box 261177, Dubai, UAE
telephone : +971.4.362 1900
facsimile : +971.4.368 5140
info@ibnbattutamall.com
www.ibnbattutamall.com

Johnny Rockets
Juma al Majid Center
Jumeirah Beach Road
PO Box 19345, Dubai, UAE
telephone : +971.4.344 7898

Dubai Marina
Marina Walk South Side, Dubai, UAE

Mall of the Emirates
Sheikh Zayed Road
PO Box 72999, Dubai, UAE
telephone : +971.4.3411 2380
www.johnnyrockets.com

LunarLand
Encounter Zone
3rd Floor, Wafi City, PO Box 721, Dubai, UAE
telephone : +971.4.324 7747
facsimile : +971.4.324 9977
www.waficity.com

Magic Planet
Mall of the Emirates
Sheikh Zayed Road
PO Box 72999, Dubai, UAE
telephone : +971.4.341 4444
www.malloftheemirates.com

Marina Market
Dubai Marina, Dubai, UAE
telephone : +971.50.244 5795
facsimile : +971.4.367 4868
info@marinamarket.ae
www.marinamarket.ae

Rampworks Skatepark
Jumeirah, Dubai, UAE
telephone : +971.50.465 7004

Ski Dubai
Mall of the Emirates
Sheikh Zayed Road
PO Box 72999, Dubai, UAE
telephone : +971.4.409 4000
facsimile : +971.4.409 4101
www.skidxb.com

The Big Bus Company
Double Decker Bus Tours LLC
PO Box 116250, Dubai, UAE
telephone : +971. 4. 340 7709
facsimile : +971.4.341 6553
infodubai@bigbustours.com
www.bigbustours.com

The Jam Jar
Street 17A, Al Quoz, PO Box 27554
Dubai, UAE
telephone : +971.4.341 7303
facsimile : +971.4.341 7304
gallery@thejamjardubai.com
www.thejamjardubai.com

Wild Wadi Water Park
Jumeirah Beach Road
PO Box 26416, Dubai, UAE
telephone : +971.4.348 4444
facsimile : +971.4.348 0275
info@wildwadi.com
www.wildwadi.com

Wonder Bus Tours
telephone : +971.4.359 5656
facsimile : +971.4.359 6959
info@wonderbusdubai.com
www.wonderbusdubai.net

Wonderland Amusement Park
PO Box 28844, Dubai, UAE
telephone : +971.4.324 1222/3222
facsimile : +971.4.324 3526/1623
info@wonderlanduae.com
www.wonderlanduae.com

ONWARDS AND UPWARDS

Al Burj
PO Box 17777, Dubai, UAE
telephone : +971.4.390 3333
facsimile : +971.4.390 3314
info@nakheel.com
www.nakheel.com

Al Sufouh Tram
Road & Transport Authority of Dubai
PO Box 118899, Dubai, UAE
telephone : +971.4.284 4444
facsimile : +971.4.206 5555
info@rta.ae
www.rta.ae

Asia-Asia
telephone : +971.4.330 3839
info@bawadi.ae
www.bawadi.ae

Burj Dubai
telephone : +971.4.367 5568
facsimile : +971.4.367 5555
www.burjdubai.com

Dubai Healthcare City
Oud Metha Road, Ibn Sina Building
Block C, Ground Floor
PO Box 66566, Dubai, UAE
telephone : +971.4.324 5555
facsimile : +971.4.324 9000
www.dhcc.ae

Dubai Mall
telephone : +971.4.367 5588
facsimile : +971.4.367 5589
enquiry@thedubaimall.com
www.thedubaimall.com

Dubai Metro
Road & Transport Authority of Dubai
PO Box 118899, Dubai, UAE
telephone : +971.4.284 4444
facsimile : +971.4.206 5555
info@rta.ae
www.rta.ae

Dubai World Central International Airport
Dubai World Central
Emarat Atrium Building - Block B,
Sheikh Zayed Road, Ground Floor - 038
PO Box 74241, Dubai, UAE
telephone : +971.4.321 4040
facsimile : +971.4.343 5505
info@dubailogisticscity.ae
www.dubaiworldcentral.net

Dubailand
PO Box 66366, Dubai, UAE
telephone : +971.4.368 0000
facsimile : +971.4.368 0011
www.dubailand.ae

Falcon City of Wonders
PO Box 120660, Dubai, UAE
telephone : +971.4.335 5539
facsimile : +971.4.335 6703
www.falconcity.com

Mall of Arabia
City of Arabia
Capricorn Tower, 10th Floor,
Sheikh Zayed Road, PO Box 114444
Dubai, UAE
telephone : +971.4.331 1022
facsimile : +971.4.332 2311
info@cityofarabia.ae
www.cityofarabiame.com

Restless Planet
City of Arabia
Capricorn Tower, 10th Floor, Sheikh Zayed Road, PO Box 114444, Dubai, UAE
telephone : +971.4.331 1022
facsimile : +971.4.332 2311
info@cityofarabia.ae
www.cityofarabiame.com

The Great Dubai Wheel
Dubailand
PO Box 66366, Dubai, UAE
telephone : +971.4.368 0000
facsimile : +971.4.368 0011
www.dubailand.ae

The Palm Jumeirah
Sales Office
PO Box 17777, Dubai, UAE
telephone : +971.4.390 3333
facsimile : +971.4.390 3314
info@nakheel.com
www.nakheel.com

The World
PO Box 17777, Dubai, UAE
telephone : +971.4.390 3333
facsimile : +971.4.390 3314
info@nakheel.com
www.nakheel.com